THE SAINT

THE SAINT

TONY MECHELE AND DICK FIDDY

Boxtree

First published in 1989 by Boxtree Limited

Copyright © 1989 Boxtree Limited

Illustrations copyright © RKO Pictures; Exclusive Films (Hammer Pictures).

The publishers wish to thank Hodder & Stoughton and Pan books. London for permission to reproduce jackets from their titles.

ACKNOWLEDGEMENTS

The authors would like to thank the following people for their contributions:

Alan Austin (Heroes).
Sharon Hill. Peter Harrington. Paul James
David Lomazoff. J. Fred MacDonald. Jo Parbles.
Richard Wilcox. Jacqueline Debs. Neil Alsop.
Maggie Hurt. Richard Dacre. Joyce Copper.
The British Film Institute.
Robin Osbourne of Flips Pages for some wonderful material. and finally. a special thank you to Bruce Campbell. without whose help this project would not have been started and certainly never completed.

British Library Cataloguing in Publication Data
Mechele. Tony
  The Saint.
  1. Fiction in English. Charteris. Leslie. 1907–.
  Characters Saint. the
  I. Title II. Fiddy. Dick
  832'.912

  ISBN 1–85283–259–2

Edited by Christopher Stocks
Designed by Julia Lilauwala
Typeset by Action Typesetting Ltd. Gloucester
Printed and bound in the UK by Redwood Burn. Trowbridge
For Boxtree Limited. 36 Tavistock Street.
London. WC2E 7PB.

THIS BOOK IS RESPECTFULLY DEDICATED TO
LESLIE CHARTERIS AND ALL SAINT FANS.

CONTENTS

ENTER THE SAINT

THE FAMOUS Simon Templar entered the world as a fully-formed 27 year old in the first Saint book, *Meet The Tiger*, published in 1928, where his arrival heralds mayhem and murder for a sleepy village on the North Devon coast. Templar's creator entered the world some 21 years earlier – half a world away – in Singapore.

Leslie Charteris was born Leslie Charles Bowyer Yin on 12 May 1907. His mother was English while his father was a respected surgeon who claimed direct descendancy from the Shang Dynasty (*c*.1766–1123 BC). The young Charteris's formative years were certainly as colourful as any of the fictional heroes and villains he would later create. He spoke both Chinese and Malay before learning English and travelled with his parents having been round the world several times by the time he was 12. He was a bright child and received a first-class education at the hands of various governesses and tutors. When he was

seven or eight he was given a typewriter; a year later he was producing a regular magazine that he sold to his parents and friends for a few pennies. The magazine included a comic-strip that Charteris drew which featured – because of his lack of artistic prowess – stick men. Later he would use the stick man image, with the addition of a halo, as the internationally recognisable sign of The Saint. When Charteris entered his teens his parents sent him to Falconbury Prep. School in England; in 1922 he moved on to Rossall School in Fleetwood, Lancashire. During this period he read many detective novels and began to toy with the idea of becoming a writer. When he was 16 he made his first sale, under the name of Leslie C. Bowyer. It was a short story, now sadly lost. His earliest traceable published work was *The Crowded Hour* sold to the *Sovereign Magazine*. However his parents wanted him to join the legal profession and with this in mind he

The first Saint Novel, *Meet the Tiger*, alongside one of the four non-Saint works by Charteris

The various Saint publications of the 1950s

The *Thriller*, the crime and mystery magazine of the 1920s

entered King's College, Cambridge in 1925. Nevertheless the lure of the pen was still strong and after just a year at Cambridge he left to pursue a career as a full-time writer – much to his father's chagrin: he considered all writers to be no better than 'rogues and vagabonds'. He made it clear that he would not give his son any financial assistance with such an irresponsible career choice.

But the young Charteris had made his mind up, and the following year (1927) his efforts were rewarded with the publication of his first novel, *X Esquire*, which decades later he was to describe as 'a lousy, imitative thing . . . thankfully long out of print.' At the time however, he was thrilled with his success and redoubled his efforts, publishing four more novels in the next two years: *Daredevil, White Rider, The Bandit* and The Saint's debut, *Meet The Tiger*. Regular publication, however, did not bring much in the way of financial reward and Charteris took a number of odd jobs to make ends meet, including a short stint as an auxiliary police constable and as a bus driver before returning for a while to South-East Asia. Here he prospected for gold in the jungle, tried pearl-fishing and worked on a rubber planation. On moving back to England he was employed as a barman, played bridge professionally and joined a travelling funfair in a job that consisted mainly of blowing up balloons for a sideshow.

By this time Leslie Yin had changed his name legally to Charteris, choosing the name partly because it was similar to his middle name Charles but also out of admiration for Colonel Francis Charteris, a rogueish gambler, lover, duellist and founding member of the Hellfire Club. Shortly after, Charteris was contacted by a London editor, Monty Haydon. Haydon told him he was starting a new magazine and invited Charteris to write for it. The magazine, called *Thriller*, was launched with much excitement as a weekly and the first edition contained a 'full-length novel' (at around 25,000 words these could better be described as novellas) by the leading popular crime-writer of the time, Edgar Wallace. The fourth issue's 'full-length novel' was by Leslie Charteris, it was called *The Story Of A Dead Man* and featured a character called Jimmy Traill and a policeman called Chief Inspector Teal. Charteris, a great admirer of Wallace's work, was understandably proud to be writing for the same organ as the master, although as he pointed out, "they had to pay Wallace about ten times what they paid me". Issue 9 featured another Charteris story, *The Secret Of Beacon Inn*, dealing with the exploits of Rameses Smith, but after this Charteris made a momentous decision. Realising that he was hooked on a certain type of character, he reasoned that it was a waste of time and effort constantly to invent new names and slightly different traits and physical characteristics for his leading man. He decided to pick one and chronicle this character's exploits in a series of adventures. Astutely he realised that now when a reader enjoyed one of his books, that reader would be likely to chase up the previous stories starring that character and keep a keen eye out for his next escapade. It meant that each book was like a salesman working for all the rest – a bonus enjoyed by any novelist regularly employing the same fictional character. Charteris went back over his output and decided that Simon Templar, The Saint, should be his recurring hero. Issue 13 introduced The Saint to *Thriller* magazine in the first of a series of stories called *The Five Kings*, where it is revealed that Templar is the head of a gang of 5 crooks working on the side of law and order but using unlawful techniques.

Writing for *Thriller* was hard work and the pay was dreadful but Haydon was a fine editor, encouraging and stimulating his authors. He kept newspaper clippings of interesting items that he thought might inspire storylines and certainly some of the early Saint adventures started life this way. Charteris and Haydon struck up a firm friendship that lasted till the latter's death. The Saint's popularity increased with every appearance in *Thriller* and the novellas were regularly gathered in groups of three and published in book form, issued alongside entirely new Saint novels which appeared every year or so. Aside from his *Thriller* magazine assignments, Charteris also had Saint stories published in similar crime-fiction magazines including a couple of tales that appeared in the famous *Black Mask*. However the majority of Saint material appeared in The Saint's own magazines.

The Saint Magazine (USA) was published nine times a year by the Fiction Publishing Company in New York. Each issue would contain a selection of crime and mystery stories (and occasionally articles) by the top writers of the day, and almost always of course a Saint adventure. The magazine was published between 1953 and 1967 and was edited by Hans Stefan with Leslie Charteris as supervising editor.

A British Empire edition was published monthly by Magazine Enterprises in Australia. This was edited by James Grant with Charteris again getting the supervising editor credit. It ran from November 1954 to December 1959. From January 1960 it changed its name to *The Saint*

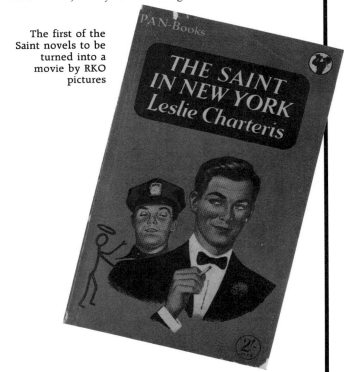

The first of the Saint novels to be turned into a movie by RKO pictures

Mystery Magazine and increased its price slightly but apart from this continued as before until 1967.

In 1931 Charteris married Pauline Schiskin and although he was becoming more successful, he was still not earning a great amount. This fact, coupled with his urge to travel caused him in 1932 to journey to New York and pursue his writing career in the US. His first American sale was a short Saint adventure, *Judith*, but major success came with the sale of *The Saint in New York* to the *American*

Magazine. Charteris spent a few weeks in New York then, in 1933, he was hired by Paramount as a screenwriter and moved to Hollywood. Charteris enjoyed his time in Hollywood but was later to become disillusioned with the machinations of the film industry (of which more in the chapter 'The Saint on Film'). He divorced his first wife in 1937 (they had a daughter) and married Barbara Meyer in 1938. They divorced in 1943 and the same year he married Elizabeth Bryant Borst. In 1946 he became a naturalised American citizen, losing his Anglo-Chinese nationality. He divorced again in 1951 and the following year married Audrey Long, with whom he found lasting happiness. Eventually he moved back to Europe, dividing his time between Britain and France; finally, thanks to Simon Templar he was a wealthy man. Throughout this period he continued to write Saint adventures regularly but also wrote screenplays, comic-strips and radio scripts, translated a bullfighter's biography, invented Paleneo, an international sign language, wrote a column for *Gourmet Magazine* and edited various fiction periodicals.

What of The Saint's formative years? How did the lifestyle and changing fortunes of his creator affect the development of the famous Simon Templar? The Saint himself ages hardly ten years throughout his entire career, but has enough adventures to fill several lifetimes. The most precise description of Templar puts him at 6ft 2in, and 175lb (12 ½ stone), blue eyes, black hair brushed back, permanently tanned, with a bullet scar on his upper left shoulder and an eight inch scar on his right forearm. He is an incorrigibly whimsical type, constantly composing rhymes, making puns, telling awful humorous stories and turning phrases into double entendres by using the 'as the actress said to the bishop' routine. Charteris chose his hero's name carefully: Simon because it would remind crooks he wasn't simple, and Templar to conjure up images of the religious order of the Knights Templar who protected pilgrimages to the Holy Land in the twelfth century. Like Charteris, he speaks several languages fluently, is an immaculate dresser, a connoisseur of food and wine and a licensed pilot. He is definitely *not* an all-round sportsman: his tennis is poor, his cricket appalling and an attempt at baseball once moved a crowd to tears; but put a fencing foil in his hand, throw him into dangerous water, sit him on a wildly bucking horse or ask him to climb a tree or the side of a house and an altogether different character appears. Although superbly adept with a gun, his preference (early on) is for knives, and he carries one at all times in a sheath strapped to his forearm. A 6in curved, leaf-shaped blade with a 3in ivory hilt; a weapon that makes him lethal and of which he is so fond that he even gives it a name, Anna. A blade similar to Anna, Belle, is occasionally lodged in a sheath on the Saint's leg. He is also very attached to his silver cigarette case, a useful and tricky object that houses a flash and smoke bomb device, and is polished to a mirror finish, enabling The Saint to view scenes taking place behind him. More than once it is used to hurl at a lightbulb, plunging a room into darkness. Tremendously handy with his fists, he's also a savage master of street-fighting and is not averse to using karate to overcome opponents; his athleticism and stamina seemingly unimpaired despite the fact that he's a heavy smoker (four cigarettes an hour, regular as clockwork) enjoys the odd beer, and takes liberal amounts of Peter Dawson Whisky. The cigarettes may have begun to take their toll. Later both Charteris and Templar gave up smoking.

From his very first appearance in print The Saint's style is defined: he's portrayed as a ruthless, somewhat egotistical latterday Robin Hood, stealing from the unworthily rich and more often than not keeping the money (or the reward) for himself. Often described as a cross between Raffles and Bulldog Drummond, this character is actually nearer in spirit to the French thief-turned-detective, Arsene Lupin, but such comparisons, although inevitable, mask interesting differences. What set The Saint apart from his contemporaries in the thriller fiction of the day was his choice of adversaries and his direct and murderous methods. Not for Simon Templar the thick-eared thug or malformed psychopath – his villains are the immoral financiers who pay the wages of sin and anonymously reap the benefits. War-mongerers, gun-runners, drug-barons, vice-kings, power-crazed dictators: all are haunted by the mysterious and deadly Saint! Working on the wrong side of the law and driven by his own desire for moral justice, Templar declares war on those who set themselves up above the law: the gang-leaders so far removed from their nefarious crimes that they can never be brought to court, the unscrupulous international businessmen making money out of misery, the crooked politicians, the corrupt judges, the bent cops. The Saint brings his own relentless form of justice to bear: robbing from the robbers, conning the con-men and, without hesitation, killing the killers. He operates as judge, jury and executioner, totally sure of his verdicts and untroubled by conscience or second thoughts. Obviously these methods bring him frequently into conflict with the world's lawmen.

Simon Templar's relationship with the upholders of law and order is understandably ambiguous. On the one hand, this freewheeling vigilante helps their cause by efficiently eliminating some of the nastier and legally untouchable criminal elements in their midst; on the other hand, this man is himself a murderer and a thief. The Saint's most famous official adversary is the gum-chewing, bulky Scotland Yard investigator, Inspector Claud Eustace Teal. Teal plots tirelessly to ensnare Templar but The Saint is always one step ahead. In one adventure, *The Story of a Dead Man*, (featured in *Alias The Saint*, a reworking of Charteris' first non-Saint story for *Thriller*, Teal saves Templar's life and puts his own in danger as he drags The Saint's unconscious body from a gas-filled room. Templar returns the favour many times, often transferring the credit for cracking a particularly difficult case to the hapless policeman. Although the two cross swords often, there seems to be an underlying respect between them, despite the fact that The Saint mercilessly taunts the portly policeman as a dim-witted plodder. Charteris himself has admitted to abhoring stupidity and his impatience with dull thinkers is passed on to The Saint who is often exasperated that the various police representatives he encounters seem unable to make the same dazzling deductions he does. But then next to the lightning-fast Templar any policeman seems a plodder, even the seasoned, street-wise New Yorker, Inspector John Fernack.

The Saint first encounters Fernack, America's answer to Teal, in *The Saint in New York*. Here Templar is confronted by a totally different police outfit from the one he's used to. In a force riddled with corruption, the few honest cops find themselves forced into using underhand and ruthless methods to make any headway against the gang-leaders whose men slip through the nets with ease, helped by bought-off politicians and crooked judges. The adventure starts with a letter from Teal at

Scotland Yard warning the Chief of Police in New York that the Saint is believed to be in America. Shortly afterwards Inspector Fernack comes to realise the importance of the missive when a gangland leader is bumped off as he walks free from a courtroom – a killing heralded by a message bearing the stick-man calling-card of The Saint. Fernack and Templar meet soon afterwards, with the Inspector finding himself on the wrong end of a gun, but soon a truce of sorts is called and New York witnesses a series of audacious escapades, involving the rescue of a kidnap victim and the gory culling of a bevy of gang bosses. As with Teal, Fernack's respect for The Saint is tempered by his respect for the law and inevitably Templar goes too far. In the subsequent years Fernack finds himself chasing shadows as he labours to bring The

villains he has wronged plot hideous revenge and the cops populate his exploits as obstacles needing to be overcome. Throughout all this is there anyone on Templar's side? Although later in his career he's seen as a loner, his earlier adventures find him very much the leader of the gang: The Saint's 'Haloes'. Even on his first outing (*Meet The Tiger*) Templar is accompanied by his slow-witted, loyal retainer Orace who walks with a lopsided gait since picking up a German bullet in his right hip at Zeebrugge during the Great War. Orace is on call for many of The Saint's future escapades, as is the 'slim fair-haired vision' Patricia Holm whom Templar meets and falls in love with in that first adventure. Pat Holm becomes more or less The Saint's permanent girlfriend, devoted to him and determinedly modern in her attitude to his various affairs,

A 1950s reprint of the 1931 book. In *The Saint Around The World*, Simon solves mysteries from London to the Bahamas

Saint to justice. The American Inspector is a tougher, harder man than his London counterpart, and he earns The Saint's respect for being a decent, honest man when so many around him are not. Nevertheless despite their similar aims their different methods condemn them to be on opposite sides.

The Saint's other police acquaintances are less memorable: Scotland Yard's Detective Inspector Carn, New York's Detective Duncarry – who bears a permanent limp thanks to The Saint but is a friend nonetheless, Nice's Inspector Lartingent, Scotland's Inspector MacKenzie and many more. All tread warily round The Saint who manages, especially later in his career, to leave no proof of his various misdemeanours. Finally, in the story *The Talented Husband* (featured in *The Saint Around the World*) Teal retires, never having added Templar's scalp to the Yard's collection. His failure epitomises the failure of all The Saint's pursuers.

So The Saint has adversaries on both sides of the law:

greeting new females whenever they're introduced with a resigned 'welcome to the harem'. Despite his constant conquests (surely an occupational hazard for someone so suavely handsome as The Saint) Pat remains his favourite and a brave and resourceful member of his team. Others that drift on and off the payroll are, from Templar's own description: Norman Kent, the most darkly attractive; Archie Sheridan, the most delightfully irresponsible; Roger Conway, the most good-looking; and dark and handsome Dicky Tremayne. Later members include Hoppy Uniatz (an American slow-witted ex-gangster), and the reliable Peter Quentin. Gradually they are all phased out, Norman Kent most poignantly, being killed by a foreign Secret Service man and war-promoter Dr Rayt Marius. Charteris comments on the playing down of the gang, claiming that they were getting in the way of the adventure, and that Patricia Holm was a block to the Saint getting involved romantically – although her presence had never seemed to be much of an inhibition to him.

When Charteris moved to the States, Templar and his gang moved too. Things were getting too hot for The Saint in Britain: it had all been so much simpler in the early days, Templar confesses at one point. Although he earned the nickname Saint when he was 19, as much for his angelic looks as his initials, for many years the general public and Scotland Yard in particular didn't know that the audacious and deadly Saint and the elegant, debonair Simon Templar were one and the same person. Hence The Saint could leave his calling card logo at the scene of the most spectacular crimes and yet go about his daily life unhindered as Simon Templar. It was a blissful arrangement that was not to last, especially with Inspector Teal growing more suspicious by the minute. Finally, with evidence stacked up against him and the boys in blue closing in, Templar flees the country, only to return after a few months to do battle once again with Dr Marius, an adventure that ends with The Saint receiving a free pardon for frustrating an attempt to wreck the Royal train and kill the King. But still Templar refuses to temper his criminal activities and soon things hot up again. He manages to spirit himself out of the country with his accumulated fortune (estimated to be nearly half a million pounds), and £100,000 in stolen diamonds in his pocket. Adventures in Europe follow. In Madrid Templar meets William K. Valcross who lures him to New York on a quest for revenge against some of the meanest gangsters Templar will ever encounter. (*The Saint in New York*). At the end of that particular escapade The Saint returns to London and Pat Holm, and the next few years find him commuting almost full-time back and forth across the Atlantic and around Europe. But as war beckons, Templar's path becomes clear and he brings his particular brand of justice to bear on Nazis and the profiteers of war, sometimes working undercover for officialdom. Both *Prelude for War* and *The Saint in Miami* cover this subject. In the former, a dangerous interlude for Simon Templar begins when he rushes into a blazing building in an attempt to save a man who turns out to be already dead. The ensuing investigation pitches The Saint against a deadly fascist organisation called The Sons of France. In the latter, an exploding ship opens a tale that brings our hero into contact with the brave Karen Leith, who infiltrates a Nazi organisation operating in the US, while America ponders over whether to join the war. The war years see a different, more mellow Saint with, as he himself puts it, 'an almost dreary respectability'. It is only after the war is over and Templar begins acting more-or-less as a single agent again that the image of the lone wolf which many associate with The Saint is finally established.

Today, over 60 years since his debut, the lure of The Saint is as strong as ever. Charteris has been criticised for glorifying a character who operates outside the law, considering himself to be above it, but whenever confronted by such observations the author has made it clear that the novels were intended as adventures and not as philosophical texts. The stories move at a breakneck pace and display a vigorous use of language. Charteris takes relish in using long, unusal words where shorter common ones would have done. He never underestimates his hero's abilities or undersells the effect the name of the Saint has on the villains, although as the years pass he craves the readers' indulgence as yet another crook gasps in terror at the mention of the name. His descriptions of place are suitably enthusiastic and authentic, in particular his superb description of Manhattan in what is probably his best work, *The Saint in New York*. His plotting in the longer tales is flawless and the shorter stories are well-crafted, usually with a smart twist in the tail. In his introductions to the later editions of his earlier works, Charteris explains that the stories are rarely 'modernised' and are best read as historical pieces and not as contemporary thrillers, which is fair enough comment.

The later Saint books are adaptations from the episodes of the Sixties television series that *weren't* based on original Charteris stories. Charteris, a long-standing member of the high IQ society MENSA, wanted fellow members to adapt the episodes. The results are tamer than Charteris's own output but occasionally capture the barnstorming cut and thrust of the master.

THE SAINT
ON RADIO

TUNE IN TO Radio Eireann for Luck' was the cheery motto that greeted wireless listeners when they tuned to 531m 565kcs in the late 1930s. Radio Eireann (which had changed its name from Radio Athlone in 1938) was a commercial station usually only broadcasting for an hour a day between 9.30 and 10.30pm. Although its output was mostly gramophone records, this station became the unlikely venue for the first radio Saint.

Brothers Derrick and Terence De Marney were good-looking British actors who had worked on the stage before making their feature film debuts: Derrick in *Music Hall* (1935) and Terence in *The Mystery of the Marie Celeste* (1936). In 1939 Terence De Marney gave a voice to Charteris's Happy Highwayman, The Saint, in a series of adventures for Radio Eireann. His brother Derrick directed some of the episodes along with Harold Cooper, and Arthur La Bern was the main scriptwriter.

The following year Terence De Marney took his version of Simon Templar to BBC Radio for a short series of 25-minute adventures. During the war many famous fictional heroes came to radio, some on the normal BBC wavelength and others on the BBC forces' band. The Saint series, featured on the latter, ran for six weeks from the 18th October 1940 and was produced by Peter Creswell with scripts adapted from original Charteris stories by James Parrish.

By this time, The Saint had also become a movie hero and Charteris himself was living and working in the States. The Thirties and Forties were the golden age of action/adventure thriller series on American radio with heroes plucked from the pages of pulp fiction alongside those specially created for the medium. The Lone Ranger brought justice to a lawless West; The Shadow stalked terrified criminals down dank, dark alleyways; Flash Gordon eluded death rays and fought alien monsters on distant planets; Perry Mason and Ellery Queen solved impossible crimes — all sorts of cops and private eyes waged war on evil-doers everywhere. The world's greatest detective, Sherlock Holmes, was an obvious choice for radio adventures and a long-running series was already well established when Leslie Charteris was invited to work on its scripts. Charteris, using the pseudonym Bruce Taylor, assisted scriptwriter Edith Meiser from 1943 and Basil Rathbone and Nigel Bruce recreated their film roles as Holmes and Watson for the series. Charteris's own creation was to make its US radio debut two years later.

With the US airwaves full of dashing adventurers and an American audience with an apparently limitless appetite

Radio Pictorial was the European radio journal of the 1930s and 40s

for such fare, it was only a matter of time before Simon Templar came to the airwaves. The Saint series made its debut on 6 January 1945 on the NBC network, with American film and stage actor Edgar Barrier in the lead role. Each show began with the sound of footsteps echoing down a lonely street and the melancholy whistling of a strange and haunting tune. The Saint's whistle became the aural equivalent of the stick man logo; a melodic calling card for Simon Templar. Former American Football star John Brown played Inspector John Fernack, and Ken Christy voiced the leaden-brained Hoppy Uniatz. The show was sponsored by Bromo Seltzer and aired on Saturday nights.

Edgar Barrier as Simon Templar takes charge of the murder weapon in another exciting radio adventure of The Saint

Brian Aherne prepares with Jane Wyatt for the next adventure of The Saint

CBS was the next station to feature The Saint in a series that started on 20 June 1945 and starred the highly regarded British actor Brian Aherne. Aherne had moved to America in 1933 and divided his time between Hollywood and New York; on stage and on screen he was the American ideal of the sophisticated Englishman. The Saint was his first regular radio role and by all accounts he was well suited to the part of the suave Simon Templar. Louise Arthur played The Saint's girl-Friday, Patricia Holm.

The most fondly remembered of the radio Saints was first heard in 1947 when Vincent Price brought his rich tones to the part in a summer series for CBS. His version of the character later turned up on the Mutual Broadcasting Company in 1949 where the series ran for a while under the sponsorship of the Ford Motor Company before moving back to NBC, where it ran for a further couple of years. The Vincent Price Saint was a sardonic, witty ladies' man, a patron of the arts and a lover of good food and wine. He was usually to be found dining at a superb restaurant when adventure beckoned, causing him to interrupt one of his favourite pastimes for another fight against crime.

The opening announcement for the Mutual Broadcasting's Saint show was typical of the day: 'The Adventures of The Saint, starring Vincent Price. The Saint; based on characters created by Leslie Charteris and known to millions from books, magazines and motion pictures. The Robin Hood of modern crime is now transcribed for radio, starring Hollywood's brilliant and talented actor, Vincent Price as . . . The Saint.'

The closing routine went: 'You have been listening to another adventure of The Saint, the Robin Hood of modern crime. And now here is our star, Vincent Price.' Price would then make a public service announcement, finishing with: 'This is Vincent Price inviting you to join us again next week at this same time for another exciting adventure of . . . The Saint.'

This would be followed by the famous whistle, fading footsteps and the announcer reading the particular credits for that episode, closing the show with: 'The Saint, based on characters created by Leslie Charteris, is a James L. Saphier production. All you Saint fans will be glad to know that The Saint comic books are on sale at your local news stand. This is the Mutual Broadcasting Company.'

The Price Saint shows were specially written for radio and didn't use Charteris stories. The famous Saint whistle, though, was a Charteris creation, a variation on the six notes that he probably dreamed up originally for the Saint movies.

Some sources, notably Vincent Terrace in his book *Radio's Golden Years: The Encyclopedia of Radio Programmes 1930–1960*, also include Tom Conway and Barry Sullivan as having voiced The Saint, but we can find no dates or recording information relating to their involvement.

Vincent Price becomes the most popular and memorable of the radio Saints

Terence de Marney as 'The Saint'

The second episode of the radio serial based on the adventures of the Leslie Charteris hero will be broadcast this evening at 7.10.

Terence de Marney as the first of the radio Saints and the only version of the Saint to be played over the British airwaves

THE SAINT ON RADIO:

A RESUME.

Radio Eirrann 1939 GB
Starring Terence De Marney as The Saint.
Directed by Derrick De Marney and Harold Cooper.
Scripts by Arthur La Bern.

BBC Forces Band 1940 GB
Starring Terence De Marney as The Saint.
Produced by Peter Creswell.
Original Charteris stories adapted by James Parrish.

1. *Prince Shamyl of Cherkessia (18 October 1940)*
What is Simon Templar's interest in the fabulous new crown being made for the mysterious Prince Shamyl of Cherkessia?

2. *The Policeman with Wings (25 October 1940)*
The Saint adds Impersonation of a Police Officer to his list of crimes.

3. *The Five Thousand Pound Kiss (1 November 1940)*
Can The Saint pull off an audacious Jewel robbery?

4. *The Inland Revenue (8 November 1940)*

5. *The Benevolent Burglary (15 November 1940)*
An arrogant millionaire throws down a challenge to The Saint.

6. *The Man Who Liked Ants (22 November 1940)*
The Saint crosses swords with a mad scientist and his giant ant.

National Broadcasting Company 1945 US
Starring Edgar Barrier as The Saint.
with John Brown as Inspector John Fernack and Ken Christy as Hoppy Uniatz.
Series broadcast from 6 January 1945.

Columbia Broadcasting Systems 1945 US
Starring Brian Aherne as The Saint,
with Louise Arthur as Patricia Holm.
Series broadcast from 20 June 1945.

Columbia Broadcasting Systems 1947 US
Starring Vincent Price as The Saint
Series broadcast from Summer 1947.

Mutual Broadcasting System 1949 US
Starring Vincent Price as The Saint.
Announcer – Merrill Ross.
Music score by Harry Zimmerman.
Directed by Thomas A. McAvity.
Produced by James L. Saphier.
Series broadcast from July 1949.

The Radio Showcase company of America has released many classic 'Golden Age' radio shows commercially. The following lists credits and storylines to their Saint episode releases:
The Conolly Silver Mine (31 July 1949)
In Mexico, a gypsy fortune teller warns The Saint to beware of meeting a young blonde girl – she could mean death to him. Nevertheless, soon afterwards Templar finds himself helping a young blonde girl with her silver mine.
Writer – Michael Cramoy
Featuring – Harry Bartell, Barney Phillips and Coleen Collins.

The Old Man's Car (14 August 1949)
The Saint steps in when two men try to steal a car belonging to an elderly man. The car, a virtual wreck, seems worthless, but then why did the two men try and steal it?
Writer – Michael Cramoy
Featuring – Lurene Tuttle, Barney Phillips and Daniel O'Herlihy.

The Color-Blind Killer (13 September 1949)
Simon Templar is relaxing on board a luxury cruise liner where he meets Barbara, a beautiful actress. One foggy evening Barbara is pushed overboard and Templar is coshed. When he regains consciousness, The Saint investigates.
Writer – Michael Cramoy.
Featuring – Betty Lou Gerson, Jean Baters, Bill Conrad and Barney Phillips.

Prove I Killed Carter (7 November 1949)
Potts has murdered his business partner Carter; or so Potts claims when he calls on The Saint. Later, the supposed 'dead man' Carter also visits Templar. Later still, Carter is killed for a second time.
Writer – Louis Vittes
Featuring – Betty Lou Gerson and Larry Dobkin.

The Fake Amnesia Killer (13 November 1949)
In San Francisco a young girl rushes up to The Saint and throws her arms around him, although Templar has never seen her before. She has mistaken him for someone she was supposed to meet – but she doesn't know who. Come to that, she doesn't know who she is herself . . .
Writer – Louis Vittes
Featuring – Peggy Webber, Tom Brown and Dan O'Herlihy.

The Purloined Pastry (Broadcast 1950)
The Saint goes to a local bakery shop for a loaf of bread. Suddenly the assistant thrusts a cake at him as two men enter the shop, one of them with a gun. Templar is forced to leave at gunpoint and taken for a taxi ride. Later The Saint returns to the shop and breaks in. Inside he finds a body.
Writer – Louis Vittes
Featuring – Peter Leeds, Dan O'Herlihy, Larry Dobkin and Betty Lou Gerson.

National Broadcasting Company 1950 US
Starring Vincent Price as The Saint.
Announcer – Don Stanley
Music score by Von Dexter
Directed by Helen Mack
Series ran from early 1950.

Vincent Price as the famous Simon Templar

Murder in the Theater (22 March 1950)
As The Saint walks past a theatre, shots ring out from inside and a man is killed. An actress rushes out of the theatre just as Templar is climbing into a cab. The girl jumps in with him and The Saint is off on another adventure.
Writer – Sidney Marshall
Featuring – Frances Chaney, Eleanor Audley and Frank Gerstle.

Mercer Bennet (14 January 1951)
The Saint goes to see the latest play starring famous stage actor Mercer Bennet. Backstage, after the performance, Bennet confesses to Templar that he's worried that his real life seems to be imitating his stage roles – and in his next play he is to portray a wife-murderer. He asks the Saint for help.
Writer – Dick Powell
Featuring – Ed Begley and Maggie Morley.

THE SAINT ON FILM

LESLIE CHARTERIS conceived and worked out the plot of *The Saint in New York* just prior to the ending of Prohibition in the States in 1933. It was at that time, before its publication, that Hollywood's movie-makers took an interest in the character of The Saint in general and his adventure in New York in particular. A script for *The Saint in New York* was written and the leads were cast. The Saint was to be played by the well-known and highly respected American actor, Frederick March, and the alluring 'bad girl' of the story, Fay Edwards, was to be played by the hypnotic Barbara Stanwyck. Alas, it was not to be – The Saint was up against an unlikely but formidable enemy: an unremarkable-looking, bespectacled man whose shadow loomed large over Hollywood, Will H. Hays. Hays was the President of the Motion Picture Producers' and Distributors' Association of America, and the author of their Production Code (published in 1930). This set of guidelines for Producers, more familiarly known as the Hays Code, was contrived to curtail the (allegedly) immoral, anti-social and sacrilegious excesses of the film-makers. The numerous gunfights essential to the barnstorming plot of *The Saint in New York* fell foul of the Hays Code, and that opposition put paid to the project. This was a great pity as any reservations one might have had as to the amiable Frederick March as the lethal Simon Templar would have been outweighed by the prospect of Stanwyck, an archetypal film noir femme-fatale, as the doomed anti-heroine.

Just under five years later in 1938, with attitudes to censorship relaxing, *The Saint in New York* was filmed. RKO Radio Pictures Inc. became base camp for the movie adventures of Simon Templar. The studio, one of Hollywood's 'Big Five' production outfits, struggled throughout most of its life against severe financial problems, but still managed gamely to issue a stream of well-crafted, well-performed, fondly remembered productions and even, occasionally, to offer up a true masterpiece such as *King Kong* or the classic *Citizen Kane*. RKO's most popular series of films were the dance romances featuring the inspired pairing of Fred Astaire and Ginger Rogers, but The Saint movies became the studio's second most successful series. South African-born Louis Hayward was loaned from Universal to play the role of Templar (Frederick March was now unavailable) and Kay Sutton took the female lead. Ben Holmes directed from a Charles Kaufman/Mortimer Offner screenplay, which remained faithful to Charteris's original novel of New York's gangland. The film was a huge hit with Saint enthusiasts and film fans alike and was one of the top five earners out of RKO's 42 releases that year. Immediately negotiations were started for the purchase of more of Charteris's Saint material.

Louis Hayward and Kay Sutton face romance and danger in, *The Saint in New York*

The following year Simon Templar's second movie appeared: *The Saint Strikes Back* based on Charteris's novel *She Was a Lady* (called *Angels of Doom* in the US). This time the urbane British actor George Sanders (borrowed from 20th Century Fox) stepped into Templar's immaculate shoes. He would play The Saint in five movies altogether. *The Saint Strikes Back* was another winner with its eponymous hero pitched against the San Francisco underworld. Sanders seemed perfectly suited to the role and effortlessly suggested the authority,

George Sanders takes up the role of The Saint and becomes the most famous of the cinema's Simon Templars

George Sanders and Sally Grey, *The Saint In London*

Paddy Carstairs (author, playwright, painter, director, etc.) finds The Saint working undercover for a government department to crack an international currency fraud case. The Lynn Root/Frank Fenton screenplay fairly crackles along and Sanders puts in another smooth performance, playing along nicely with the romantic interest, Sally Gray. The film, made as part of a quota plan arrangement, was another financial success earning $140,000 for RKO. Charteris himself was particularly happy with this interpretation of his work and remained a close friend of director, John Paddy Carstairs. Indeed, years later, it was Carstairs that set up the crucial meeting between Charteris and producer Robert Baker that led directly to the Sixties TV series of *The Saint*.

By the Forties the movie Saints were RKO's most popular series and the decade kicked off with *The Saint's Double Trouble*, a sub-standard entry that Charteris himself hated; he described the film years later as 'appalling'. With the emphasis on comedy, laughs were mined from the device of confronting Templar with an evil identical twin. The cracks were beginning to show by this time – although the fans kept on coming.

Later that same year (1940) came the release of the fifth movie in the series and the first one *not* to be based on an original Charteris story. *The Saint Takes Over* was conceived by screenwriters Root and Fenton but was very much in the Charteris style with its story of race-track tricksters who frame Inspector Fernack. Sanders by this time was becoming so laid back in his portrayal of Templar that occasionally he appeared to be about to drop off in mid-sentence. He was to make only one more appearance in the role of Templar in the next instalment released the following year. *The Saint in Palm Springs* was a decidedly low-key affair, the spring definitely missing in Saunders' suave step. The story was based on a Charteris original but the production failed to capture the essence of

confidence and suaveness that the Templar character commanded. The direction, by John Farrow, was tight and the script by John Twist was suitably lean and tense.

Later that year the production team travelled to England and returned with the fast moving *The Saint in London* based on the Charteris story, *The Million Pound Day*. The tale, competently directed by Renaissance Man John

Paul Guilfoyle and Jonathan Hale join up with George Sanders for *The Saint Takes Over*, the fourth Sanders Saint movie

the character in the way the earliest films had. Despite this the film was a considerable success at the box-office, netting a handy $90,000 profit for the studio.

Sanders' reign as The Saint finally came to an end and he handed over the halo to a fellow Brit, Hugh Sinclair. Sinclair's first appearance as Templar was in the 1941 offering, *The Saint's Vacation*, produced in England by William Sistrom from RKO's frozen funds. Despite the fact that Sanders had practically sleepwalked his way through the later movies, Sinclair still had quite an act to follow as, by this time, Sanders *was* The Saint to many of the movie-going public and throughout he managed to maintain that suggestion of absolute authority and confidence. Nevertheless Sinclair coped well enough in a modest little story of a murder mystery surrounding a music-box. Sally Gray co-starred as she had done in *The Saint in London* but as a different character. Almost immediately Sistrom began work on the next instalment in the series going back to the Saint's first published

Hugh Sinclair takes up the role of Simon Templar and co-stars with Sally Grey in *The Saint's Vacation*

adventure for *The Saint Meets the Tiger*, produced in England in 1941 for RKO Radio British Productions. RKO company executives viewed the finished film and considered it an unmitigated disaster with wooden acting, impenetrable British accents and a ludicrous plot. Washing their hands of the whole mess, RKO turned it over to Republic for US distribution and the movie finally sneaked out in 1943.

But even as *The Saint Meets the Tiger* was in production in England, back in the States a plot was being hatched which was unlikely enough to find its way between the pages of any of the Saint's adventures. George Sanders, still warm from the persona of Simon Templar turned up as another urbane and suave mystery-solving hero in *The Gay Falcon*. The character of crime-buster Michael Waring (known as The Falcon) had been created by Michael Arlen for the short story *The Gay Falcon* published in 1940. On screen, played by Sanders with a screenplay by Saint scripters Root and Fenton and with Saint series regular Wendy Barrie in the cast, the adventures of The Falcon bore more than a little similarity to the adventures of Simon Templar. Charteris certainly thought so – he brought a legal action against RKO, accusing them of plagiarism – and he had a good case. (RKO later settled out of court). The Falcon films took over from The Saints' as RKO's top grossing series and when Sanders finally tired of playing sophisticated sleuths he was killed off in *The Falcon's Brother*, the fourth film in the series, and replaced by Sanders' real-life brother Tom Conway as The Falcon's equally adept sibling.

Louis Hayward returns to the role of The Saint fifteen years after the first Saint movie

After the unpleasantness of the legal tussles had been forgotten RKO had one more involvement with The Saint. By the early 1950s, due to rising costs and a shrinking market, US companies were finding it difficult to produce the kind of 'B' Movies that had been their bread and butter in the decades before. British production companies, however, could provide such movies at reasonable costs and RKO took advantage of this, commissioning Hammer Films to provide *Whispering Smith Hits London* in 1952, and the following year they repeated the arrangement in

an attempt to revive The Saint series with *The Saint's Return* (US title: *The Saint's Girl Friday*). Louis Hayward, the first screen Saint, was despatched to play the role in which Templar investigates the murder of a girlfriend in London and tries to prevent a similar fate happening to his current ladyfriend, Lady Carol Denbeigh (played by Naomi Chance). The film wasn't successful enough to warrant any more sequels and is notable mainly for a brief appearance by the young and attractive Diana Dors, looking not unlike Marilyn Monroe. Interestingly the British version ran some five minutes longer than the US release.

So after nine films RKO's interest in The Saint came to an end. This wasn't the end for Simon Templar's large-screen adventures, although his next outing would find him demonstrating his command of foreign languages by speaking fluent French for the entire movie in *Le Saint Mene La Danse* (*The Saint Leads the Dance*).

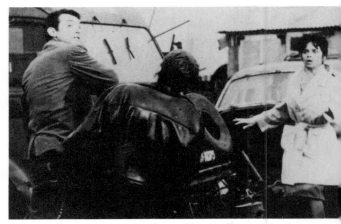

Felix Marten as Simon Templar tackles a villain as the Saint movies go off in a new direction

The Saint books, translated in over 15 languages, have always had a strong international following, particularly in France where the character was very nearly as popular as he was in Britain and the US. In 1959 the French production company, Lux Films, announced a new Saint movie, *Le Saint Mene La Danse*, to star Felix Marten as Simon Templar with direction by the young Jacques Nahum from his own script written with Albert Simonin and based on the Charteris story, *The Saint in Palm Springs*. The film, a comedy thriller, was released the following year to generally friendly reviews, Marten commended for his nonchalant Templar and mention made of the 'trois jolies femmes'.

Five years later (1965), with the British TV series of *The Saint* in full swing, the French released another large-screen adventure of Simon Templar, *Le Saint Prend L'Affut* (*The Saint Lies in Wait*), this time with French swashbuckler Jean Marais in the lead role (at 52 by far the oldest screen Saint). This was an Intermonde Production directed by Christian Jacque from a screenplay by Jean Ferry and Henri Jeanson. Charteris made no secret of his low opinion of the French efforts and no further exploits of *Le Saint* were made.

By the end of the Sixties the internationally syndicated *Saint* TV series had established Roger Moore as the definitive Simon Templar. The Saint's next large-screen outings would consist of two-part episodes from the TV series released theatrically (these are dealt with in the chapter, 'The Saint on TV').

THE MOVIES

THE SAINT IN NEW YORK
(RKO Radio Pictures 1938)

Simon Templar	**Louis Hayward**
Fay Edwards	**Kay Sutton**
Hutch Rellin	**Sig Rumann**
Inspector Fernack	**Jonathan Hale**
Red Jenks	**Jack Carson**
Hymie Fanro	**Paul Guifoyle**
William Valcross	**Frederick Burton**
Papinoff	**Ben Weldon**
Vincent Nather	**Charles Halton**
Sebastian	**Cliff Bragdon**
Screenplay by	**Charles Kaufman,**
	Mortimer Offner
Directed by	**Ben Holmes**
Produced by	**William Sistrom**

A committee organised by a man called Valcross, enlists the help of Simon Templar in getting rid of the gangsters that rule the city. Using the cover of his mysterious personality as The Saint. Simon starts to work on a list of six criminals. His first victim is a man called *Irboll*. He then wrests some cash out of *Irboll's* crooked lawyer, Nather.

As Simon's investigations continue he discovers that there is a seventh crook, an unknown leader of the gang. Seeking him, Simon becomes trapped in a nightclub by the gang, but he manages to escape by killing one of his captors, and then manages to release a young girl, Fay, who was being held for ransom.

Simon trails another crook, Papinoff, who is marked for death after letting The Saint escape from the club. Suddenly Simon is overtaken by two gunmen, Red and Hymie, who shoot Papinoff and are about to kill him when they are interrupted by Fay. Seeing his chance, Simon tackles the two men and they are both killed.

Fay promises to reveal the identity of the top man to Simon, but while he is recuperating from his wounds from the battle with Red and Hymie, Inspector Fernack arrives and proceeds to arrest him. Simon makes a deal with Fernack. He arranges to bring in 'Mr Big', or else he will surrender himself for trial. Simon's next victim is a 'hood' called Rellin. A surprise is in store for Simon as Fay leads him to 'Mr Big'.

Running Time 69 mins.

Louis Hayward and Kay Sutton

THE SAINT STRIKES BACK
(RKO Radio Pictures 1939)

Simon Templar	George Sanders
Val Travers	Wendy Barrie
Inspector Fernack	Jonathan Hale
Cullis	Jerome Cowan
Allan Breck	Neil Hamilton
Zipper Dyson	Barry Fitzgerald
Webster	Robert Elliott
Harry Donnell	Russell Hopton
Pinky Budd	Edward Gargan
Commissioner	Robert Strange
Martin Easton	Gilbert Emery
Secretary	James Burke
Mrs Fernack	Nella Walker
Screenplay by	John Twist
Directed by	John Farrow
Produced by	Robert Sisk

The Saint is in San Francisco to investigate the mysterious suicide of a police inspector, who had been dismissed from the force for receiving stolen bank notes. Simon is looking into the case at the request of his old friend, Inspector Fernack, of the New York Police Department. Fernack believes his colleague was framed, possibly by one of his fellow officers.

Simon's investigations lead him to clash with Valerie Travers, the strong-willed daughter of the dead man. She plans to take her revenge her own way. She starts up her own gang in an attempt to bring the crooks to justice. After she comes up against Simon a couple of times she discovers that Simon is an expert in dealing out justice to the ungodly.

Running Time 64 mins.

Based on the novel, *She was a Lady*.

The novel was set in London, with Simon involved once again with Inspector Teal. The movie location switched to the more glamorous San Francisco, with Teal being replaced by his New York counterpart, Inspector Fernack.

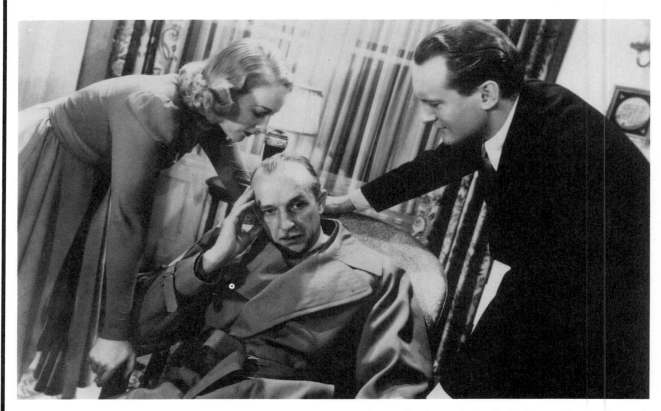

George Sanders and Wendy Barrie console Jonathan Hale

THE SAINT IN LONDON
(RKO Radio Pictures 1939)

Simon Templar	George Sanders
Penny Parker	Sally Grey
Dugan	David Burns
Inspector Teal	Gordon McLeod
Bruno Lang	Henry Oscar
Kusella	Ralph Trueman
Stengler	Carl Jaffe
Mrs Morgan	Nora Howard
Blake	Ballard Berkley
Wilkins	Ben Williams
Mrs Buckley	Athene Seyler
Count Duni	John Abbott
Screenplay by	**Lynn Root, Frank Fenton**
Directed by	**John Paddy Carstairs**
Produced by	**William Sistrom**

Simon Templar returns to England and becomes involved in a mysterious mission with Blake, an old acquaintance. At his friend's request Simon visits the Morgan's, and meets Penelope Parker, an attractive American girl, and Bruno Lang, another visitor.
As Simon leaves the house he finds a card on the wheel of his car bearing the message 'Bruno Lang vs. The Saint'. As Lang leaves Simon follows him, and as Lang retires,

Simon enters the house and takes some papers out of his safe. Suddenly, Lang enters the room and demands the return of the papers. Simon outwits him and as he returns to his car he finds Penelope waiting for him.
As Simon is about to take Penelope home they hear a scream and a man rushes into the beam of the car's headlights. Simon recognises the man as Count Duni, a noted diplomat, who has been held captive at the Lang

A publicity poster from the movie

residence. Duni is followed by one of Lang's men, whom Simon deals with swiftly.

Lang telephones *Kussella* and tells him of Duni's escape, and of Simon's involvement. Simon returns home and places Penelope in the care of Duggan, his general handyman. Later he takes Duni to the home of Mrs Buckley, an old friend who runs a boarding house. Later Count Duni tells Simon of Lang's plans to cheat his government out of a million in a currency fraud.

Inspector Teal receives an account of the incident outside Lang's house from a local constable, and traces the car to Simon. Meanwhile The Saint hands the document he took from Lang's safe to his friend, Blake. Shortly afterwards Simon returns home to discover from *Duggan* that Penny had left the flat to follow *Kussella*, and has been captured by him.

Kusselli telephones Simon and offers to exchange Penny for Count Duni, but before the trade can go ahead, *Kusselli* holds Simon along with Penny. It's up to Duggan to rescue them, which he does, but returning home, Simon finds Count Duni dead and Inspector Teal waiting for him. The evidence points to Simon having murdered the Count, and the Inspector arrests him. Simon convinces Teal that he is innocent and that if he is allowed to go free he will catch the real killers. Simon visits Mrs Buckley and discovers that Duni telephoned a man called Stengler at a foreign Embassy. Simon visits Stengler, but the man refuses to reveal what the Count told him over the telephone.

A few more people will die before the case is closed, and Simon can leave to continue his eternal struggle against crime.

Based on the story, *The Million Pound Day*.

Running Time 73 mins.

George Sanders with Gordon McLeod as Inspector Teal

THE SAINT'S DOUBLE TROUBLE
(RKO Radio Pictures 1940)

Simon Templar	George Sanders
Anne Bitts	Helena Whitney
Inspector Fernack	Jonathan Hale
Partner	Bela Lugosi
Bohlen	Donald MacBride
Limpy	John F. Hamilton
Professor Bitts	Thomas W. Ross
Monk	Elliott Sullivan
Express Man	Pat O'Malley
Card Player	Donald Kerr
Screenplay by	Ben Holmes
Directed by	Jack Hively
Produced by	Cliff Reid

The Saint finds he has more trouble than usual when he is faced with a criminal who is his exact double.

An Egyptian mummy containing stolen uncut gems is shipped to a college professor by the leader of a gang of jewel thieves. When the professor discovers the gems, he is killed by the gang leader, a man who is the spitting image of Simon Templar.

The Professor's daughter, Anne, asks Simon to help her uncover the killers of her father. Partner, the mystery man who shipped the mummy from Egypt, arrives on the scene.

It is not long before Simon assumes the identity of his double in an attempt to bring the killers to justice. Several complex twists occur before the diamonds are recovered, and The Saint is able to close another case.

Running Time 68 mins.

Simon Templar discovers another corpse

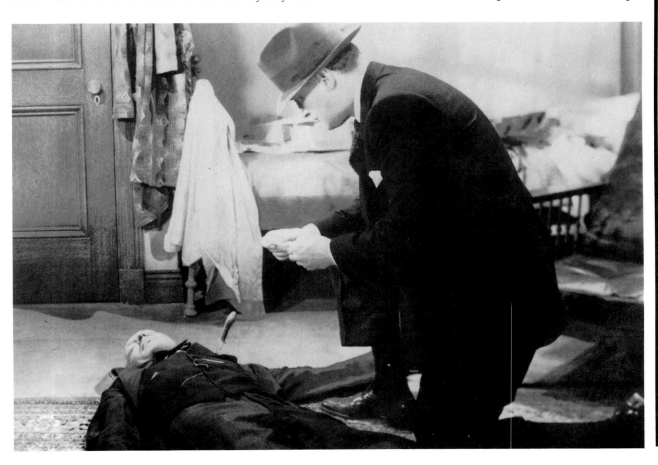

THE SAINT TAKES OVER
(RKO Radio Pictures 1940)

Simon Templar	George Sanders
Ruth	Wendy Barrie
Inspector Fernack	Jonathan Hale
Pearly Gates	Paul Guilfoyle
Sam Reese	Morgan Conway
Leo Sloan	Robert Emmett Keane
Max Bremer	Cyrus W. Kendall
Mike	James Burke
Captain Wade	Robert Middlemass
Weldon	Roland Drew
Lucy Fernack	Nella Walker
Egan	Pierre Watkin

Screenplay by	Lynn Root, Frank Fenton
Directed by	Jack Hively
Produced by	Howard Benedict

Simon Templar returns to New York after a stay in London and he finds that his old friend, and sometime enemy, Inspector Fernack, is in trouble – $50,000 has been found in his safe.

A publicity poster from the movie

A short time earlier Fernack had arrested 'Rocks' Weldon, a criminal. The case had fallen apart when the chief witness, Johnnie Summers, had been killed. It now appears that someone had bribed Fernack to try and convict Weldon.

Simon knows his old friend well enough to realise that he has been framed. He later discovers that the man behind the frame is Big Ben Egan, along with his cohorts, Weldon, Bremer and Reese. Egan, collected $90,000 to cover the cost of framing Fernack. That night Weldon sends Pearly Gates to rob Egan's safe. Pearly is surprised by Egan, who sends him back to Weldon, and after that night when Simon breaks into Egan's house, he finds him dead. Fernack arrives a few seconds later.

Simon finds a camera rigged up near the safe, and when the film is developed it shows Pearly Gates in the act of opening the safe. With this evidence Simon forces Pearly to help them in their efforts to clear Fernack.

Weldon is killed before Simon and Fernack can question him. They then kidnap Sloan, but an unknown assassin kills him and while he is being held at Fernack's house, Simon meets up with Ruth, a young girl he met on board the ship, crossing over from England. Simon soon realises that she is involved in the case, and may be responsible for the deaths of Egan and the others. He finds out that she is the sister of Johnnie Summers, and she is out to avenge the death of her brother.

Ruth agrees to help Simon in trying to bring the gang to justice and clear Fernack. Meanwhile Inspector Fernack has been arrested when he is found by the police with Sloan's corpse.

Simon enlists Pearly's help in tricking Reese and Bremer into confessing that they killed Johnnie Summers and framed Fernack. A couple more people will die before the Saint is able to clear Fernack.

Running Time 69 mins.

THE SAINT IN PALM SPRINGS
(RKO Radio Pictures 1941)

Simon Templar	**George Sanders**
Elna Johnson	**Wendy Barrie**
Pearly Gates	**Paul Guilfoyle**
Inspector Fernack	**Jonathan Hale**
Margaret Forbes	**Linda Hayes**
Mr Evans	**Ferris Taylor**
Chief Graves	**Harry Shannon**
Detective Barker	**Eddie Dunn**
Whitey	**Richard Crane**
Mr Fletcher	**Charles Quigley**

Screenplay by	**Jerry Cady**
Directed by	**Jack Hivley**
Produced by	**Howard Benedict**
Cameraman	**Harry Wild**

An old friend of Inspector Fernack of the New York police has died abroad and left three rare vintage stamps to his daughter Elna, who is staying at Palm Springs.

Inspector Fernack calls on The Saint for help when several attempts are made on the life of Peter Johnson, the man who is transporting the stamps to Elna. Simon calls on Johnson to collect the stamps. Johnson goes into the next room to collect a locket in which the stamps are enclosed, and suddenly, he is killed. Simon rushes into the room and struggles with the killers, but they make their escape without the locket.

Travelling to Palm Springs, Simon is attracted to a beautiful young girl, Margaret Forbes. He later discovers that she has ransacked his stateroom. As Simon checks into his Palm Springs hotel, he discovers that the house detective is Pearly Gates, a reformed pickpocket and old friend of Simon's.

After a fight with three unknown men, Simon finally gets to meet Elna, and hands over the locket to her. She opens it and discovers it to be empty. Simon enlists the aid of Pearly, who picks the pockets of all the hotel guests. The stamps are eventually discovered in the bottom of a pill box, but unfortunately, Pearly can't remember from which of the guests he stole the box.

Simon arranges with the police to advertise the stolen pill-box to be reclaimed and during this time a policeman is stabbed and the box disappears. Simon, however, had removed the stamps, and the crooks are led to believe that the stamps are in the hotel safe. Meanwhile, Elna visits Simon's home, and is stopped by Margaret, who demands the stamps. Margaret is shot dead by a mysterious criminal, and Simon devises a plan to bring the criminal to justice. He writes a note to Elna arranging to meet her with the stamps in the desert the following evening. Three of the hotel guests, headed by a man called Evans, intercept the note before passing it on.

That night, Simon sends Pearly with Elna to the desert. While he arranges to have a drink with Evans, Evans drugs Simon's drink, and while he is unconcious Evans searches him but fails to find the stamps. Evans and his men capture Elna and Pearly. Simon, who replaced the dope tablets with aspirin, sets out after them to bring them to justice and return the stamps to their rightful owner, Elna Massen, and then move on to his next adventure.

Running Time 66 mins

Paul Guilfoyle, George Sanders and Wendy Barrie check in to a Palm Springs hotel to find murder and mystery

THE SAINT'S VACATION
(RKO Radio Pictures 1941)

Simon Templar	Hugh Sinclair
Mary Langdon	Sally Grey
Monty Hayward	Arthur Macrea
Rudolph	Cecil Parker
Valerie	Leueen MacGrath
Inspector Teal	Gordon McLeod
Gregory	John Warwick
Emil	Ivor Barnard
Marko	Manning Whiley
Leighton	Felix Aylmer
Screenplay by	Jeffry Dell, Leslie Charteris
Directed by	Leslie Fenton
Produced by	William Sistrom

The Saint decides to take a vacation and he takes along with him his friend, Monty Howard. They arrive at Dover en route for the continent, and at the dockside, Simon evades a party of curious reporters, but Mary Langdon, a beautiful and persistent newswoman, decides The Saint is news, and worth following.

Later at a Swiss mountain resort Simon spots a British secret agent, Valerie, hand a small box to her companion, Gregory. The exchange is also observed from an upper window by two men, Rudolph and Marko, members of a notorious international gang.

Mystery and suspense are found on *The Saint's Vacation*

When Gregory leaves with another man, Emil, Rudolph and Marko follow with Simon and Mary close on their heals, and during a struggle, Simon captures Emil and the box.

Later, Emil is mysteriously killed, and then Rudolph and Marko gain possession of the box. Simon follows them to their hide-out, and sees Gregory being tortured to reveal the combination that will open the key to its contents. Simon enters the room, gun in hand, and tackles the men. Monty joins in the fight, but once again Simon is forced to part with the mysterious package. Monty thinks that they have lost out, but Simon reveals to him that he handed the crooks an imitation box.

The following morning, in full view of Valerie, Marko and Rudolph, Simon posts a parcel which is placed in a mail bag and put on a train. Later on the train, Gregory is knifed by Rudolph, who later bribes the police to arrest Simon. Mary poses as Simon's wife and is allowed to see him. She reveals to The Saint that Monty has been captured by Rudolph. Simon, who has hidden the real package in Monty's suitcase, evades the police guard and goes to Rudolph's house.

Simon talks Rudolph into releasing Monty, and then confronts him with evidence that will send him to prison for a long time. Rudolph admits defeat, and Simon returns to Dover with Monty, Mary and Valerie. He is met at the port by his old friendly enemy, Inspector Teal. Teal arrests Simon, and takes him to the Yard, where it is discovered that the mysterious box is the key to a secret sound detector sought by the British Government. Teal, as in so many times before, receives orders to release Simon.

Whistling, Simon leaves; he has a dinner invitation with Valerie and Mary, and for The Saint the vacation is over.

Running Time 78 mins.

THE SAINT MEETS THE TIGER
(RKO Radio Pictures 1943)

Simon Templar	Hugh Sinclair
Patricia Holmes	Jean Gillie
Inspector Teal	Gordon McLeod
Sidmarsh	Clifford Evans
Horace	Wylie Watson
Bently	Dennis Arundell
Bittle	Charles Victor
Aunt Agatha	Louise Hampton
Merridon	John Salew
Police Constable	Arthur Humbling
Screenplay by	Leslie Arliss and Wolfgang Wilhelm
Directed by	Paul Stein
Produced by	William Sistrom

The Saint finds the dead body of a small-time gambler, and suddenly he is involved in a case of mystery and suspense. His investigations into the murder take him to Barcombe, a small town on the Cornish coast. There, The Saint comes up against, the Tiger, the deadly leader of a gang of smugglers. The Tiger is actually a man called Sidmarsh, who uses his cover as a newspaper reporter to hide his smuggling activities. That is until The Saint comes along, in a case which ends up with a mysterious ship loaded with gold bullion.

With the help of his man, Horace, and assistance from the lovely Patricia Holmes and with a fair amount of hinderance from the plodding, Inspector Teal, when The Saint meets the Tiger you can be sure that it won't be fur that flies.

The Saint's man Horace holds a gun on a suspect while Simon questions him

THE SAINT'S RETURN (THE SAINT'S GIRL FRIDAY) (Exclusive Films 1953)

Simon Templar	Louis Hayward
Carol Denby	Naomi Chance
Max Lennar	Sidney Tafler
Chief Inspector Teal	Charles Victor
Katie French	Jane Carr
Jarvis	Harold Lang
Keith Merton	Russell Enoch
Margie	Diana Dors
Irish Cassidy	Fred Johnson
Hoppy Uniaty	Thomas Gallagher
Screenplay by	Allan MacKennon
Directed by	Seymour Friedman
Produced by	Julian Lesser, Anthony Hinds
Music by	Ivor Slaney
Cameraman	Walter Harvey

The Saint returns to London in response to a telegram from Judy Fenton. He arrives, only to learn that Judy has been killed in a car 'accident'. Simon is convinced that her death was no accident and decides to investigate, much to the annoyance of Inspector Teal. Simon believes her death was connected somehow with some crooked gamblers to whom she had lost large sums of money. His efforts to solve the mystery lead him to the River Mob, a group of crooks operating from a luxurious barge.

Simon is aided by Carol Denby, a victim of the crooked gamblers, who is forced by them to lure the gullible into the club, to help pay off her gambling debts.

Running Time 73 mins.

Carol Denby (Naomi Chance) watches The Saint as he prepares to play for big stakes

LE SAINT MENE LA DANSE

(The Saint Leads The Dance)
(Films Du Cyclope [Roland Girard] – Lux Films. 1959)
Released 1960.

Simon Templar	**Felix Marten**
Fred Pellmann	**Jean Desailly**
Gina	**Nicole Mirel**
Norma	**Francoise Brion**
Dany	**Michele Mercier**
Le Maitre d'hôtel	**Jean-Roger Caussimon**
Le valet.de chambre	**Clement Harari**
Le chauffeur	**Henri Nassiet**
Le policier	**Andre Valmy**
Un voyou	**Jean-Marie Riviere**

Directed by Jacques Nahum
Script by Albert Simonin and Jacques Nahum
Music by Paul Durand

FREDDIE PELLMANN. who has inherited $5,000,000 employs Simon Templar as a bodyguard to protect him against possible assassination by the friends of an American gangster Pellmann had had arrested two months previously in New York. Simon moves into Pellmann's luxury property and is immediately suspicious of the millionaire's three servants and the three beautiful women who act as his girl-fridays.

But murder strikes the household. despite The Saint's presence. when the chauffeur is asphyxiated by car fumes. a dog is poisoned and one of the girls. Dany. is nearly knifed in bed.

The Saint must visit a cemetery and descend into a hidden cavern before he is able to throw some light on this shady affair and save not only Dany's life. but also his own as well.

Quite well received as a comedy-thriller in France but it failed to impress Charteris who blocked its release in English-speaking territories. Later. after seeing the second French attempt with Jean Marais. Charteris could take no more and refused to license further Saint movies to the French.

Felix Marten as The Saint views the case from a different angle

LE SAINT PREND L'AFFUT
(THE SAINT LIES IN WAIT)
Intermondie Prods France 1966

Simon Templar	Jean Marais
Hoppy Uniatz	Jess Hahn
Sophie	Daniele Evanou
Oscar	Henri Virlojeux
Fat Man	Dario Moreno
German	Jean Yanne
Screenplay by	Jean Ferry, Henri Jeanson
Directed by	Christian Jaque
Cameraman	Pierre Petit
Film Edited by	Jacques Desagneaux

This light-hearted adventure with The Saint has Simon Templar and his simple-minded companion. Hoppy Uniatz. chasing after a secret cache of American dollars that were hidden after the completion of a secret undercover operation during the war.

Several enemy agents are also after the loot. and Simon has to battle his way through a series of escapades and beautiful women until the money is recovered.

Running Time 90 mins.

Jean Marais takes up the role of The Saint in this light-hearted adventure of a middle-aged Simon Templar

THE SAINT BOOKS

(reissue titles in brackets)

Meet the Tiger, London, Ward Lock, 1928; New York, Doubleday, 1929 (*The Saint Meets the Tiger*, New York, Sun Dial Press, 1940).

The Last Hero, London, Hodder & Stoughton; New York, Doubleday, 1930 (*The Saint Closes the Case*, New York, Sun Dial Press, 1941).

Enter the Saint (3 Novellas) London, Hodder & Stoughton, 1930; New York, Doubleday, 1931.

Knight Templar, London, Hodder & Stoughton, 1930 (*The Avenging Saint*, New York, Doubleday, 1931).

Featuring The Saint (3 Novellas) London, Hodder & Stoughton; New York, Douleday; New York, Avon, 1931.

Alias The Saint (3 Novellas) London, Hodder & Stoughton, 1931.

Wanted for Murder, (Comprising *Featuring The Saint* and *Alias The Saint*) New York, Doubleday, 1931 (*The Saint – Wanted for Murder*, New York, Sun Dial Press; New York, Triangle, 1943).

She Was a Lady, London, Hodder & Stoughton, 1931 (*Angels of Doom*, New York, Doubleday, 1932, *The Saint Meets His Match*, New York, Sun Dial Press, 1941)

The Holy Terror (3 Novellas) London, Hodder & Stoughton, 1932 (*The Saint vs. Scotland Yard*, New York, Doubleday, 1932).

Getaway, London, Hodder & Stoughton, 1932 (*The Saint's Getaway*, New York, Doubleday, 1933).

Once More The Saint, London, Hodder & Stoughton, 1933 (*The Saint and Mr. Teal*, New York, Doubleday, 1933).

The Brighter Buccaneer (Short Stories) London, Hodder & Stoughton; New York, Doubleday, 1933 (*The Saint: The Brighter Buccaneer*, New York, Avon).

The Misfortunes of Mr. Teal, London, Hodder & Stoughton; New York, Doubleday, 1934 (*The Saint in London*, New York, Sun Dial Press, 1941; *The Saint in England*, New York, Avon).

Boodle(Short Stories) London, Hodder & Stoughton, 1934 (*The Saint Intervenes*, New York, Doubleday, 1934).

The Saint Goes On (3 Novellas) London, Hodder & Stoughton, 1934; New York, Doubleday, 1935.

The First Saint Omnibus: An Omnibus of Saintly Adventures (Compilation) London, Hodder & Stoughton, 1934; New York, Doubleday, 1939 (*Arrest The Saint*, New York, Permabooks, 1951).

The Saint in New York, London, Hodder & Stoughton; New York, Doubleday, 1935.

The Saint Overboard, London, Hodder & Stoughton; New York, Doubleday, Sun Dial Press, 1936 (*The Pirate Saint*, New York, Triangle, 1941).

The Ace of Knaves, London, Hodder & Stoughton; New York, Doubleday, 1937 (*The Saint and The Ace of Knaves*, New York, Avon, 1937, *The Saint in Action*, New York, Sun Dial Press, 1938).

Thieves' Picnic, London, Hodder & Stoughton; New York, Doubleday, 1937 (*The Saint Bids Diamonds*, New York, Triangle, 1942, *The Saint and the Thieves' Picnic*, New York, Avon).

Prelude for War, London, Hodder & Stoughton; New York, Doubleday, 1938 (*The Saint Plays with Fire*, New York, Triangle, 1942).

Follow The Saint (3 Novellas) London, Hodder & Stoughton, 1938; New York, Doubleday 1939.

The Happy Highwayman (Short Stories) London, Hodder & Stoughton; New York, Doubleday, 1939.

The Saint in Miami, Doubleday, 1940; London, Hodder &Stoughton, 1941.

The Saint Goes West (3 Novellas) New York, Doubleday; London, Hodder & Stoughton, 1942.

The Saint Steps In, New York, Doubleday, 1943; London, Hodder & Stoughton, 1944.

The Saint at Large (Short Stories) New York, Sun Dial Press, 1943.

The Saint on Guard (2 Novellas) New York, Doubleday, 1944; London, Hodder & Stoughton, 1945 (1 Novella published as *The Saint and the Sizzling Saboteur*, New York, Avon, 1956).

The Saint Sees It Through, New York, Doubleday, 1946; London, Hodder & Stoughton, 1947.

Call for The Saint (2 Novellas) New York, Doubleday; London, Hodder & Stoughton, 1948.

Saint Errant (Short Stories) New York, Doubleday, 1948; London, Hodder & Stoughton, 1949.

The Second Saint Omnibus (Compilation), New York, Doubleday, 1951.

The Saint in Europe (Short Stories) New York, Doubleday, 1953; London, Hodder & Stroughton, 1954.

The Saint on the Spanish Main (Short Stories), New York, Doubleday; London, Hodder & Stoughton, 1955.

The Saint Around the World (Short Stories), New York, Doubleday, 1956; London, Hodder & Stoughton, 1957.

Thanks to The Saint (Short Stories). New York. Doubleday. 1957; London. Hodder & Stoughton. 1958.

Senor Saint (Short Stories) New York. Doubleday. 1957; London. Hodder & Stoughton. 1959.

Concerning The Saint (Short Stories). New York. Avon. 1958.

The Saint to the Rescue (Short Stories). New York. Doubleday. 1959; London. Hodder & Stoughton. 1961 (New Edition. 1970).

The Saint Cleans Up (Short Stories from: *The Brighter Buccaneer. The Happy Highwayman* and *The Saint on The Spanish Main*) New York. Avon. 1959.

Trust The Saint (Short Stories) New York. Doubleday; London. Hodder & Stoughton. 1962 (New Edition London. Coronet Books. 1978).

The Saint in the Sun (Short Stories). New York. Doubleday. 1963; London. Hodder & Stoughton. 1964.

Vendetta for The Saint. New York. Doubleday. 1964; London. Hodder & Stoughton. 1965.

The Saint and the Fiction Makers ** (Adaption of TV script). New York. Doubleday; London. Hodder & Stoughton. 1968.

The Saint on TV ** (Adaption of two TV scripts). London. Hodder & Stoughton. 1968.

The Saint Returns ** (Adaption of two TV scripts). New York. Doubleday. 1968.

The Saint Abroad ** (Adaption of two TV scripts). London. Hodder & Stoughton. 1969.

The Saint in Pursuit (Novelisation of comic-strip). NewYork. Doubleday. 1970.

The Saint and the People Importers ** (Adaption of TV script). New York. Doubleday. 1971.

Saints Alive (Compilation) London. Hodder & Stoughton. 1974.

The Saint and the Hapsburg Necklace *** New York. Doubleday. 1975.

Catch The Saint. New York. Doubleday; London; Hodder & Stoughton. 1975.

The Saint's Sporting Chance (Short Stories). New York. Doubleday. 1975.

Send for The Saint **** (Adaptation of two TV scripts). London. Hodder & Stoughton. 1977; New York. Doubleday. 1978.

The Saint in Trouble ***** (Adaptation of two TV scripts). New York. Doubleday. 1978.

The Saint and the Templar Treasure ***** New York. Doubleday. 1978.

Count on The Saint. New York. Doubleday. 1980.

The Fantastic Saint (Short Story collection chosen by Martin Harry Greenberg and Charles Waugh). New York. Doubleday 1982.

Salvage for The Saint **** (Adaptation of TV script) London. Hodder & Stoughton. 1983.

* This is (virtually) the third volume of a trilogy begun by *The Last Hero* and *The Avenging Saint*.

** By Fleming Lea.

*** By Christopher Short.

**** By Peter Bloxham.

***** By Graham Weaver.

THE COMIC-STRIP SAINT

THE STYLE OF the character of The Saint lent itself well to comic-strip interpretations and numerous versions appeared over the years. Probably the most collectable are the 12 comics issued by Avon in the US between 1947 and 1952, which seem to include specifically-written new Saint adventures as well as collections of newspaper strips. Stories for these comics are by I. Ulmer and Walter Johnson among others, with Charteris himself scripting the newspaper strips drawn by Mike Roy, which appear in the later issues and which are reprints of the strips originally syndicated in 1944 and 1945. Charteris, incidentally, wrote for the syndicated strip *Secret Agent X-9* in the mid-thirties.

The syndicated *Saint* newspaper strip from the late 1940s

A selection of covers from the U.S. comic version

The mid-1950s British version of *The Saint* comic

In the 1950s the combination of Charteris as writer and John Spranger's artwork was seen in many newspapers and these strips have recently been reissued in comic-book form under Eternity Publishing's title *Private Eyes*. These are stylish adaptations, wittily plotted with a nice vein of black humour running throughout.

Also in the Fifties we find the *Super-Detective Library*, a pocket-sized comic featuring a number of different heroes. Six Saint stories were featured during the comic's run, and they appeared as follows:

Issue 1: *Meet The Saint in the Case of the Contraband People*.
Issue 15: *The Saint in the Case of the Vanishing Policeman*.
Issue 28: *You Can't Stop The Saint*.
Issue 33: *Danger, The Saint at Work*.
Issue 38: *The Saint Plays The Joker*.
Issue 59: *The Saint's Sunken Gold*.

During the heyday of the Roger Moore TV series in the Sixties, The Saint comic-strips were actually adaptations of the TV series, using that as their basis and not the character from the books. The small-screen-celebrating *TV Tornado* ran numerous strips of this type between 1967 and 1968. They were fairly primitive, but their cover-artwork (when it featured The Saint) was fine. The TV spin-off *Annuals* that accompanied both the Moore and Ogilvy series featured comic-strip interpretations of the programmes as well as specially-written short stories.

Translations and original adaptations of The Saint, turn up worldwide – especially alongside the international success of the TV series.

A variety of Saint publications

THE SAINT ON TV

The Roger Moore Years

I N 1961, INDEPENDENT Producer Robert S. Baker and ex-cameraman Monty Berman became partners in a new production company called New World, with offices in Jermyn Street in London. Shortly after the company opened an old acquaintance of theirs, director and writer John Paddy Carstairs, popped in to the office

Leslie Charteris, creator of The Saint. His creation is about to take shape on the small screen as The Saint comes to television

for a chat. He talked about Leslie Charteris, an old friend of Carstairs, and Baker suggested that The Saint would make a marvellous television series. Carstairs then arranged a meeting between Charteris, Baker and Berman which resulted in Charteris agreeing in principle to license The Saint for a television series. Baker took this agreement to Brian Tesler at ABC Television but he considered Baker's budgeting of each episode at £15,000 to be far too expensive for the company. Tesler suggested they take the idea to Lew Grade, whom they approached some time later at a charity function. They told him that they could offer the TV rights to all The Saint stories and Grade

arranged to see them at his offices the following Monday, when he agreed to buy the worldwide TV rights for £500,000. Baker flew to Florida and spent a week with Charteris ironing out the details and returned with Charteris's signature on the contract. Grade committed £30,000 to finance each episode (hour-long episodes being decided on) and the search was on to find an actor to play the television Saint.

Charteris had long wanted Cary Grant to portray Templar but when this suggestion proved unworkable he took no further part in the casting, although it was made clear that his ultimate approval in the matter was of paramount importance. The production team's first choice for the role was the Irish American actor Patrick McGoohan, currently a 'hot' property due to his compelling performance as Agent John Drake in *Danger Man* — a series then in limbo pending a decision on its future. McGoohan, however, scuppered the idea when he made it clear he wouldn't be prepared to play Templar in the style the producers outlined, as he considered the character too promiscuous. So with their first choice out of the running the search for a star was on. Many actors were considered, with the American Craig Stevens reputedly a major contender at one time, but the part went to the handsome British actor Roger Moore who, conveniently, was with one of Lew Grade's own theatrical agencies. Moore was taken to meet Charteris, who had no objections to the decision.

Moore was an inspired choice. The actor was no stranger to TV series, having played lead roles in *Ivanhoe*, *Maverick* and *The Alaskans*, and a few years previously had looked into buying the TV rights to The Saint, as he had always had a hankering to play the character. With the lead cast and the Canadian-born Hollywood teleplay writer Harry W. Junkin on board as script-editor, the show was ready to roll. At a press conference in Spring 1962, Lew Grade launched the series and introduced Roger Moore to the assembled representatives of the press. He announced that Moore was to play the famous Simon Templar in a series of 26 one-hour shows. This was news to Moore, who thought the episodes were going to be half-hour long and said as much at the launch. He realised in horror he had agreed to a salary he considered appropriate to half-hour shows for ones twice that length. Despite this, Moore launched himself energetically into the role and the series' subsequent success owed much to his portrayal of the famous Simon Templar. Moore brought a persuasive authority to the role that easily

Leslie Charteris visits Roger Moore on the set of *The Saint*

rivalled the efficient style of George Sanders in his early Saint movies. The TV Saint was often criticised for being a cleaned-up, diluted version of the lethal assassin of the Charteris books, but a curtailment of the character's more murderous activities was always inevitable considering the comparatively narrow boundaries of the TV guidelines. It is of more interest to view the TV version as quite a different character from his literary antecedent, and a well-rounded character in his own right. Although Charteris's stories were adapted for most of the TV episodes, it is a different Simon Templar that strolls through these plots. This one is a less egotistic, less whimsical, more likeable type, equally competent but less deadly to know than his precursor. He still has an innate sense of justice that is sometimes at odds with official views on the subject, but although he may still break the law, he now does it only as an expedient to obtain that justice and almost never for personal gain. The activities of this Templar are more often sanctioned by some legal body using The Saint as an undercover agent, but apart from this occasional link-up with covert organisations, this one is very much a lone-wolf and doesn't surround himself with a gang. (Although Hoppy Uniatz and Dicky Tremaine (sic) are featured in one segment apiece and Italian taxi-driver Marco Di Cesari reappears several times.

The character of Chief Inspector Claud Eustace Teal, however, did remain faithful to the books with Ivor Dean best remembered as the portly, gum-chewing Scotland Yard man.)

The Saint was a fast-moving, tightly plotted, good-looking action/adventure series which soon proved highly popular with the public and a little later with the critics as well. Roger Moore was lauded for his portrayal and even got his own fan club quite early on in the show's run. Grade sensing an 'in' to the US market flew over to the States in 1963 to try and persuade one of the major US networks to purchase the series. At NBC, Grade showed Vice-Chairman Mort Wener two of the best Saint episodes. Werner was appalled. As the second segment began he told Grade, 'I've never seen so much crap in all my life.' With NBC uninterested Grade tried CBS and ABC but to no avail: they found the show, 'too English' and 'too old-fashioned'. Disappointed, Grade had no choice but to deal with local TV stations and to sell the show for syndication where it might easily be lost in the schedules at some bizarre hour or find itself without a regular timeslot, being shown as a 'filler' whenever required.

Back in England production of *The Saint* was going from strength to strength. By all accounts the assembled company were having a good time making the series, which helped tremendously towards the smooth-running that is necessary for the assembly line nature of long-running series. Moore himself, an amiable practical joker, was instrumental in fostering the happy atmosphere. Not content with just playing the lead, he also tried his hand at directing a few of the episodes (starting with *Sophia* in 1964) and he enjoyed this task immensely, approaching each assignment with enthusiasm. The show was highly popular, the viewing audience appreciating its breezy pace, well-known guest stars and consistently entertaining episodes. Because the producers had the choice of 100 Charteris stories on which to base their episodes, the series never became predictable; on the contrary. Some weeks it would be a murder mystery, some weeks a morality tale, some weeks a romance, some weeks a whodunit and some weeks sci-fi or fantasy-related. All these factors combined to make *The Saint* a great success in its home territory, but Templar as a character always won through in whatever country he found himself and this trait seemed to carry through to his TV persona in the battle for a network showing in the States.

The syndicated showings of *The Saint* in the US, despite their irregular airings outside prime time, had still attracted some good reviews and a dedicated cult following in the two years since Grade's sale. One critic in the *New York Times* went as far to say that it was an excellent series compared with the lacklustre dross on the three main networks. In 1965 NBC found themselves with a trouble spot in their schedules. Late on Saturday nights CBS were showing old Hollywood movies which trounced all the opposition in the ratings. At an NBC board meeting when this was being discussed someone suggested that they should try running *The Saint* on the strength of its syndicated performance. The series could be bought relatively cheaply, so if it flopped it wouldn't be a financial disaster for the corporation.

NBC tried out *The Saint* in New York as an experiment and to their astonishment the series crushed the opposition. At first they assumed this was a freak result but when they ran episodes from the series at the same time for the next six weeks, the outcome was the same: victory for Simon Templar. NBC, though jubilant at their success, were still reluctant to believe that their initial verdict on the series could have been so wrong. Maybe they were witnessing a New York phenomenon and they suspected that the show's popularity wouldn't stretch across the country. But they repeated the New York experiment on their Los Angeles station and found the same result; likewise in Chicago. The US public loved *The Saint*.

Back in England, with the series 71 episodes completed, its future became the subject of discussion. Moore, like all actors in long-running series, had expressed concern about playing the same role for so long, but those thoughts never affected his sturdy performances. However with NBC now understandably very keen on the series Lew Grade flew out at the earliest opportunity to negotiate the sale of more episodes. All *The Saint* stories up to this time had been filmed in black and white, but NBC, like all the US networks, were now operating fully in colour with no new shows being produced in black and white. They did a deal with Grade for 43 new episodes of *The Saint* to be filmed in colour. Grade flew home and work commenced. The main difference in the organisation by this time was that Baker and Berman had gone their separate ways and Baker and Moore had formed their own company,

acquiring TRI (Television Reporters International Ltd) an all-but-defunct production company that had been set up in 1962 by a breakaway group of journalists from BBC's *Panorama* (Robert Kee, James Mossman and Ludovic Kennedy) with Malcolm Muggeridge and Lord Francis-Williams, to make current affairs programmes. They traded under the name Tribune (the name stemming from the TRI) and sometimes as Bamoore. Eventually 47 episodes were made in colour before Moore and the crew decided to call it a day. Towards the end of the run, one episode, *The Ex-King of Diamonds*, looks very much like a pilot for *The Persuaders*, Baker and Moore's next TV outing following their unhappy big-screen attempt *Crossplot*. The series was still popular when it finished and just prior to the end Moore received a Spanish TV award for his role as *El Santo*. The show was watched in 86 different countries including, eventually, Italy which had held out on the show since one early episode (*The Latin Touch*) portrayed the Rome Chief of Police as a secret Mafia member. The series made Roger Moore a rich man and a household name; it created a demand for British produced action/adventure series, and forged a definitive physical image for The Saint in the eyes of the public.

The Saint novels have been translated into many languages. This French edition contains stories taken from different novels

Comparisons between Simon Templar and James Bond are often made, and not just because Moore went on to play 007 a few years later. Both characters have become immensely popular twentieth-century heroes, enjoying larger-than-life adventures and proving irresistible to women. Both are elegant dressers and admirers of good food and wine. Both are quick-witted, physically adept, formidable at hand-to-hand combat and lethal with weapons. Both kill efficiently. But Charteris considered them very different types. In a 1967 interview he addresses such comparisons: 'Personally, I can't see any resemblance whatever. Just to take two major points: Bond had a "licence to kill" and the Saint always did it at his own risk. But The Saint always had fun with his adventures, while Bond always seems to take his so glumly and grimly. In the books. I mean – the movies are handled quite differently.'

Charteris is obviously quite right about this: indeed the filmed adventures of James Bond have probably got more in common in spirit with The Saint books than the Fleming books. and although there were obvious similarities between Moore's Bond and his Templar, those similarities were undoubtedly Moore's own characteristics. not traits pinched from The Saint.

THE SAINT – EPISODE GUIDE

A total of 118 episodes of *The Saint* were made: 71 in black and white. 47 in colour. The episodes took between 10 and 14 days to produce.

Many notable writers worked on the series with scripts by Michael Pertwee. John Kruse. Terry Nation. Norman Hudis and script-editor Harry W. Junkin among others.

Well-known names such as John Paddy Carstairs (who. of course. directed *The Saint in London* with George Sanders in 1939). Peter Yates. Roy Ward Baker. Leslie Norman. John Llewellyn Moxey and Freddie Francis all sat in the director's chair.

Moore enjoyed doing most of his own stunts. but for particularly dangerous moments he had a stunt double. Les Crawford.

The two two-part stories. *Vendetta for The Saint* and *The Fiction Makers* were both released theatrically in some territories.

A sample original script is reproduced on the following pages.

Script editor for the series, Harry W. Junkin

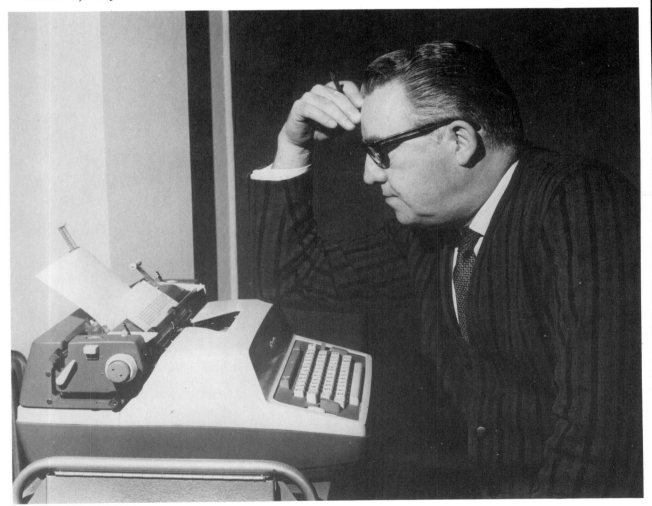

The Talented Husband

SET LIST

STUDIO OR LOCATION

THE SAINT
JOHN CLARRON
MADGE CLARRON
DR. SPRAGUE
ADRIENNE HALBERD
MR. HANKS
MRS. MARY JAFFERTY
MARIO
TICKET COLLECTOR
CHEMIST
GILBERT

NO LINES

BARTENDER IN COOKHAM PUB

PLAINCLOTHES POLICEMAN NO. 1
PLAINCLOTHES POLICEMAN NO. 2
DETECTIVE

EXTRAS

IN COOKHAM PUB BAR
IN COOKHAM RAILWAY STATION
IN COOKHAM RAILWAY STATION, FOUR
  HOURS LATER
GETTING OFF BUS IN COOHKAM HIGH
  STREET
IN SAVOY GRILL (WAITERS AND
  CUSTOMERS)
IN THEATRE BAR

THE TALENTED HUSBAND

ACT ONE
Fade in:
1   EXT. PICCADILLY CIRCUS NIGHT. (STOCK)
SHOWING THE ELECTRIC SIGNS, THE WHIRLING
TRAFFIC, ETC.

MIX TO:

2   EXT. A WEST END THEATRE. NIGHT. (STOCK)
*Any theatre will do. Crowds of opening night
playgoers, most of them in evening clothes, are
entering the theatre.*

MIX TO:

3   INT. THEATRE. NIGHT. (STOCK)
*Showing the curtain coming down at the end of an
act. The audience applauds, begins to leave the stalls
for an intermission.*

MIX TO:

4   INT. THEATRE BAR. NIGHT. (STUDIO)
*It is a typical small bar in a west end theatre and it
is crowded with people sipping drinks, smoking and
discussing the play. Since it is an opening night,
most of the people are in evening clothes.*

*The Saint, immaculate in a black tie, stands slightly
away from the crowd. He leans against an 'exit'
door, holds a full highball glass.*

CUT TO:

CLOSE SHOT: THE SAINT
*He drinks the entire highball without a pause for
breath. Then he turns, confidentially, to the camera*
SAINT: (*Low, Conversational*) Sorry to gulp my
drink. It's sheer self-defence . . . I'm bored
absolutely numb. It's taken two whole acts for an
inhibited young man with long hair and a bad
complexion . . . to ask a terribly dreary
overweight girl to marry him. I'm told that in Act

three she rejects the poor twit and goes to live in a tree house. (HE SHUDDERS) I call it the 'nothing-ever-happens-next' school of theatre. The drama of calculated inertia. Me . . . I like action. You know . . . murders, duels, battles, suicides, ghosts, explosions, thunderstorms . . . *and sex . . .* like Shakespeare. (*HE LOOKS OUT OF FRAME, REACTS NERVOUSLY*) Here comes the Producer's wife. What'll I say?

CUT TO:

MED. LONG SHOT: THE ROOM

Madge Clarron is working her way through the crowd towards the Saint. She is forty-seven years old and thinks about it constantly. Her figure is superb. She spends a great deal of time in beauty salons and looks it. She wears a stunning short evening dress, a diamond necklace, diamond bracelet, diamond earrings. She has a sort of younger Claudette Colbert quality and at the moment is flushed with happiness and excitement.

MADGE: (*Calling*) Simon! Darling!

CUT TO:

MED. TWO SHOT: MADGE and the SAINT

SAINT: (*He likes her*) Hello Madge.
MADGE: You're as wickedly handsome as ever! Now tell me honestly! *What* do you think of it?
SAINT: (*Straight*) Madge . . . I can honestly say I've never seen a play like this in my entire life! Never!
MADGE: (*Delighted*) Isn't it thrilling? Now you stay right here. I want you to meet John. He's so very clever. He was an actor once, you know.
SAINT: (*Sighing*) I know.

Madge moves out of the crowd towards her husband, John Clarron. John is actually forty-five but he looks ten years younger. He is extremely handsome in a rather 'actorish' way, with wavy black hair that is streaked with grey at the temples. He is of medium build with a trim athletic figure. He is a somewhat shorter and considerably younger edition of Walter Pigeon. He wears perfectly tailored tails.
He is surrounded by a crowd of admirers, is flushed and excited.

MADGE *moves to his side.*

MADGE: (*To the crowd*) I have to steal him from you for a moment . . . come, darling.

JOHN and MADGE move back towards THE SAINT.

CUT TO:

TWO SHOT : JOHN AND MADGE
PAN WITH THEM AS THEY MOVE THROUGH THE CROWD:

MADGE: (Bubbling) I want you to meet the most outrageously gorgeous fantastic man. I've told you about him. John, this is . . . Simon Templar.

CUT TO:

CLOSE UP: THE SAINT. (HEAD AND SHOULDERS) THE HALO INSTANTLY APPEARS, HOVERING OVER HIS HEAD.
INSTANTLY WE SUPER THE TITLE:

THE SAINT

SAINT MUSIC
DISSOLVE QUICKLY TO:
SAINT LINE DRAWING:
AND OVER THIS THE OPENING TITLES:
(AFTER TITLES)
FADE IN:

THE TALENTED HUSBAND (1962)

Simon Templar	**Roger Moore**
John Clarron	**Derek Farr**
Adrienne Halberd	**Shirley Eaton**
Madge Clarron	**Patricia Roc**
Mario	**George Roderick**
Dr Sprague	**Donald Churchill**
Mr Smith	**Norman Mitchell**
Gilbert	**John Kelland**
Chemist	**Clemence Bettany**
Screenplay by	**Jack Saunders**
Directed by	**Michael Trueman**

SIMON TEMPLAR travels to Cookham, a small town on the Thames, to visit an old friend, Madge Clarron. Madge has recently married John Clarron, an ex-actor and unsuccessful playwright. Madge has been recently confined to her bed after a near fatal accident, and according to Clarron is not well enough to see Simon yet. The main reason for Simon's visit is to investigate Clarron, whose two previous wives died in mysterious circumstances. Simon, staying at the local inn, meets Adrienne Halberd, a young lady who has taken the next house to Clarron so that she can keep a close watch on him. Simon and Adrienne team up, and take turns watching the house. Clarron employs an elderly Irish woman to help out with the cooking and cleaning while Madge is bedridden. The next day when Clarron travels up to London to discuss the script of his next play, Simon decides to search the house for clues, but where is the strange housekeeper, and can Simon prevent Madge from becoming the next victim of the talented husband?

Though not featured in the first episode of the TV series, in the 1957 book version, Chief Inspector Teal retires after The Saint helps him solve his last case, and he gives up trying to catch The Saint, after nearly 30 years.

Shirley Eaton becomes the first of the Saint's ladies, a handful of actresses who would return in different roles throughout the series.

THE LATIN TOUCH (1962)

Simon Templar	**Roger Moore**
Hudson Inverest	**Alexander Knox**
Maude Inverest	**Doris Nolan**
Tony Unciello	**Bill Nagy**
Marco	**Warren Mitchell**
Inspector Buono	**Peter Illing**
Signora Unciello	**Marie Burke**
Sue Inverest	**Susan Farmer**
Benson	**Robert Easton**
Screenplay by	**Gerald Kelsey and Dick Sharples**
Directed by	**John Gilling**

THE SAINT IS IN Rome, at the Colosseum, and goes to the aid of a young American girl who is being overcharged by a taxi-cab driver. Simon introduces himself to the girl, Sue Inverest, tells off the driver, Marco, but then offers to pay him a decent sum if he will wait while Simon shows Sue around the Colosseum. As Simon shows Sue round he is suddenly attacked by two men and knocked out. He comes to in a cell in the local police station next to Marco the cab driver. Inspector Buono charges Simon and Marco as accomplices in Sue's disappearance. US Governor Hudson Inverest and his wife are staying at the Embassy with the Consul, Benson, when they hear that Sue has disappeared, and that The Saint is under arrest. Inverest knows the Saint's reputation as a crime-fighter and orders Inspector Buono to release him. Simon joins them at the Embassy to help trace Sue, and later that day Inverest receives a telephone call from Tony Unciello, an American gangster who demands to see Inverest at a lonely rendezvous. Simon goes along with Inverest, posing as his chauffeur. Unciello is not after money; what he wants is the release of another gangster, Mick Keston, who is Tony's brother from death row and who is due to be executed in 48 hours. Only Inverest can order Keston's reprieve and Unciello gives the Governor 24 hours to order Keston's release or Sue will die. Unciello leaves and is followed by Marco, who trails him into town but then loses him in the traffic. Marco returns to the Embassy to report his failure to shadow Unciello. However, he has managed to find the address of Unciello's mother. Simon pays her a visit but she tells him that she has not seen her son for some time. Simon returns to the Embassy where he finds Inspector Buono with Inverest discussing the plans for Keston's release. Simon tells them that he has traced Unciello's hiding place through one of his men. Later that evening Simon goes to see Maria, Tony's ex-girlfriend. She has not seen Tony for some time and she shows Simon a deep scar on her face, a present from Tony. As Simon leaves he is picked up by Unciello's men, taken to see the mobster and held prisoner along with Sue. Time is running out for The Saint and Sue. Will Inverest give in to Unciello's demands and free a killer? Simon has just one chance to save the pair of them: he must employ the Latin touch.

Warren Mitchell makes the first of several appearances as Marco Di Cesari, a taxi driver.

Based on the 1954 short story.

THE CAREFUL TERRORIST (1962)

Simon Templar	Roger Moore
Nat Grindel	Peter Dyneley
Hoppy	Percy Herbert
Inspector Fernack	Allan Gifford
Jenny Hallam	Sally Bazely
Herman	David Kossoff
Lester Boyd	Gary Cockrell
Clinton	Robert Ayres
Dr Grant	Nicholas Stuart
Verna	Dorinda Stevens
Ricci	George Sperdakos
Floor Manager	Clay Johns

Screenplay by	Gerald Kelsey and Dick Sharples
Directed by	John Ainsworth

THE SAINT, relaxing in New York, watches a TV broadcast by his friend, the crusading newsman Lester Boyd. In his programme Boyd attacks Nat Grindel, the powerful boss of a crooked labour union. After the programme is over Boyd returns home and is killed when a bomb devastates his apartment. Simon decides to bring Grindel to justice and he replaces Boyd on his TV show. Just before the first broadcast an attempt is made on the life of Grindel. Simon is the prime suspect but he has been at the studio all day rehearsing the programme. That evening, Simon continues with the attack on Grindel and his union. Grindel decides that the Saint must be eliminated. After the broadcast, Simon receives a visit from Boyd's fiancée, Jenny. She was the person who made the attempt on Grindel's life, but she was shot while escaping. Simon calls a local doctor who tends to Jenny. The next day Simon confronts Grindel and threatens to expose him on the next broadcast with evidence left by Boyd. Grindel brings in 'Herman', a professional killer, and the man who planted the bomb in Boyd's apartment. 'Herman' perfects a double bomb, and Grindel's men posing as telephone repairmen, plant the bombs while the Saint is out. Simon returns to find the first bomb and calls in the police. Can Simon find the second bomb in time, or will he become the next victim of the careful terrorist?

Based on the 1957 short story.

Hoppy Uniatz was the Saint's general handyman in many of the earlier stories; this is the only episode of the TV series in which he appears.

Alan Gifford as Inspector Fernack questions Simon Templar while Percy Herbert as Hoppy Uniatz ponders on the future of his character

THE COVETOUS HEADSMAN (1962)

Simon Templar	**Roger Moore**
Valerie North	**Barbara Shelley**
Inspector Quercy	**Eugene Deckers**
Georges Olivant	**George Pastell**
Sergeant Leduc	**Robert Cawdron**
Josie Clavel	**Carole Grey**
Madame Duras	**Josephine Brown**
Kaplan	**Michael Spear**
Air Hostess	**Barbara Roscoe**
Antoine Louvois	**Esmond Knight**
Mario	**André Boulay**
Matron	**Natalie Benesch**
Screenplay by	**John Roddick**
Directed by	**Michael Truman**

ON A FLIGHT from New York to Paris The Saint is seated next to Valerie North, an attractive young woman who is on her way to see her long-lost brother. On arriving in Paris, Valerie discovers that her brother is dead and she is informed by Inspector Quercy that he was murdered. Simon takes Valerie for a drink in the hotel bar and on returning to her room she surprises a burglar going through her luggage, she screams and Simon races to her rescue. After a brief struggle the man escapes. Simon escorts Valerie to see Inspector Quercy to try and identify the man. On her return to the hotel Valerie is kidnapped by Georges Olivant, an ex-Nazi who is after a pair of St Christophers. One was taken from the dead man, and Valerie had the other, but now it is in the hands of The Saint. Simon visits Antoine Louvois, a good friend and one of the Resistance leaders during the war. Antoine examines the St Christopher and discovers strange markings on it. Simon must then bargain with Olivant for Valerie's life in exchange for the St Christopher, and a 20-year-old debt has to be paid before the case of the covetous headsman is closed.

Based on the 1954 short story.

Robert Cawdron makes the first of several appearances throughout the series as the harassed policeman, Sergeant Leduc.

THE LOADED TOURIST (1962)

Simon Templar	**Roger Moore**
Helen Ravenna	**Barbara Bates**
Fillipo Ravenna	**Edward Evans**
Oscar Kleinhaus	**Guy Deghy**
Galen	**Michael Ritterman**
Inspector Coudot	**John Dearth**
Jacques	**Andrew Sachs**
Butler	**Raymond Ray**
Alfredo Ravenna	**Joseph Cuby**
Carlo Visconti	**Norman Florence**
Garcia	**David Cargill**
Screenplay by	**Richard Harris**
Directed by	**Jeremy Summers**

THE SAINT IS AT Rome airport, about to take a flight to Geneva. He boards the plane and is seated next to a young man, Alfredo, whose father and stepmother are emigrating to the United States. Alfredo is upset because he does not want to leave his home. The Ravenna family stop off in Geneva for a couple of days on business before flying on to America. They are stopping at the same hotel as Simon and that evening as Simon relaxes on the veranda of the hotel he sees Fillipo attacked by a man in the hotel grounds. Simon goes to Fillipo's aid and chases

Guy Deghy as the mysterious Kleinhaus talks to The Saint about the murder of Fillipo Ravenna

off the man. Fillipo was stabbed and is dead. Simon is taken to the police station and questioned by Inspector Coudet about Ravenna's attacker. The Inspector believes that Simon is involved and they also question him about Ravenna's briefcase, which he was carrying. Simon returns to the hotel where he is stopped and questioned by a man called Oscar Kleinhaus, a man who was around at the time of Ravenna's murder. Simon goes to the bar and is joined by Helen Ravenna who offers him $5000 for the return of the briefcase. Simon returns to his room and finds Alfredo waiting for him. He tells Simon that he believes his stepmother is involved in his father's death. Simon decides to search the grounds where Fillipo was killed and with Alfredo's help he finds the briefcase. Back in his room Simon opens the case and finds diamonds worth a small fortune, and also an introduction to a man called Galen. The next day as he is leaving the hotel Simon runs into Kleinhaus again. He travels to the countryside to visit Galen, and posing as Ravenna he offers him a sample of the jewels. Galen is impressed but wants to see the rest of the diamonds. Simon agrees to see him that evening with the remainder of the jewels. Garcia, the man who killed Ravenna, breaks into Simon's room but he is interrupted by Kleinhaus who enters pointing a gun at him. Garcia panics and tries to escape onto the balcony; he slips, and falls to his death. Simon returns to his hotel, is again questioned by the police and identifies Garcia as the man who killed Ravenna. Simon returns to his room to find Kleinhaus waiting for him with a gun. Can Simon uncover the identity of the mysterious Kleinhaus, and find out who was really behind the plot to kill the loaded tourist?

Based on a 1954 short story.

THE PEARLS OF PEACE (1962)

Simon Templar	**Roger Moore**
Consuelo	**Dina Paisner**
Joss Hendry	**Erica Rogers**
Brad Ryan	**Bob Kanter**
Harry Tiltman	**Robin Hughes**
Pedlar	**John Barrard**
Mike Harris	**Warren Stanhope**
Screenplay by	**Richard Harris**
Directed by	**David Greene**

THE SAINT IS IN Mexico, where he runs into an old friend, Brad Ryan, who asks him to loan him some money so that he can organise an expedition to search for some fabled jewels, the pearls of San Domingo. Simon advances him $3000. Brad's fiancée, Jocelyn, a mercenary and ambitious young lady also lends him $500. Brad leaves on his quest with his partner Harry Tiltman, but he soon discovers that Harry is a crook. When they are in an isolated area, Harry attacks Brad. The two men fight and Brad is knocked down, hitting his head on a rock. Several years pass by and Simon finds himself back in Mexico. Out of the blue he receives a visit from Jocelyn who shows him a letter that she had recently received from Brad saying that he has found the pearls. Jocelyn is anxious to return to San Domingo to see Brad, and more importantly the pearls, and she persuades Simon to accompany her. Jocelyn believes that if Brad has found the pearls, she can relieve him of them. They reach San Domingo and Simon is shocked to find that Brad has lost his sight as a result of the bump on the head when he fought Tiltman. Simon discovers that for the last few years he has been cared for by a very plain girl called Consuelo, who is nothing compared to Jocelyn, but she has cared for and looked after Brad constantly since the accident. Brad is convinced that he has the pearls, but they are just worthless stones. Consuelo has been afraid to tell him, and has worked day and night to raise the money each time Brad decides to sell a pearl. Consuelo is saving desperately for an operation for Brad, in the hope that he may regain his sight, although she believes that if he does he will no longer want her. Jocelyn is recently divorced and quite wealthy, and she decides to break up the affair between Brad and Consuelo. Simon has a plan to teach Jocelyn a lesson and succeeds in turning some worthless stones into the pearls of peace.

Based on the 1958 novelette.

THE ELEMENT OF DOUBT (1962)

Simon Templar	**Roger Moore**
Carlton Rodd	**David Bauer**
Inspector Fernack	**Alan Gifford**
Agnes Yarrow	**Margaret Vines**
Joe Sholto	**Bill Nagy**
Gilroy	**Ken Wayne**
Mary Hammond	**Anita West**
Stan Johnson	**Robert O'Neil**
Nurse	**Sarah Brackett**
Screenplay by	**Norman Borisoff**
Directed by	**John Ainsworth**

SIMON IS IN America, reading about the exploits of Carlton Rodd, a brilliant, but crooked, attorney. In a matter of months Rodd has won freedom for all his clients, from embezzlers to murderers. He is not concerned with their guilt, just the size of his fee. Simon decides it's time he took him in hand so he visits Rodd and warns him that the next case he takes he will take a personal interest in, and make sure the courts have a conviction. Rodd's next case is defending Joe Sholto, a man who burned down his warehouse for the insurance money. Cleaning woman Agnes Yarrow saw the fire, banged her head, and as a result lost her sight. A policeman investigating the fire was also killed. With Agnes's evidence the case comes to court, but on the witness stand Rodd's ruthless questioning of Agnes leaves her in a confused state and she is unable to identify Sholto's voice on a tape recorder. The case is dismissed and Sholto released. The case is over as far as the court is concerned, but not for Simon. He devises a plan to turn the tables on Rodd and Sholto, and comes up with the idea of making Sholto think Rodd is about to shop him to the police for a large reward. Sholto decides he must take action and take care of Rodd, now that Simon has put the element of doubt in his mind.
Based on the 1958 short story.

THE ARROW OF GOD (1962)

Simon Templar	**Roger Moore**
Lucy Wexall	**Elspeth March**
Herbert Wexall	**Ronald Leigh-Hunt**
Pauline Stone	**Honor Blackman**
John Herrick	**Tony Wright**
Floyd Vosper	**Anthony Dawson**
Janet Blaise	**Anne Sharp**
Arthur Gresson	**Gordon Tanner**
Major Fanshire	**John Arnatt**
Astron	**John Carson**
Dr Ralph	**Alex Mango**
Screenplay by	**Julian Bond**
Directed by	**John Paddy Carstairs**

THE SAINT IS IN THE Bahamas, in the town of Nassau, where he is a guest at a party given by the wealthy Lucy and Herbert Wexall. One of the guests at the party is Floyd Vosper, a vicious newspaper columnist, who digs out the dirt and scandal on the rich and famous. Most of the guests at the party are potential 'victims' of Vosper's scandal column. Among the guests are Lucy's sister, Janet, who is engaged to tennis star John Herrick. There is also

an Indian mystic, called Astron, and Wexall's secretary, Pauline. Throughout the day Vosper is gathering information on his 'victims' as he listens in on conversations. Later that evening after dinner Vosper is found dead in the gardens: he has been shot through the heart with an arrow. John Herrick is the prime suspect, as his future as a tennis player had been threatened by Vosper. As Simon investigates he finds 'skeletons in the cupboards' of almost everyone. Lucy may be a bigamist, and Vosper knew that. Simon also discovers that Arthur Gresson has been selling phoney stock and that Janet offered Vosper money to keep quiet about her affair. Astron is a charlatan and almost everyone has a secret to keep and a reason to want Vosper dead. Can Simon uncover the guilty party and if Vosper deserved killing who fired the arrow of god?

Based on the 1955 short story.

THE EFFETE ANGLER (1962)

Simon Templar	**Roger Moore**
Gloria Uckrose	**Shirley Eaton**
Clinton Uckrose	**George Pravda**
Patsy O'Kevin	**Patrick McAlinney**
Vincent Innutio	**Paul Stassino**
Superintendent Marsh	**Jack Gwillim**
Dan Morrow	**Roland Brand**
Des	**Kevin Scott**
Housekeeper	**Gladys Taylor**
Bartender	**Ronald Wilson**
Screenplay by	**Norman Borisoff**
Directed by	**Anthony Bushell**

THE SAINT, on vacation in Miami Beach, Florida, decides to relax on a fishing trip. Unable to find a free charter boat, Simon decides to visit one of the local night-spots. Simon meets the lovely Gloria Uckrose who invites him to join her on a fishing trip the next day. After losing a 36lb marlin the boat docks at Bimini, a small pleasure island, where Simon meets the unpleasant Mr Uckrose and his right hand man, Vincent. Simon believes the Uckrose party are up to no good, and suspects them of smuggling but cannot prove it. Gloria offers to leave her husband if Simon will go away with her, but the Saint suspects it's just a plot to get him to leave the island. Gloria asks Simon to leave the island first and says that she will follow on the next flight. Simon pretends to leave and moves into a small hotel, but he is followed by Vincent who tries to kill him. Simon calls in the local police and Uckrose is arrested along with Vincent on a charge of attempted murder. Gloria escapes to the fishing boat, but Simon catches up with her only to discover there are still bigger fish to catch, before the case of the effete angler is closed.

Based on the 1955 short story.

Honor Blackman as Pauline Stone is one of several murder suspects that The Saint must question

Shirley Eaton is about to get into hot water when she tries to trick The Saint

THE GOLDEN JOURNEY (1962)

Simon Templar	Roger Moore
Belinda Deane	Erica Rogers
Woodcutter	Paul Whitsun Jones
Hotel Manager	Roger Delgado
Guardia Civile	David Lawton
Guitarist	Ricardo Cortes
Head Waiter	Richard Montes
Joan West	Stella Bonheur
Screenplay by	Lewis Davidson
Directed by	Robert S. Baker

SIMON TEMPLAR, IS ON THE Costa Brava, relaxing, awaiting the wedding in ten days' time of a good friend, Jack Easton, to the lovely (but very spoilt and wealthy) Belinda Deane. Simon decides to teach Belinda a lesson, so with the cooperation of her aunt he sneaks into Belinda's room and takes her passport, jewellery and money. Belinda turns to Simon in desperation, but finds only an offer of a walking holiday from The Saint, which she rejects. She then attempts to steal a motor scooter, and is arrested by the local constable. Simon pays her fine and they start off the long walk to Torremolinos. After a series of painful mishaps Belinda slowly begins to see the error of her ways and realises that Simon is only trying to help her by teaching her a useful lesson. By the time they reach Torremolinos, Belinda is a changed person, having learned from The Saint a golden lesson on the golden journey.

Based on a 1954 short story.

Erica Rogers as the spoiled heiress, Belinda Deane, receives a painful lesson from the hands of Simon Templar

THE MAN WHO WAS LUCKY (1962)

Simon Templar	Roger Moore
Lucky Joe Luckner	Eddie Byrne
Inspector Teal	Campbell Singer
Jane	Vera Day
Marty O'Connor	Harry Towb
Eddie Toscelli	Charles Houston
Bailey	Nicholas Selby
Sergeant Stevens	John Forbes Robertson
Frank	Jack Taylor
Harry	John Sullivan
Cora	Delphi Lawrence
Screenplay and Directed by	John Gilling

SIMON RECEIVES A telephone call from a bookmaker friend, Marty O'Connor. He and his partner Bailey are in trouble because they are being forced to pay protection money to a vicious gangster called 'Lucky' Joe Luckner. Before Simon can offer them aid, Bailey is murdered. Marty is persuaded by his girlfriend Cora to go into hiding. Cora works in one of Lucky's nightclubs, and she believes that Marty will be killed next because Lucky wants her to be his girl. The Saint steps into the case, visits Lucky's club and speaks to Cora's friend, Jane, who tells Simon that Cora has borrowed some money from her so that she and Marty can get away to the country. Jane takes Simon to see Cora, and he works out a plan with them to help Eddie get out from under Luckner's clutches. Following Simon's instructions Cora telephones Lucky and tells him that she is going away with Marty. As part of the plan, Simon visits Lucky and offers to take him to Marty's hideout for $5000. Luckner agrees, and Simon tells him he will fix up a meeting for later that evening, and take him to Marty. Simon has come up with an ingenious plan to make Lucky Joe pay for Bailey's death. When Luckner crossed the Saint's path, it was an unlucky day for the man who was lucky.

Based on the 1939 short story.

Roger Moore questions Vera Day about her association with gangster, Lucky Joe Luckner

THE CHARITABLE COUNTESS (1962)

Simon Templar	**Roger Moore**
Countess Rovagna	**Patricia Donahue**
Aldo Petri	**Nigel Davenport**
Marco De Cesari	**Warren Mitchell**
Father Fellini	**Anthony Newlands**
Enrico Vespa	**Anthony Jacobs**
Princess De Ribes	**Marie Burke**
Count Alzemo	**Victor Rietti**
Signora Vespa	**Irene Prador**
Franco	**Philip Needs**
Screenplay by	**Gerald Kelsey and Dick Sharples**
Directed by	**Jeremy Summers**

THE SAINT IS IN Rome attending a charity ball given by the Countess Kristina Rovagna who is raising money for Father Bellini's mission for the homeless. One of the street orphans, Franco, is organising his gang of street urchins to rob the cars outside the Countess's house. As Simon leaves the house his taxi accidentally knocks down Franco as he is dashing across the road. Simon takes Franco to his flat. The boy is not hurt, just scared. Simon makes him take a bath, and then gives him a solid meal. Later Simon goes to see Father Bellini whom he persuades to take young Franco in but when Franco hears about it he refuses to go unless the other eight members of his gang can go as well. Simon discovers from talking to Father Bellini that only a small percentage of the money the Countess collects is passed on to the mission. Simon knows that the Countess used to be a stripper in a New York nightclub and he goes to see her. He accuses her of running a charity racket. He then finds that he has another problem on his hands when Father Bellini agrees to take in the boys and discovers one of them is a girl. (The mission is strictly for boys.) Simon has a plan to make sure that the Countess pays enough money to take care of the boys' future, but the Countess pulls a fast trick, leaving Simon at a disadvantage. Will the Countess win, or will Simon come up triumphant, and teach a lesson to the charitable Countess?

Based on the 1939 short story.

Simon Templar with the Countess Rovagna, played by Patricia Donahue, who will get the upper hand

THE ROMANTIC MATRON (1963)

Simon Templar	**Roger Moore**
Beryl Carrington	**Ann Gillis**
Ramon Venino	**John Carson**
Police Inspector	**Patrick Troughton**
Ernesto	**Joby Blanshard**
Commissionairi	**Victor Spinetti**
Landlady	**Madge Bradley**
Juanito	**Laurence Taylor**
Miguel	**Peter Diamond**
Chico	**Kaplan Kaye**
Manuel	**Peter Elliott**
Bernabe	**Christopher Rhodes**
Screenplay by	**Larry Forrester**
Directed by	**John Paddy Carstairs**

A SECURITY VAN travelling along the road is hijacked by two men. They block off the van when it enters a tunnel, the men are gassed, and their load of gold bullion stolen. The Saint is in Buenos Aires on vacation, staying at the Hotel Cordova. A middle-aged American woman, on holiday, Beryl Carrington, checks into the hotel. Shortly after she is followed by Ramon Venino; his car bumps into Beryl's and scratches her bumper, and he insists on taking it away and having it repaired for her. Ramon returns a few hours later with the car as good as new. He apologises again and offers to show her the sights of the town. For the next few days Ramon takes her all over the place, sight-seeing by day and dining by night. Beryl notices that for the last few days they have been followed by two men. Ramon says that they are after him, but will not say why. That evening in the hotel bar Beryl recognises Simon, and tells Ramon that he could help, but Ramon refuses. The next day Beryl calls on Ramon at his house because she is worried about him. Suddenly a shot is fired through the window which just misses Ramon. He tells her that he has a list of party members of an illegal movement that is planning to overthrow the present government. Ramon tells her that his life is in danger as long as he has the list. Beryl offers to take the list out of the country for him when she leaves in a couple of days. He gives her the list in a briefcase, and she returns to the hotel. Beryl spots Simon in the hotel bar and she asks him for help. He agrees and they put the briefcase in the hotel safe. Later that day Simon talks to the hotel manager about the state of the country, and is told that the people are happy and the government is good. Simon returns to his room and is attacked by two men who question him about the briefcase. Simon gets the upper hand and then calls the police to take care of the men. He then pays a visit to Ramon's house. He is out but the landlady says that he has only been there a couple of days. Simon goes to the garage to check up on Beryl's car. He is questioned by a big man there who suddenly attacks Simon and knocks him out. When Simon recovers he is tied up and strung up on a hoist in the garage. He is a prisoner of the men who committed the armoured car robbery. Can Simon escape from his captors and aid the romantic matron before she gets into any more trouble?

Based on the 1958 novella.

When The Saint tries to help a middle-aged matron with her love life, he soon comes up against the local gangsters

THE INVISIBLE MILLIONAIRE
(1963)

Simon Templar	**Roger Moore**
Rosemary Chase	**Katherine Blake**
Dr Quintus	**Michael Goodliffe**
Jim Chase	**Nigel Stock**
Nora Prescott	**Eunice Gayson**
Ellen Chase	**Jane Asher**
Marvin Chase	**Basil Dignam**
Bertrand Tamblin	**Mark Eden**
Inspector Welland	**Charles Morgan**

Screenplay by	**Kenneth Hayles**
Directed by	**Jeremy Summers**

THE SAINT IS IN London at the Stock Exchange, the heart of the financial world. Simon runs into Nora Prescott, an old friend who tells him that she is working for Marvin Chase, a very wealthy businessman. At the Chase country home Jim Chase calls on his brother Marvin. Jim is the black sheep of the family and he has come to see Marvin to borrow some money. Marvin refuses and Jim leaves. Marvin Chase has to drive into town on business taking with him his personal assistant, Bertrand Tamblin. Marvin knows that Tamblin is involved with his wife, Rosemary, and as they drive along the narrow country roads Chase increases the speed. The next day, Simon reads in the local paper that Marvin Chase and his assistant were involved in a major car crash. Tamblin was killed and Chase was severely burned on the face and hands. Simon rings up Nora and offers his assistance to the family. Jim calls to see his brother, but Rosemary and Dr Quintus say that he is too ill for visitors, heavily bandaged and constantly attended by his doctor. Chase starts to resume his affairs and Rosemary receives instructions from him to sell off certain of his business interests. When Nora receives the instructions to sell she goes to see Chase to confirm it. Worried, she telephones Simon and asks him to help. She arranges to see him later that evening in the local pub. When she arrives she sees Jim standing at the bar near Simon and she slips Simon a note to meet her outside at a nearby warehouse. Nora waits in the warehouse and suddenly a man comes in. It is not Simon. He stabs her with a long knife and she screams out. Hearing the scream Simon rushes into the room, the man fires at him and runs off. Jim Chase suddenly appears, and Simon tells him to call the police. Inspector Welland takes charge of the case. Ellen Chase talks to Simon and explains that she is worried something has happened to her father. Inspector Welland calls to question Chase, but is unable to do so as he is heavily sedated. Simon visits a broker friend in the City who tells him that Chase is selling off a lot of his stock. Later that day Simon has lunch with Ellen at the local pub. She tells him about the crash and, in particular, that the car's clock stopped at nine minutes past eleven. Later Simon talks to the local postman, who says that Chase's car passed him only seconds before the crash at exactly 11pm. What happened in the missing nine minutes? Can Simon avenge the death of Nora? What is the mystery behind the invisible millionaire?

Based on the 1938 novella.

Millionaire Marvin Chase is badly injured in a car crash. His daughter Ellen (Jane Asher) calls on The Saint to help

THE GENTLE LADIES (1963)

Simon Templar	Roger Moore
Florence Warshed	Avice Landon
Ida Warshed	Renee Houston
Violet Warshed	Barbara Mullen
Alfred Powls	Philip O'Flynn
George Marsh	Anthony Nichols
Charley Butterworth	Timothy Bateson
Kathleen Howard	Christina Gregg
Joe Tracey	Frank Siemen
Miss Wilson	Gwenda Ewen
Detective Sergeant	Donald Tandy
Waiter	Barry Wilsher
Screenplay by	John Graeme
Directed by	Jeremy Summers

SIMON IS about to take a restful holiday in the quiet English village of Bosham, in the heart of Sussex. As he parks his car an elderly lady, Florence Warshed, manages to bump into his car, even though the rest of the car park is empty. As they start to exchange names and addresses Simon gives her his famous card, and she reacts in terror. The main reason Simon has come to Bosham is to visit Kathleen Howard, an attractive young lady. He tells her of his meeting with Florence and her reaction, but Kathleen isn't surprised. She later introduces him to George Marsh, the Warshed sister's lawyer. George tells Simon that the ladies are the sweetest people around, but he does not tell Simon that he is in love with Florence. Later that day Florence and her two sisters, Violet and Ida, receive a visit from a young man called Alfred Powls who threatens them with a dark secret from their past. He demands to stay at the cottage and insists on a payment of £2000 a year to stay quiet. The ladies are terrified their secret will come out and so they have no option but to give in to Powls' demands. Later that day Simon is at Kathleen's estate agents' office when Powls comes in looking for a house. Simon is suspicious of him and manages to get a sample of his fingerprints, which he sends off to Scotland Yard. When Florence asks Kathleen to cash a large cheque for her, Simon is convinced that the sisters are being blackmailed. How will Simon deal with Powls, and what possible dark secret could be hidden by the gentle ladies?

Based on the 1958 short story.

Barbara Mullen, Avice Landon, and Renne Houston, as *The Gentle Ladies*, are questioned by lawyer Anthony Nichols, while The Saint looks on

THE EVER-LOVING SPOUSE (1963)

Simon Templar	**Roger Moore**
Otis Q. Fennick	**Barry Jones**
Liane Fennick	**Jeanne Moody**
Norma Upton	**Jacqueline Ellis**
Brent Kingman	**Paul Carpenter**
Vern Balton	**David Bauer**
Alec Misner	**Alexis Kanner**
Det. Williams	**Robert Arden**
Miss Grinshaw	**Janet Brandes**
Desk Clerk	**Max Faulkner**
Bartender	**Hal Gallili**
Pete	**Stuart Nichol**
Screenplay by	**Norman Borisoff**
Directed by	**Ernest Morris**

IT'S CONVENTION TIME in San Francisco, and Simon's hotel is full of party guests from the candy makers and confectionary companies. Otis Q. Fennick, wealthy sweet manufacturer and his associate Brent Kingman return from a party in the hotel bar. Kingman leaves and Fennick retires for the evening. There is a knock on the door and as Otis opens it, a young girl rushes in wearing a slip and puts her arms around Otis, just then a photographer snaps the two in a clinch and rushes off with the girl. The girl, Norma Upton, returns to her boyfriend, Alec Misner, and the photographer, Vern Balton, returns to his studio. Simon is in his room when he sees Otis climbing down the fire escape. He pulls him into the room and Otis explains about the incident. Simon offers to help Otis. He leaves him in his room while he goes looking for Norma. He checks with the hotel barman and gets the address of Balton's studio. Simon returns to the room to find Otis has left. Fennick's wife Liane is in town. She goes to Balton's studio where she pays him a thousand pounds for the photo of Otis and Norma. Vern gives her the picture, but holds onto the negative. He wants ten thousand for it. Liane calls on Kingman. She shows him the picture. She has been trying to divorce Otis for the past three years and now she has evidence. She asks Brent for his help in getting the negative back. Alec pays a visit to Balton. He warns him not to get Norma involved in his shady business. The next day Otis sees Simon. He apologises to him for running out, and once again asks Simon for his help. Simon pays a call on Balton at his studio, and finds him dead. Suddenly Norma appears. She asks Simon not to call the police as she believes that Alec killed Balton. Suddenly a man fires at Norma through the door hitting her in the shoulder. Simon calls the police and Detective Williams takes charge of the case. He tells Simon not to leave town. Brent Kingman visits Otis on a business matter. Otis tells him he knows about the affair, and that he is fired. Williams arrests Alec on the charge of murder. Simon returns to see Otis and tells him that Balton is dead. He then pays a visit to Liane who tells him that she had nothing to do with Balton's death. There are several people who wanted Balton dead. Simon must uncover the truth behind the killing, in the case of the ever-loving spouse.

Based on the 1959 short story.

THE SAINT SEES IT THROUGH (1963)

Simon Templar	**Roger Moore**
Lili	**Margit Saad**
Dr Ernst Zellerman	**Joseph Furst**
Tante Ada	**Elspeth March**
Carl Eberhard	**Guy Deghy**
John Hamilton	**Larry Cross**
Fritz Kapel	**Gordon Sterne**
Police Captain	**Carl Duering**
Otto	**Peter Perkins**
Policeman	**Graeme Bruce**
Screenplay by	**Ian Martin**
Directed by	**Robert S Baker**

SIMON TEMPLAR IS AT Idelwild Airport, New York. He is there at the request of John Hamilton, a government man. He tells Simon that there is a delicate matter which he needs The Saint's help with. Hamilton tells Simon that someone had recently stolen the Rafael miniatures from the Kremlin, and they are being smuggled into the US by German sailors. The Russians have asked the Americans to help them recover them. Simon flies to Hamburg where he waits at his hotel to be contacted. The telephone rings and Fritz Kapel arranges to meet him in a local nightclub. Later that evening the two men meet and Kapel tells Simon that another boat will be leaving in a couple of days. In the nightclub Simon meets up with Lili, a young woman he was once in love with. As they talk their reunion is interrupted by Dr Ernst Zellerman, who tries to make Lili leave with him. She refuses and after a brief struggle with the Doctor, Simon leaves taking Lili with him. After they have left, Ernst has a meeting with the club's owner Tante Ada and her henchman Carl Eberhard. She tells them that she has found another sailor to make the delivery, Fritz Kapel. Simon asks Lili about Dr Zellerman, but their talk is interrupted by a visit from Tante Ada who apologises to Lili about the trouble at the club. Tante Ada returns to the club, where she and Zellerman instruct Kapel on how he is to hide the miniatures in his baggage. Kapel leaves and is followed by Eberhard. Kapel is packing when he is paid a visit by Eberhard who saw him send a telegram to Washington. Eberhard knows he is a spy and kills him. Simon returns to see Lili who tells him that she is a patient of Dr Zellerman's. Simon leaves and vistis Eberhard, and warns him that he is out to get him. Simon receives a telephone call from Dr Zellerman. He apologises to Simon about the incident the other evening and invites him round to lunch. Simon has a drink in Zellerman's office before they go to lunch. He admits to breaking into the Doctor's office the night before, not realising that the police are listening outside the door. Zellerman has laid a trap for Simon, and the police officers take Simon off to a prison cell. If Simon is in prison how will he be able to stop the rest of the Rafael miniatures from being smuggled out of the country, and how will his reunion with Lili turn out? This is one time the Saint must see it through.

Based on the 1946 novel.

THE FELLOW TRAVELLER (1963)

Simon Templar	Roger Moore
Magda Vamoff	Dawn Adams
Superintendant Kinglake	Glyn Owen
Nick Vashetti	Neil McCallum
Joe	Michael Bates
Mactavish	Angus Lennie
Mrs Matson	Jeanne Watts
Henry Matson	Brian Oulton
Gower	Charles Simon
Marsh	Ray Austin
Sergeant Lashbrook	Fred Ferris
Receptionist	Janine Grey
Screenplay by	Harry W. Junkin
Directed by	Peter Yates

SIMON CHECKS in to the Cromwell Hotel in Stevenage, where he receives a telephone call from Henry Matson, who asks him to meet him at an isolated bus stop. Matson starts to tell Simon why he sent for him. He is in trouble: he works at a top security plant that makes components for satellites and he has been asked to steal blueprints. A van drives along past the couple, and suddenly a man fires a gun at Matson, killing him. The police are called in and Superintendent Kinglake takes charge of the case. The Inspector takes Simon's statement, and then he leaves to pay a call on Mrs Matson. Simon questions Mrs Matson to try to find out if she knew what her husband was up to. She tells him that Henry had received a couple of cryptic phone calls lately, and that he had been seeing a woman called Magda Vamoff in a club called the Blue Goose. Simon drives to the firm that Matson worked for, Watford Williams, where he talks to the manager who is unaware that secret plans have been stolen. Simon leaves, and as he drives along a narrow country road, a lorry driver tries to force him off the road. The Saint narrowly avoids crashing. That evening Simon goes to the Blue Goose, and there he meets Magda and talks to her about Matson. Later on he drives her home and she warns him to be careful. The next day Simon receives a call from Inspector Kinglake, who warns Simon not to interfere. Simon visits Mrs Matson again and she says she remembers her husband mentioning the name of a man called Maris. Simon receives a note from a man called Nick Vashetti. He tells The Saint that he knows who the mysterious man called Maris is, and that he will call round later that evening. Simon goes out to see Magda, but before he leaves he orders a bottle of whisky to be sent to his room. Later that evening Simon returns to the hotel and meets Vashetti. They go up to his room, and as Vashetti starts to tell him about Maris, Simon pours them both a glass of whisky. He is unaware that it has been tampered with and now contains a deadly poison. Has the mysterious Maris won? Is this the end of the road for the happy highwayman, on a journey that started when he met a fellow traveller.

Based on the 1945 novella, *The Sizzling Saboteur*.

STARRING THE SAINT (1963)

Simon Templar	Roger Moore
Byron Ufferlitz	Ronald Radd
Teal	Wensley Pithey
Jack Groom	Alfred Burke
Peggy Warden	Monica Stevenson
Orland Flane	Alexander Davion
Vic Lararoff	Paul Whitson-Jones
Bob Kendricks	Jerry Stovin
David Brown	Ivor Dean
Sergeant Graham	John Dunbar
Cabbie	Brian Weske
April Quest	Jackie Collins
Barman	John Gayford
PC Burns	Bryan Marshall
Screenplay by	Harry W Junkin
Directed by	James Hill

THE SAINT IS IN London when he reads the newspaper that a movie is to be made about his life by producer Byron Ufferlitz, and he wants Simon to star in it. When Ufferlitz offers him £1000 a week, Simon accepts. Byron Ufferlitz has many enemies including Orland Flane, a star who has now been dropped in favour of the Saint. Simon's first assignment is to be seen in public with April Quest, a glamorous actress. The evening is interrupted when Simon receives a note from Ufferlitz asking him to go to the studio at once. Simon arrives at Byron's office where he finds him dead. His secretary Peggy is in the room terrified. She came back to collect her dictation and discovered the body. The police arrive and Simon is the prime murder suspect. One thing is clear to the Saint: the note wasn't written by Ufferlitz, but was just a trick to get him into the office with the body. If Peggy hadn't been there by accident, he would have had no alibi. With the death of Ufferlitz, Simon's career as a film star is over before it has begun. Simon decides to investigate the case in order to clear himself, and he starts questioning people. The name Trilby Andrews comes up. Simon discovers that she was engaged to one of Byron's directors, Jack Groom. Byron took her away from him with promises of a film career, and she later committed suicide after Byron dropped her. Groom has good reason to want Ufferlitz dead, and as Simon's investigations continue he finds others, in particular Orland Flane, who is later arrested by the police. Simon is not convinced that Flane is guilty. There may not be a movie starring The Saint, but Simon will bring down the curtain on Byron Ufferlitz's killer.

Based on the 1942 novella, *Hollywood*

JUDITH (1963)

Simon Templar	Roger Moore
Judith	Julie Christie
Burt Northwade	David Bauer
Ellen Northwade	Margo Johns
Dr Northwade	John McLaren
Inspector Lavin	John Serret
Sergeant Soustelle	Ross Parker
Tom Mackinnon	Warren Stanhope
Hal Sinfield	Robert MacLeod
Jim Wallace	William Greene
Garner	Andre Boulay
Desk Clerk	Ronald Wilson
Screenplay by	Leonard Grahame
Directed by	Robert Lynn

THE SAINT IS IN Canada. As Simon drives along the road heading for Montreal a young girl suddenly backs her car out of a side road, hits Simon's car and drives off without stopping. Immediately afterwards Simon is accused of trespassing on the estate of wealthy businessman, Burt Northwade. Northwade is a ruthless tycoon on the verge of a big business deal over a new production engine, but his wife Ellen accuses him of having stolen the plans from his brother, Dr Northwade. Burt Northwade was given the plans as security against a loan he made his brother and now the time limit for the repayment is almost up. Burt despises and envies his brother partly because he has a young daughter Judith, whereas his own marriage is childless. When Simon finally traces the girl who bumped into his car, she tells him that she is Judith Northwade, and that she was trespassing on her uncle's estate with a view to robbing it.

Judith takes Simon to see her father. Simon sympathises with the Northwades and decides to help them, but Dr Northwade forbids them to go ahead with their plans. Simon decides to investigate Burt Northwade and discovers a few unpleasant things about him. He tries to see Northwade, but Northwade refuses and calls in the police. Simon receives an unexpected ally in Ellen Northwade when she comes to see him. She begs Simon to steal the plans of the engine, and with Ellen's help Simon breaks into the house and takes the plans in the easiest robbery of his career. But the case is not yet over, for Simon discovers that there is still a mystery to solve, that of Judith . . .

Based on the 1948 short story.

Roger Moore and Julie Christie star in the intriguing tale of *Judith*

TERESA (1963)

Simon Templar	Roger Moore
Teresa	Lana Morris
Casemegas	Eric Pohlmann
Borota	Marne Maitland
El Rojo	Lawrence Dane
Senora Artigas	Marie Burke
Miguel Artigas	Alexander Davion
Carlos Segoia	Richard Montez
Sebastian	Paul Whitson-Jones
Café Proprietor	Alan Browning
Padron	Frank Olegario
Police Lieutenant	George Little
Lucito	Peter Exposite
Screenplay by	John Kruse
Directed by	Roy Baker

THE SAINT IS IN Mexico visiting old friend Miguel Artigas, a trapeze artist. During his performance, Miguel is shot and falls to his death. Simon learns that Miguel was to have helped Teresa, the wife of an old friend of Miguel, try and locate her missing husband, a man wanted by the police for an attempted political assassination. Simon decides to take Miguel's place and he travels with Teresa through the local villages, and across the mountains. Unknown to Simon the pair are being followed by a hired assassin, Borota, waiting to be led to Teresa's husband. The couple stop off at a local tavern for refreshments where the owner is later found dead. Simon is charged with his murder, but freed when the killer's fingerprints are found at the bar. Borota tampers with the brakes of Simon's car and the couple narrowly avoid a crash in the mountains. Later they are taken prisoner by the men of El Rojo, the leader of a mountain band of rebels. They are followed by Borota. After a meeting with the rebel leader, Simon learns the secret of El Rojo, and the real reason Teresa is desperately searching for her husband.

Based on the 1948 short story.

THE ELUSIVE ELLSHAW (1963)

Simon Templar	Roger Moore
Anne Ripwell	Angela Browne
Sir John Ripwell	Richard Vernon
Mrs Ellshaw	Ellen McIntosh
Ellshaw	Philip Latham
Martin Irelock	Antony Bate
Hugo Meyer	Walter Brown
Kenneth Ripwell	Philip Bond
Teal	Norman Pitt
Gunsmith	Arthur Hewlett
Dr Cranston	James Ottaway
Screenplay by	Harry W Junkin
Directed by	John Moxey

SIMON IS INVITED BY Anne Ripwell to stay at her father's country home for the weekend, and to join his shooting party. On the way down Anne takes him to a local gunshop run by Arthur Ellshaw and his wife, who used to be Sir John Ripwell's secretary. While Simon is selecting a gun Mrs Ellshaw suddenly rushes from the shop. She has just seen her husband go by, but he is supposed to be in Canada. She follows him to an old house, and there she confronts him. Ellshaw pleads with her not to tell anyone that she has seen him and asks her to go away without giving her any explanation. She returns to the shop and asks Simon to help. When Simon returns to the house with Anne they find it completely empty. Simon believes Mrs Ellshaw was mistaken about seeing her husband, but when they return to the shop they find her murdered. Simon learns from Anne that an attempt had been made on her father's life. Could the two events be connected? When they arrive at the house they discover that the shooting party is already out. Sir John and his son Kenneth are out with Hugo Meyer and Martin Irelock, Sir John's partner, and secretary. Suddenly the party returns as Sir John has been accidentally shot. The wound is not serious but it is not clear who fired the gun, although the evidence points to Kenneth. The atmosphere in the house that weekend is tense. Kenneth appears to be under the control of Martin, while Hugo is disagreeable, and he clearly dislikes Martin. In the event of Sir John's death his money would go to Anne and Kenneth, and the business would be taken over by Hugo; the only person who would not benefit is Martin. Kenneth disappears, and then Simon discovers that he owned the property where Ellshaw had been hiding out; so what about the elusive Ellshaw?

Based on the 1932 novella.

MARCIA (1963)

Simon Templar	Roger Moore
Claire Avery	Samantha Egger
Mike Sentinal	Kenneth Mackintosh
Johnny Desmond	Johnny Briggs
Irene Cromwell	Jill Melford
Inspector Carlton	Phillip Stone
Frank Landon	Stanley Meadows
Barry Aldon	Tony Beckley
Pearl	Janet Davies
Assistant Director	Philip Anthony
Nurse	Virginia Clay
Prop. Man	Peter Duguid
Sheila Sentinal	Marion Mathie
Screenplay by	Harry W. Junkin
Directed by	John Krish

ACTRESS MARCIA LANDON commits suicide after her face has been disfigured. This is a golden opportunity for young actress Claire Avery, who is asked to take over the leading role in Marcia's latest picture. Claire accepts the role with mixed feelings. She knows that this would be her big break, but Marcia was also a good friend. Claire goes to see Simon, and she tells him that Marcia was murdered, although legally it was suicide. She tells Simon that Marcia was alone in the studio when a man standing in the shadows called out her name, and then threw acid in her face. In a fraction of a second her career was over and she had no reason to live. Producer Mike Sentinal plans to groom Claire as Marcia's successor though his wife Sheila doesn't approve because she is as jealous of Claire as she was of Marcia. Barry Aldon also objects, he does not wish to co-star with an unknown actress. Actress Irene Cromwell is also jealous, because she was hoping to get Marcia's role in the movie. Only one person seems pleased that Claire got the part: the assistant director, Johnny Desmond. The next day Claire receives a warning note telling her that unless she leaves £5000 in an envelope on the set, the same thing that happened to Marcia will happen to her. Claire is terrified and she calls on Simon for help. The next day at rehearsal Claire's performance suffers and Simon sets a trap to catch the blackmailer, but it fails. Claire then receives a second warning note after an attempt is made on her life. The blackmail money is left a second time, and Simon waits in the darkened studio for the man to appear. He spots him and then after a chase through the set the blackmailer is caught, but is this the person who threw the acid into the face of Marcia?

Based on the 1937 novella, *The Beauty Specialist*

Roger Moore proves to co-star Samantha Egger that he's a mean artist with a piece of chalk

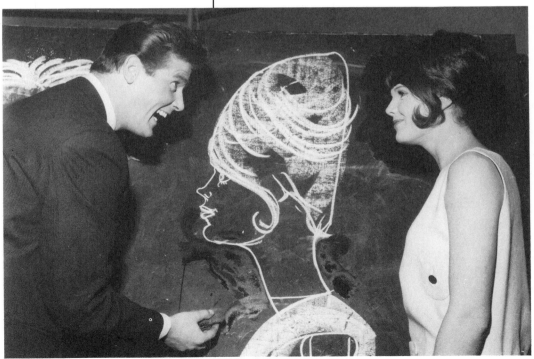

THE WORK OF ART (1963)

Simon Templar	Roger Moore
Juliette Grillot	Yoland Turner
André Grillot	Alex Scott
Major Quintana	Martin Benson
Jean Bourgrenet	John Bailey
Sergeant Luduc	Robert Cawdron
Inspector Quercy	Manning Wilson
Vladek Urivetsky	Hamilton Dyce
Mere Lafond	Hazel Hughes
Lieutenant Prevost	Neville Becker
Maria	Miki Iveria
Receptionist	Anne Sharpe
Paul Fouchet	Tom Naylor
Annette Dosterd	June Smith
Screenplay by	Harry W. Junkin
Directed by	Peter Yates

PARIS IN THE Springtime and Simon is out sightseeing with the lovely Juliette Grillot. Meanwhile, Juliette's brother André is unaware that his business partner, Jean Bourgrenet, is an undercover agent for the Algerian rebel leader, Major Quintana. Quintana has given Bourgrenet forged US bearer bonds to sell and raise money for the movement, but Jean has plans to doublecross the Major. He changes a cheque signed by André from 500 francs to 5000 francs. André discovers this when the bank telephones him to query it. André goes to Jean's apartment but the place is empty except for a suitcase that he believes contains the stolen money; what if it actually contains the bearer bonds stolen from the Major? Major Quintana tracks down Jean to his apartment, and learns that he is planning to escape with the bonds. The Major shoots him, the police are called in and André becomes the main murder suspect when his fingerprints are found all over the flat. Simon decides to help André out. He investigates the case, much to the displeasure of Inspector Quercy of the police department, who places the long-suffering Sergeant Luduc on Simon's tail for the remainder of his stay in Paris. During his investigations Simon makes several discoveries, one of them being that the dead man had been born in Algiers. He later discovers that the stolen bonds could only have been the work of Vladek Urivetsky, a Pole, known as the master forger of Europe. The only problem Simon has is that Vladek was supposed to have been killed sometime ago. He is now convinced that Vladek is still alive and that he is hiding out with Quintana. Simon plans to set out after Vladek, but first he must lose his watchdog Sergeant Luduc. With Juliette's help, he throws a wild party to distract the Sergeant, and he then sets out to trap the Major and Vladek. To prove André's innocence finally he must destroy the plates that are a work of art.

Based on the 1937 novella, *The Spanish War*

IRIS (1963)

Simon Templar	Roger Moore
Iris Lansing	Barbara Murray
Rick Lansing	David Bauer
Inspector Teal	Ivor Dean
Jack Hardy	Cyril Luckham
Stratford Keene	Ferdy Mayne
Mark Belden	John Ronane
Calder	Anthony Wager
Thatcher	Barry Linehan
Harry Blundel	Meadows White
Mary Hardy	April Wilding
Screenplay by	Bill Strutton
Directed by	John Gilling

A NEW PLAY is in rehearsal in London. Simon has read the script and realises that it will be a flop on the opening night. Actress Iris Lansing has persuaded her husband to finance the play with her in the starring role. Rick Lansing is a crook who runs a protection racket in London's Soho. He pays a visit to Harry Blundel, the owner of a small news agent shop, and warns him that if he does not pay for protection his shop will be damaged. Simon visits Mary Hardy, a young actress who has a small part in the play. She invites him along to watch the rehearsal, and as they arrive at the theatre, Simon bumps into Lansing. Both men know each other by their reputation. Lansing leaves and returns to his office. He arranges with his man, Thatcher, to deal with Blundel. Later that evening they pay a visit to Blundel, and when he refuses to knuckle down to their threats, Lansing starts a fire and leaves. Blundel is an old man, his heart fails, and he dies.

The next day Lansing receives a telephone call from The Saint. He threatens to expose Lansing unless he pays out £10,000 to him. Lansing arranges with his man Thatcher to leave the money at a post office in Kensington.

Later that day Simon receives a telephone call from the Kensington post office telling him that they are holding a parcel for him. As Simon collects the parcel he is held up at gunpoint by Thatcher and another man, and they take him back to Lansing. Simon denies all knowledge of the blackmail plot, and when Lansing opens up the parcel the money has been replaced by cut up news paper. Lansing still believes that Simon is involved, but lets him go as he does not want any more bad publicity. Later that day Mary's father, Jack Hardy, receives a telephone call from Simon threatening to expose a dark deed in his past unless he pays £10,000 to him.

The Saint does not like blackmail, especially when someone uses his name, and so sets out to discover who is behind the blackmail plot. Could it be one of the actors in the stage play — could it be . . .? Ivor Dean makes his first appearance as the long suffering Chief Inspector Claude Eustace Teal. In the novels he was famous as the gum-chewing Inspector, in the TV series he became the peppermint 'popping' Teal.

Based on the 1948 short story.

THE KING OF THE BEGGARS (1963)

Simon Templar	**Roger Moore**
Dolores Marcello	**Maxine Audley**
Joe Catelli	**Oliver Reed**
Theresa Mantania	**Yvonne Romain**
Marco Di Cesari	**Warren Mitchell**
Stephen Elliot	**John McLaren**
Leghetti	**Charles Houston**
Maria Calvetti	**Jessie Robins**
Inspector Mateoli	**Bruno Barnabe**
Nicky	**Ronald Corbett**
Policeman	**Gino Coia**
Screenplay/Directed by	**John Gilling**

THE SAINT, relaxing in Rome at a street corner cafe, sees a blind beggar deliberately run down and killed by a motorist. The next day at the same spot he runs into an old friend Marco Di Cesari, a taxi driver. While Simon is talking to Marco he sees an elderly beggar woman attacked by a thug, Joe Catelli. Simon goes to her aid and chases the man off. He follows the beggar woman and discovers that she is really Theresa Mantani, a celebrated stage actress, who is trying to find out about the death of the blind beggar, who was an ex-actor friend. The next day, Simon poses as a blind street-beggar in order to trace the leader of the beggar's protection association. He is picked up by Joe Catelli, the head thug, who works for the 'King of the Beggars'. Simon is told that each day he must take half of his daily takings to a hostel run by a woman called Maria Calvetti. Simon later returns to the place that he was taken to by Catelli and, while searching for clues, he is attacked by another thug, Carlo. Simon gets the upper hand and questions Carlo, but before he can reveal the identity of the gang leader, Carlo is shot and killed. Simon learns that the hostel is owned by a man called Stephen Elliot. Theresa invites Simon to a party given by the Contessa Marcello and Elliot. He questions Elliot but finds no further clues to the identity of the 'King'. The next day he resumes his role as the blind beggar and goes to the hostel. He is taken to a room by Maria and given a drugged drink, and while he is unconscious Theresa is kidnapped by Joe. Simon later recovers and escapes from the hostel. Can the Saint rescue Theresa in time and uncover the identity of the mysterious 'King of the Beggars'?

Based on a 1948 short story.

THE ROUGH DIAMONDS (1963)

Simon Templar	**Roger Moore**
Alan Uttershaw	**Douglas Wilmer**
Inspector Teal	**Ivor Dean**
Milton Ourley	**George A Cooper**
Tina Ourley	**Vanda Godsell**
Ricco	**Paul Stassino**
Barbara Sinclair	**Jemma Hyde**
Joe	**Ray Austin**
George Stanton	**Michael Meacham**
Gabriel Linnet	**William Dexter**
Screenplay by	**Bill Strutton**
Directed by	**Peter Yates**

THE SAINT is asked by Alan Uttershaw to escort him while he is travelling with a package of diamonds worth £100,000. The armoured car is ambushed on its way to the airport to meet Uttershaw and the security men are killed and replaced by members of the gang. On clearing Customs, Uttershaw hands the diamonds over to the phoney security men who drive off with them. The next day Simon visits Scotland Yard but is unable to identify the hold-up men. Uttershaw invites Simon to a party given by Milton Ourley, the man to whom the diamonds were to be delivered. After the party, Simon goes to see Gabriel Linnet, Ourley's partner. While attempting to break into Linnet's flat he is attacked by Joe, one of the two phoney security guards. Entering the apartment Simon finds Linnet dead. Moments later Chief Inspector Teal arrives after having received a tip-off phone call. Teal releases Simon on insufficient evidence. Simon returns to his flat where he is attacked by another of the phoney security guards, and after a brief struggle with The Saint, the man falls to his death. Simon returns to Ourley and accuses him of being involved in the crime but he has insufficient evidence. He returns to Linnet's flat where he finds a suitcase with £100,000 in it. The Saint, on his way to Scotland Yard with the money, finds he is being followed by another car, and so he returns to the flat but he finds two more members of the gang waiting. Simon subdues them and calls the police. The Saint returns to his flat for a final confrontation with the mastermind behind the plot to steal the 'rough diamonds'.

Based on the 1944 novella, *The Black Market*

THE SAINT PLAYS WITH FIRE
(1963)

Simon Templar	Roger Moore
Kane Luker	Joseph Furst
Lady Valerie	Justine Lord
Sidney Fairweather	John Robinson
Inspector Teal	Ivor Dean
Lady Sangore	Margaretta Scott
'Jacko' Jackman	Robert Brown
John Kennet	Tony Beckley
West	John Hollis
Ralph Windley	John Kellard
Sir Robert Sangore	Geoffrey Denton
Screenplay by	John Kruse
Directed by	Robert S. Baker

SIMON TEMPLAR watches as a riot slowly starts to build up at a public meeting of the revival of the British Nazi Party. At the meeting Simon bumps into an old friend 'Jacko' Jackman. editor of the *New Nation Magazine*. Jackman introduces Simon to one of his top reporters. John Kennet. the man who is working on an expose of the new Nazi Party. The next day Kennet is killed during a mysterious fire at a weekend house-party given by Sidney Fairweather. the man sponsoring Kane Luker. the new party leader. Simon. driving past. sees the fire and attempts to rescue Kennet. but he finds the door locked from the inside. Later at the inquest. Simon suggests to the Coroner's Court that Kennet was dead before the fire started. but the verdict of the court is accidental death. A couple of days later Ralph Windley is murdered. He was a close friend of Kennet and was working undercover at the Nazi party and feeding information back to Kennet. Simon decides to concentrate his attention on Lady Valerie. a mercenary young lady who was hired to lure Kennet down to the country house that fatal weekend. John Kennet left some important papers with Valerie just before he died. and Valerie decides to use the papers to blackmail Fairweather and Luker. Simon heads for a final showdown with Luker but is captured along with Valerie by Luker's henchmen. Luker decides to dispose of Simon and Valerie in another fire. Can the Saint turn the tables on Luker and his men. or will the Saint get his fingers burnt?

Based on the novel. *Prelude for War*. 1938.

The original pre-war novel *Prelude For War* was updated to the 1960s by having a Nazi revival party as the theme

THE BENEVOLENT BURGLARY (1963)

Simon Templar	Roger Moore
Elliot Vascoe	John Barrie
Bill Fulton	Gary Cockrell
Delphine Chambers	Rachel Gurney
Meryl Vascoe	Susanne Neve
Martin Grahame	Barry Keegan
Deslauriers	Neal Arden
Germaine	Ivor Salter
Colonel Latignant	Arnold Diamond
Jules Brant	Raymond Adamson
Screenplay by	Larry Forrester
Directed by	Jeremy Summers

THE SAINT IS IN Monte Carlo, at one of the Casinos, where he bumps into a friend, Bill Fulton, a musician who is down on his luck. Bill's fiancée Meryl is having trouble with her father, Elliot Vascoe, who does not want her to get involved with Bill. Later that evening Meryl joins Bill and Simon at the Casino. Bill tells Simon that he came over from London with an offer of a job, but when he arrived the job had fallen through. Simon goes to see Deslauriers, the nightclub owner for whom Bill was to work. Under pressure he tells Simon that he was forced to cancel the contract because of pressure from Vascoe. Later that day Vascoe holds a press conference to open a special exhibition of art and jewellery. Simon arrives at the showing and is suddenly confronted by Vascoe who tells him to leave. Simon and Vascoe had a previous encounter some time earlier. Vascoe is proud of his first-class security system, which he says is burglar proof, but Simon challenges him to a bet that the exhibition will be robbed within 4 days. The next day Simon receives a call from Colonel Latignant of the police department. He warns Simon that he will be followed and watched constantly by the police. The Colonel then goes to see Vascoe, who warns him not to interfere in The Saint's burglary attempt. Meryl goes to see Bill and agrees to marry him without waiting until he has the money to support her. Meanwhile

Jules Brant, a master criminal, approaches Vascoe's chauffeur and offers him a deal, if he will help him steal the jewellery. Simon returns to Vascoe's house to check out the security. That evening as Vascoe prepares to go out to the Casino his security man, Graham, checks the alarm system. Vascoe and Meryl arrive at the Casino. Shortly after, Simon cashes in his chips and leaves, fully aware that he is being followed by the Colonel's man, Germaine. Simon returns to his hotel room, where he is held at gunpoint by one of Brant's men. After a while Simon manages to distract the man and knock the gun away. He subdues him and heads for Vascoe's house. Vascoe returns home and retires for the evening. Simon is followed by Sergeant Germaine. The Colonel is in touch with his men by radio and he instructs them to close in on Simon, but the Saint has a shortwave radio on him and redirects all the Colonel's men. Back at the Vascoe house, the security guards collapse one by one. They have been drugged and someone has turned off the alarm. Will the Saint be able to stop Brant and his men from stealing the jewellery? If Simon goes through with his plan to steal the jewels, will he be arrested by the Colonel? How can the Saint turn it into a benevolent burglary?

Based on the 1933 short story.

THE BUNCO ARTISTS (1964)

Simon Templar	Roger Moore
Sophie Yarmouth	Mary Merrall
Richard Eade	Peter Dyneley
Jean Yarmouth	Justine Lord
Joyce Eade	Louise King
Charlie Lewis	Victor Platt
Vicar Stone	John Glyn Jones
Miss Emmar	Marie Makino
Mrs Rance	Barbara Ogilvie
Louis	André Maranne
Gendarme	John Standing
Colonel Latignant	Arnold Diamond
Screenplay by	Lewis Davidson
Directed by	Peter Yates

THE SAINT IS IN London, in the heart of theatreland, to visit Jean Yarmouth, a friend who is rehearsing a new play. Meanwhile in Jean's hometown, the small village of Netherdon, an American woman called Amelia Wades books into a small hotel. She is a 'bunco artist': a conwoman. Amelia stops off at the local church, which needs £8,000 for refurbishment. The vicar has left for London leaving Jean's mother, Sophie, in charge of the church funds. Amelia tries to persuade Sophie to part with the church money saying if she can prove that she has £6,000 she will give her the final £2,000 as a gift from a charity organisation. Sophie is not convinced about the offer and Amelia leaves. Simon takes Jean to lunch and she invites him to Netherdon to stay for the weekend. Shortly after Mrs Wade has left, Sophie receives a visit from a man called Henderson of the International Police. With him is the local constable, Charlie Lewis. Henderson confirms that Mrs Wade is a bunco artist, and asks Sophie to go along with his plot to catch her. The constable agrees, and Sophie draws out the money from the bank. Sophie telephones Amelia at her hotel and Amelia comes straight over. She counts Sophie's money and then makes a switch with the cash, which is observed by the constable and Henderson, who arrest Mrs Wade. Sophie is told by Henderson that the money must be taken to the police station as evidence, and while constable Lewis is writing out a receipt, Amelia and Henderson slip out with the money. Locking them in, they then take the next flight to Nice. Simon and Jean arrive at the village to find Sophie distraught. Simon goes to the local telephone exchange and traces Henderson's call to the airline. Simon and Jean return to London to take the next flight to Nice. Simon visits his acquaintance Colonel Latignant of the police, and tells him he wants to trace a couple of old friends and the Colonel comes up with the address of their hotel. Simon checks into the hotel posing as a Texas millionaire, Hiram S. Toombs, and at the hotel bar, Henderson (whose real name is Richard Eade), sees Simon as another mark. He arranges with his wife, Joyce, to drop her necklace near Simon at the bar. Simon hands back the necklace to Joyce who says its worthless. Eade tells Simon that he knows jewels and that it is worth £5,000. Simon suggests to Eade that he buy the necklace for him. The next day, Simon buys the necklace for £2,000 and he checks back with Eade who still wants to buy the necklace. What plan does Simon have? Can he teach them a lesson they will never forget? Is this the end of the road for the bunco artist?

Based on the 1957 short story.

THE WELL MEANING MAYOR
(1964)

Simon Templar	**Roger Moore**
Sam Purdell	**Leslie Sands**
Alice Purdell	**Mary Kenton**
George Hackett	**Norman Bird**
Molly Hackett	**Mandy Miller**
Jack Bryant	**Noel Trevarthen**
Alderman Greer	**Cameron Hall**
Ironside	**Kenneth Henry**
Maxin	**David Morell**
Dr Yates	**John Gill**
Screenplay by	**Robert Stewart**
Directed by	**Jeremy Summers**

THE SAINT VISITS Seatondean, a small seaside town, for a spot of fishing and relaxation. He bumps into an old friend, Jack Bryant, who is helping his future father-in-law, George Hackett, run for Mayor in the local election. Hackett loses out to Sam Purdell, a man with powerful ambitions. At the next council meeting Hackett and Purdell argue over plans for future projects. Hackett accuses Purdell of taking bribes, but he has insufficient evidence to back up his claims. After a lunchtime drink with Simon and Jack, Hackett is involved in a minor car accident, and he accuses Purdell of having arranged the accident. That evening Hackett goes to the local building site to look for proof of Purdell's double dealings. The next day Hackett is found dead on the beach, and the verdict of the inquest is accidental death. Simon decides to investigate and, posing as a supplier of electrical goods, he visits Purdell's offices and offers him a bribe in return for a contract on a new building site. Enraged, Purdell attacks Simon. After a savage fight, Simon decides that Purdell is not the crook that Hackett accused him of being. Simon and Purdell team up in an attempt to catch the real crook and they arrange a party at Purdell's house to gather all the likely suspects together. Simon approaches each man and offers him a bribe but there are no takers. As Simon leaves the party he finds a note in his car with instructions to be at the building site the next evening. Simon arranges with Purdell to call the police and he heads off to the building site for a confrontation with the killer. Simon comes face to face with the killer of George Hackett on top of the building works. Can the Saint triumph once again?

Based on the 1933 short story.

Molly Hackett (Mandy Miller) and Simon look through her father's personal things in an attempt to find his murderer

THE SPORTING CHANCE (1964)

Simon Templar	Roger Moore
Netchideff	Derren Nesbitt
Professor Mueller	Gerard Heinz
Pavan	Godfrey Quigley
Marion Kent	Carol Cleveland
Cleaver	Brandon Brady
Beaver Johnson	Harry Webster
Jack Williams	Bruce Boa
Inspector Hackett	Nicholas Stuart
Mrs Whicker	Nan Marriot-Watson
Detective Gorman	William Buck
Dr Beamish	Evan Thomas
Screenplay by	John Kruse
Directed by	Jeremy Summers

THE SAINT IS IN Canada, at Manitou Lake, Ontario, looking forward to a spot of peaceful fishing and relaxation. Meanwhile in Toronto, Professor Otto Mueller is packing to go off on holiday. He is also off on a fishing trip, or so it appears. Professor Mueller has recently perfected a new satellite guidance system, and his fishing trip is really a cover for him to defect to the East. His guidance system will be traded off in return for the release of his wife and daughter. Mueller heads north for a rendezvous with the men who hold his family. Simon, out fishing the next day, spots Mueller having trouble with his fishing equipment; he invites him for a social drink but Mueller declines. Later that day Mueller is approached by Cleaver, the man who is the go-between in the transfer. Jack Williams, a constable with the Royal Canadian Mounted Police, calls at the hotel to check up on Mueller. Williams runs into Simon, an old friend, and offers to buy him a drink. Simon sees Mueller leaving the lodge and goes to fetch him. Simon returns to the bar to find Williams dead from a knife wound. The knife is then found in Simon's jacket pocket. Inspector Hackett questions Simon about the murder but releases him for lack of evidence. Simon questions the hotel clerk and discovers that Cleaver checked out of the lodge the same time as Mueller; also that he telephoned Vancouver that evening. Simon traces the call to Julius Pavan, then heads to Vancouver. Professor Mueller is taken by Cleaver to Pavan, the middle-man who is supposed to arrange the transport. The next day Simon arrives at Pavan's offices just after the three men have left. He questions Pavan's secretary Marion Kent but finds no clues to Mueller's whereabouts. Later that evening Simon returns to search Pavan's offices but he is caught by Marion. He explains why he is there and she agrees to help him. The next day Marion overhears a conversation between Pavan and Mueller but while she is telephoning Simon she is caught by Cleaver. Pavan leaves with Mueller, taking Marion along too, but he leaves Cleaver behind to take care of The Saint. Simon arrives at the offices and is attacked by Cleaver, but after a brief struggle Cleaver falls out of the window to his death. Simon traces Pavan to a small cabin in one of the remote lake areas where Pavan is waiting to be picked up by a seaplane. Simon watches the plane land and Pavan meet up with Netchideff, a German agent. Simon attacks Netchideff but is caught off guard by Pavan, and he is tied up while Pavan goes for some gasoline. Simon informs Mueller that his daughter and wife have escaped to the West. Mueller tries to get Netchideff drunk in order to free Simon and Marion, but his attempt fails. Pavan and Netchideff prepare to leave with Mueller. Simon and Mueller try a last desperate attempt to escape using Pavan as a hostage, but Netchideff shoots Pavan and leaves with Mueller. Can Simon free himself in time to stop Netchideff escaping with Mueller? Can he cast a line and reel in the big one, or will it be a case of the one that got away?

Based on the 1957 short story.

THE WONDERFUL WAR (1964)

Simon Templar	Roger Moore
Mrs McAlister	Renee Houston
Mike Kelly	Noel Purcell
Harry Shannet	Alfred Burke
Abdul Aziz	Alec Mango
Major Hussain	Patrick Westwood
Ahmed	David Graham
Raschid	John Bennet
The Iman	Ferdy Mayne
Prince Karim	Louis Raynor
John McAndrew	Jack Lambert
Lilla McAndrew	Suzanna Leigh

Screenplay by	John Graeme
Directed by	Robert S. Baker

JOHN McANDREW is in charge of the oil rigs owned by the Iman, the ruler of a small state in the Middle East, suddenly wealthy thanks to its oil. McAndrew visits the Iman to report on the latest find. Suddenly the Prime Minister Abdul Aziz rushes in with his armed guards. They kill the Iman and McAndrew, but the Iman's son Prince Karim escapes with a bullet-wound in his shoulder. Abdul Aziz formed the revolution with the aid of Harry Shannet, an Englishman who wanted to obtain the oil rights. Meanwhile the Prince manages to sneak out of the Palace and escapes to the home of Mike Kelly, a friend and co-worker of McAndrew's. Kelly patches up the young Prince's wounds and takes him to a friend, Mrs McAlister, who hides him. Back in London, Simon reads in the local paper about the revolution. He goes to see Lilla McAndrew, the young daughter of McAndrew, because it is not clear from the article if McAndrew is alive or dead. Lilla asks Simon to help her find out. Simon and Lilla arrive in Kuwait. He takes Lilla to see Kelly, who is an old friend of Simon's, and he confirms that her father is dead. Simon works out a plan with Kelly to help the young Prince regain his throne. He goes to see Abdul Aziz, posing as J. Pierpoint Sykes, a wealthy businessman who wishes to buy the oil leases. Late that evening several men sneak into the grounds of Mrs McAllister's house to kidnap the Prince. Lilla telephones Simon (who is nearby). He rushes over and tackles the men, and after a struggle they run off. Simon decides the Prince would be safer disguised as a worker at the oil rig, and so Kelly takes him out there. Simon returns to the Palace as the mythical Sykes, and offers the Prime Minister and Shannet $5,000,000 for the oil rights. He then goes onto the oil field to see Kelly, where they start the plans for a bloodless revolution. That evening Simon arrives at the Palace and over dinner with the Prime Minister he drops a few hints that the Prince has raised an army. Then out at the field Kelly and the Prince, with radio special effects and a few explosions, convince the soldiers at the field that they are under attack. The guards telephone Abdul and he believes that the revolution has begun. The Prime Minister's man, Raschid, arrives at the Palace and is about to report his failure to capture the Prince when he recognises Simon as the man he fought with in the grounds. The Prime Minister's men attack Simon and he is knocked out and thrown into prison. Can Simon escape from the prison? Will his attempts to return the Prince to power succeed and will his attempt at a bloodless revolution manage to bring about a 'wonderful war'?

Based on the 1931 novella.

THE NOBLE SPORTSMAN (1964)

Simon Templar	Roger Moore
Lady Anne Yearley	Sylvia Sims
Lord Yearley	Anthony Quayle
Paul Farley	Francis Matthews
Bruno Walmar	Paul Curran
Rose Yearley	Jane Asher
Kelly	Russell Walters
Bates	Martin Wyldeck
Tom Crofton	Howard Douglas
Commentator	Tony Bilbow
Screenplay by	John Graeme
Directed by	Peter Yates

SIMON TEMPLAR IS IN London at a show jumping event when he is invited to a celebration party by Lord Yearley and his new young wife, Anne. Simon notices that during the party Anne leaves abruptly without Yearley knowing. She goes to the apartment of Paul Farley, a young architect with whom she has been having an affair, and she tells Farley that the affair is over as she is expecting Yearley's child. The following day Lord Yearley cancels plans to sell off a large piece of property, deciding to build on the land himself instead, making himself some powerful enemies. Lord Yearley returns home to his farm and is confronted by one of the local farmers who threatens to kill him if he continues to fox-hunt on his land. Yearley's daughter, Rose, finds an anonymous letter threatening to kill her father. She calls in Simon but Yearley refuses his help. That evening while driving home Yearley has a near-miss accident when the brakes of his car are tampered with. The next day Yearley asks Simon

for his help, and together they arrange a house party to which they invite all the suspects. Later that evening Yearley receives a second death threat. At the party he sees Farley with his wife and discovers about the affair. That evening another attempt is made on Yearley's life when a shot is fired at him in his bedroom. The weapon had been taken from his own gun collection. Simon searches Farley's apartment and discovers the blackmail notes were cut from Farley's magazines. The next day, Yearley is out fox-hunting and is again threatened by Bates, the farmer, this time with a gun. Several more twists to the plot occur before Simon unravels the full story behind the plot against 'the noble sportsman'.

Based on the 1934 short story.

Anthony Quayle (centre) as *The Noble Sportsman*, in a lighter mood just before someone tries to kill him

LUELLA (1964)

Simon Templar	**Roger Moore**
Bill Harvey	**David Hedison**
Doris Harvey	**Suzanne Lloyd**
Luella	**Su Lloyd**
Matt Joyson	**Aidan Turner**
Ted Kermein	**Michael Wynne**
Miss Hill	**Jean St Clair**
Head Porter	**John Woodnutt**
Waiter	**Julian Holloway**
Hotel Clerk	**Peter Fontaine**

Screenplay by	**Harry W. Junkin**
Directed by	**Roy Baker**

SIMON IS AT London Airport. He is there to meet a passenger off the New York flight, Bill Harvey, an old wartime friend of Simon who has come over to work in London for a year. He has brought along his wife, Doris, whom Simon has never met. Simon checks them into a Mayfair Hotel, and shortly afterwards Doris receives a call from her sister in Paris. She is expecting a baby quite soon, and Doris flies off to Paris to be with her. Simon takes Bill sightseeing around London by day, but Bill is more interested in seeing the nightlife. Simon is reluctant as he had promised Doris that he would look after Bill, but after pressure from him Simon gives in. They tour all the nightclubs with Simon keeping a close watch on Bill and keeping him out of trouble. The next evening Bill pretends to have a hangover so that he can go out on the town and really have a good time away from the watchful eye of Simon. Bill starts off the evening by having a drink in the bar, where he meets the lovely Luella, who is waiting for a friend. She is about to go off on holiday, but wants someone to look after her flat. Bill takes her out to dinner and persuades her to rent the flat to him. Luella takes Bill back to the flat, and while he fixes them both a drink, Luella slips into something more comfortable, then reappears and snuggles up to Bill. Just then a photographer appears and snaps them together, followed by Luella's irate husband. While Luella is changing, her husband tells Bill that the photo will be used as evidence in the divorce. Bill manages to persuade him with a payment of £2,000 to destroy the photo. Bill leaves and returns to the hotel, arriving only seconds before Doris, but he manages to get to the room before her. Bill appears to be fast asleep when Doris enters the bedroom, but as she hangs her coat up she finds a handkerchief in Bill's pocket with Luella's name on it. She wakes Bill up and confronts him with it. The next day Bill goes to see Simon and he tells him the whole story. Simon decides to give Bill a helping hand. He goes along to Luella's flat where he sees the porter from Bill's hotel leaving the flat. Simon approaches him and threatens him with prison unless he

follows Simon's orders. The porter reports to Luella that he has found another 'mark' and that evening Simon, posing as Samuel P. Taggart, a wealthy businessman, is approached by Luella. She goes through the same 'flat' routine with Simon, and after dinner she takes him back to her flat. Simon fixes a drink while Luella slips into something more comfortable. She returns and as she snuggles up to Simon, the door opens, and . . .

This is one of the few light-hearted episodes of the series. David Hedison was a good friend of Roger Moore's and he became one of the few Americans to guest on the show. He was then to play Felix Leiter, James Bond's American counterpart in the first, Moore 'Bond film', *Live and Let Die.*

Based on the 1948 short story.

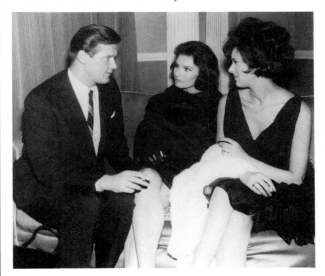

Roger Moore discusses the next scene with Suzanne Lloyd and Su Lloyd, in this light-hearted episode

THE LAWLESS LADY (1964)

Simon Templar	**Roger Moore**
Countess Audrey	**Dawn Adams**
Halloran	**Julian Glover**
Inspector Teal	**Ivor Dean**
Sanders	**Ronald Ibbs**
Jacques Boucher	**John G. Heller**
Dickie Tremaine	**David Sumner**
Photographer	**James Bellchamber**
Miss Williams	**Anthea Wyndham**
Lord Wentworth	**Kenneth Benda**
Lady Wentworth	**Dorothy Black**
George Ulrig	**Stuart Saunders**
May Ulrig	**Anne Sharp**
Sir Edras Levy	**Gerald Young**
Lady Levy	**Edith Saville**
Screenplay by	**Harry W. Junkin**
Directed by	**Jeremy Summers**

THE SAINT drives throug the City of London with one purpose in mind. His Volvo narrowly misses crashing into a Rolls which belongs to Countess Audrey Morova. While she and her driver examine the cars Simon steals a glove from her car. The Countess returns to her Mayfair house where she is interviewed and photographed by the press about her social activities. That evening she invites several wealthy friends round for dinner including Lord and Lady Wentworth. Shortly after they have left, the Countess's driver returns from robbing the Wentworth home. Later that evening Simon calls on the Countess on the pretext of returning her glove. Simon persuades her to go dancing with him, and later when they return to her house he accuses her of. stealing the Wentworth jewels and he invites her to join him as a partner in crime. The Countess is not sure about Simon and so she puts him to the test by arranging for him to steal some jewellery. Simon is interrupted by the butler. whom he locks up in the cupboard before returning with the jewels to the Countess. Simon returns home to find Inspector Teal waiting for him. Simon had telephoned the Yard earlier to inform them about the robbery. He tells Teal that he has joined the gang with the intention of breaking it up and bringing the Countess's driver. Halloran. to justice. The next day Saunders. another one of the Countess's men,

leaves for Amsterdam to fence the jewels that Simon stole. and Simon arranges with Teal to pick him up when he lands at Amsterdam Airport. Simon returns to see the Countess. and Halloran accuses him of being involved with the police but cannot prove it. The Countess does not believe it as she is attracted to Simon. The next day Simon. the Countess and the rest of her men leave for Cannes. They are preparing to go on a cruise that they have organised. taking with them several wealthy couples. whom they plan to rob when they are at sea. While the boat is still tied up. Simon goes into town where he meets a young friend. Dickie Tremaine, whom he asks to help him out. Simon notices that he is being watched by Halloran. The next day the boat leaves. The Countess plans to rob them after they have had dinner by serving them with a drugged coffee. Halloran receives a cable giving him information about Simon. That evening just before dinner Simon is enjoying a cigarette on deck when Halloran sneaks up behind him and knocks him out. and then with the help of another man they lift Simon and prepare to throw him overboard. Is it to be the deep blue sea for Simon. or are the Saints watching over him? How will he succeed in bringing to justice the 'lawless lady'?

Based on the 1930 novella.

THE SAINT ON TV 77

THE GOOD MEDICINE (1964)

Simon Templar	**Roger Moore**
Denise Dumont	**Barbara Murray**
Phillipe Dumont	**Anthony Newlands**
Maria	**Jean Marsh**
David Stem	**Bill Nagy**
Count Alfredo	**John Bennet**
Madame Dumont	**Veronica Turleigh**
Jacques	**Bruce Montagne**
Mathilde	**Alexandra Dane**
Screenplay by	**Norman Borisoff**
Directed by	**Roy Baker**

SIMON TEMPLAR IS IN Paris where he meets an old journalist friend called David Stem for lunch. David points out to Simon Denise Dumont. a very wealthy woman. who has had a quick rise to power and fame. David tells him the background story to Denise's rise to wealth. She started out as a chemist's assistant to Phillipe Dumont. in a small village. Phillipe was a brilliant chemist. but not ambitious. Denise wormed her way into Phillipe's life pretending that she cared for him and his elderly mother. and when his mother died she persuaded Phillipe to marry her although she did not love him. She constantly badgered him to develop and expand the business. spending the next few years developing and building up her cosmetic business until she was at the top of her league. Phillipe took a back seat and as Denise became more powerful she decided that she no longer needed him, so she divorced him and he returned to the small town he came from. a broken man. As Simon and David finish the meal Denise comes over to see them. David introduces The Saint as 'Simon Toombs'. Denise is taken with him and invites him to dinner the next day.

David takes Simon to the small village to see Phillipe who is down on his luck and living with his sister. Maria. Maria had tried to call on Denise but she had refused to see her and Simon decides it's time someone taught Denise a lesson. That evening Simon takes Denise out for a meal, and then after the meal he takes her home. Later that evening in a fit of temper she fires her maid over a trivial item. and Simon finds a replacement for her, Maria. He tells Denise that he must go to London for a few days to see a chemist who is developing a new formula for him. Denise is curious and sends her friend Count Alfredo to follow him. Simon knows that he is being followed and leaves the Count in David's charge. A couple of days later Simon returns to see Denise telling her that his chemist has developed a new anti-bug pill. Denise realises that there is money in this, and she plans to cheat Simon out of the formula. He strings her along and she gives him a cheque for 650.000 francs. Simon plans to use the money to help Phillipe. and give Denise a good dose of her own medicine.

Based on the 1957 short story.

THE HIGH FENCE (1964)

Simon Templar	Roger Moore
Inspector Pryor	James Villiers
Gabby Forest	Suzanne Lloyd
Inspector Teal	Ivor Dean
Enderby	Reginald Beckwith
Bob Stryker	Stanley Meadows
Johnny Anworth	Harry Towb
Mrs Anworth	Claire Kelly
Jim Fasson	Dyson Lovell
Quincy	Peter Jeffrey
Mrs Stewart	Hazel Hughes
Robbins	Richard Poore
Screenplay by	Harry W. Junkin
Directed by	James Hill

Ivor Dean as Inspector Teal questions Claire Kelly as Mrs Amworth about the murder of her husband

Imogen Hassal as Sophia helps The Saint bring justice to a small Greek fishing village

SIMON TEMPLAR calls on Gabby Forest, an attractive young actress, with whom he has a theatre engagement. After discovering that she has left the tickets behind, Gabby and Simon return to the flat. Gabby enters the flat and discovers burglars going through her things. She screams and Simon rushes into the flat. After a brief struggle the two men escape; Simon pursues them but loses them in the traffic. Simon calls in the local police, and Inspector Pryor takes charge of the case. At the local station Simon identifies one of the two men as Johnny Anworth, a small-time crook. Anworth is brought in for questioning by Pryor and his men. After several hours of questioning Anworth is given a rest and some tea is fetched from the local café, but unseen by the police, poison has been slipped into Anworth's tea. Anworth is just about to reveal whom he is working for when the poison takes effect. Inspector Teal takes charge of the case and accuses Pryor of neglect. Simon teams up with Bob Stryker, a former Scotland yard man now working for an insurance company, and together they question Mrs Anworth, who tells them that her husband and his partner Jim Fasson worked for a criminal known only as 'the high fence'. Simon arrives at Fasson's house just as he is about to leave. After a brief struggle Fasson is shot by an unknown gunman but before he dies he tells Simon that the high fence's rendezvous point is a café called the Cosy Corner. Simon persuades Gabby to get a job as a waitress in the café so she can keep a watch on its customers. The next day she spots the suspicious exchange of a package between two men, one of whom turns out to be Quincy, the gunman who killed Fasson; the other man is Enderby, a jeweller. Simon follows Enderby back to his shop after a signal from Gabby, but he is caught by Quincy, and taken to the mysterious leader of the gang. Will the police arrive in time to assist Simon when he jumps the 'high fence'?

Based on the 1954 novella.

SOPHIA (1964)

Simon Templar	**Roger Moore**
Aristides	**Oliver Reed**
Sophia	**Imogen Hassall**
Nico	**Peter Kriss**
Stavros	**Tommy Duggan**
Professor Hamish Grant	**John Wentworth**
Joe Martin	**Hal Gallili**
Gorgo	**Wolfe Morris**
American Tourist	**Donna Pearson**
Photographer	**Raymond Ray**
Greek Villagers	**Andreas Malandrinos**
	Tony Arpino

Screenplay by	**Robert Stewart**
Directed by	**Roger Moore**

SIMON IS ON holiday in Athens, and is being shown around the Parthenon by a friend, Professor Hamish Grant, who invites Simon to stay with him for a couple of days and to visit the excavation site in a small village nearby where he is working. In Athens town, Aristides, a small-time crook, is packing to leave. He is running out on his partner, Joe Martin, but suddenly Joe appears and Aristides pulls a gun on him and shoots him. Simon arrives at the small village where the Professor is staying; he checks into the local inn run by Stavros and his daughter, Sophia. He arrives right at the moment Sophia is telling her father off for giving free drinks to the locals. She takes Simon to his room and apologises to him for her outburst. Later that day Stavros receives a call from his nephew Aristides, who tells him that he will be coming to stay for a couple of days. The Professor shows Simon round the site telling him he is on the verge of a big discovery. The next day Aristides arrives and is given a cool reception by his uncle, who years ago lent his sister a large sum of money. When she died Aristides should have repaid it, but he ignored his uncle. Aristides plays up to Sophia and is warned by Stavros to stay away from her. Meanwhile, at the site, Professor Grant has discovered a valuable gold statue. That evening at supper Stavros tells them he plans to retire soon to a farm and leave the inn to Sophia. Simon realises that Aristides is a petty crook and warns Sophia about him. Aristides questions the Professor about the statue, and then it is locked up in Stavros's safe. The next day Simon talks to Stavros about his financial problems, and he then talks to Sophia's fiancé Nico. That evening he follows Aristides when he sneaks off into the woods to meet a man called Gorgo. The two men plan to steal Professor Grant's statue. The following day Aristides goes off with Sophia when she takes lunch to the men at the site, so that he will have an alibi when Gorgo steals the statue. Gorgo opens the safe but before he can steal it Simon tackles him and ties him up. Aristides returns after lunch without Sophia, and Nico goes looking for her. She is missing, and Aristides says she left him at the excavation site. A search party is organised but they fail to find her. The search party returns to the inn to find a note written on the wall: Sophia will be returned for 500,000 drachmas. Aristides swears to Simon that he knows nothing about it. If that is true, who has kidnapped Sophia?

Based on the 1948 short story, *Lucia*.

THE MIRACLE TEA PARTY (1964)

Simon Templar	**Roger Moore**
Geraldine McLeod	**Nanette Newman**
Dr Sandberg	**Conrad Phillips**
Aunt Hattie	**Fabia Drake**
Commander Richardson	**Basil Dignam**
Norton	**Charles Houston**
Inescue	**Viktor Viko**
Osbett	**Patrick Westwood**
Atkins	**Robert Brown**
Franklin	**Edward Jewesbury**
Wilson	**Neville Whiting**
Barlow	**Michael Standing**

Screenplay by	**Paddy Manning O'Brien**
Directed by	**Roger Moore**

THE SAINT IS AT Waterloo railway station awaiting the delivery of his car. As there is no sign of the car Simon telephones the garage to enquire about it, but while he is telephoning the man in the next booth collapses. Simon and the man's companion a young girl called Geraldine, rush to his aid but it is too late – the man is dead. Simon discovers a small broken phial of glass on the floor of the phone booth, and he learns that the man and Geraldine worked at a naval base nearby. He takes her to dinner and later, back at his flat, Geraldine discovers a packet of herbal tea that her companion must have slipped into her bag. Inside the packet is £500. A man attempts to break into the flat and while Simon pursues him another man attacks Geraldine and snatches the packet of tea. Simon calls in Commander John Richardson of Naval Intelligence, who tells Simon that the dead man was working undercover at the base to try to stop a leakage of secret information. Simon agrees to help the Navy and the next day he drives down with Geraldine to the Portland Navy Yard. Geraldine's Aunt Hattie agrees to help and puts Simon up at her house. Hattie is an avid photographer and agrees to take photos of everyone entering and leaving the Naval Base. Simon discovers that the Miracle Tea adverts on the radio are being used to transmit stolen, secret information to the enemy, and that the spies' headquarters are based at the local chemist shop. Dr Sandburg, the Naval Base's doctor, is the head of the spy ring, and fearing discovery he kidnaps Geraldine and takes her to London to his apartment. Simon follows one of the spies to London, while Aunt Hattie telephones the police. Can the Saint rescue Geraldine in time before the final broadcast of secret information is passed on to the enemy by Dr Sandberg? Will the police arrive in time to assist Simon break up the case of the 'Miracle Tea Party?

Based on the 1939 novella.

LIDA (1964)

Simon Templar	Roger Moore
Joan Wingate	Erica Rogers
Lida Verity	Jeanne Moody
Bosun	Barry Keegan
Maurice Kerr	Peter Bowles
Esteban	Marne Maitland
Pebbles	Aubrey Morris
Inspector Maxwell	Robert Raglan
Mara	Maggie Wright
American Man	Henry McCarthy
Screenplay by	Terry Nation
Directed by	Leslie Norman

RELAXING IN THE Bahamas, Simon Templar runs into an old friend, Joan Wingate, who tells him that her sister, Lida, is in trouble and needs help. That evening at dinner with Joan, Simon receives an urgent phone call from Lida asking him to meet her at a nearby nightclub. On arrival at the club Simon hears a shot and shortly afterwards discovers Lida dead. The police are called in and suicide is suggested, but Simon thinks otherwise. Returning to her apartment he looks through her things in search of clues, and finds evidence of blackmail. The evidence leads Simon to Maurice Kerr, a friend of Lida's and also the owner of the murder weapon. Simon questions Kerr and uncovers a vicious blackmail plot. Kerr is killed by an unknown assassin before he can reveal to Simon the name of the gang leader. Simon is accused by Inspector Maxwell, of the crime but released on insufficient evidence. He returns to the girl's apartment where he discovers that Joan has been kidnapped. She has been taken by Pebbles, a photographer at the club where Lida was killed. Simon sets out for the club to rescue Joan and for a final showdown with the man who killed Lida.

Based on the 1941 short story.

Roger Moore and
Erica Rogers try to
solve the murder
of *Lida*

JEANNINE (1964)

Simon Templar	Roger Moore
Jeannine Roger	Sylvia Syms
Madam Chen	Jacqui Chan
Sergeant Luduc	Robert Cawdron
Inspector Quercy	Manning Wilson
Lo Yung	Eric Young
Jerome	Martin Miller
Kwan Li	Peter Elliott
Fouquet	John Dearth
Peyrac	Peter Diamond
Hotel Manager	Michael Anthony
Receptionist	Maggie Wright
Screenplay by	Tery Nation
Directed by	John Moxey

THE SAINT is in Paris, and as usual his old sparring partner, Inspector Quercy has his eye on Simon. As he waits for him to break the law, the Inpsector puts the long suffering Sergeant Luduc on The Saint's tail. The Inspector starts to worry when Simon turns up at a reception at the same time as the dictatorial, Oriental diplomat, Madam Chen, who is wearing her famous pearl necklace. Simon has a reason for being interested in Madam Chen's party. He recognises her public relations officer, Jeannine Roger, whom Simon knows to be a crook, but Jeannine assures him that she has reformed. Madam Chen is charming, but ruthless and she is a dangerous woman. Her violent temper is unleashed on her Minister, Kwan Li, when he fails to arrange a meeting for her with a French Minister. She later stands up well at a press conference when she is asked how the US grant to her country is being used. Madam Chen's presence in Paris has also been noted by a couple of crooks, Fouquet and Peyrac, who plan to relieve her of her jewels. They are not the only ones; there is also Lo Yung, one of her countrymen – he is the first to make an attempt to steal the pearls. Lo Yung is nearly caught, but he makes his escape, and hides in Simon's room. The Saint catches him and he explains that his people are starving and the money the pearls would have fetched would have brought some relief to them. Simon has a task ahead of him, because he must prevent the two crooks from stealing the pearls and then help Lo Yung and his countrymen. This means more trouble for the long suffering Sergeant Luduc, and then Simon finally has to foil the plot by Jeannine to substitute the pearls.
Based on the 1948 short story.

THE SCORPION (1964)

Simon Templar	Roger Moore
Karen Bates	Catherine Woodville
Patsy Butler	Nyree Dawn Porter
Eddy	Dudley Sutton
'Long Harry' Garrett	Philip Latham
Inspector Teal	Ivor Dean
Montgomery 'Birdie' Bird	Leon Cortez
Wilfred Garniman	Geoffrey Bayldon
Mark Deverest	Ronald Leigh-Hunt
Cynthia Deverest	Eve Lister
Screenplay by	Paul Erickson
Directed by	Roy Baker

LATE ONE EVENING, The Saint receives a phone call from a petty criminal called Long Harry. The man is terrified and asks for Simon's help, and so Simon tells Harry to come over straight away. Harry tells Simon that he was paid to steal documents from a man called Deverest for the purpose of blackmail by a criminal known only as the Scorpion. Harry has seen the Scorpion and fears for his life. Simon leaves Harry at his flat and goes to see Deverest, who denies that his flat has been

The Saint comes up against a deadly criminal called The Scorpion, when he tries to help a friend who is being blackmailed

burgled, and during his conversation with The Saint receives a phone call from a girl called Patsy Butler who is involved in the blackmail plot. Karen. Deverest's secretary, listens in on the extension and she tells Simon that Mark arranged to meet Patsy at a club called the Bird's Nest for the first blackmail payment. Simon and Karen go to the club where they see Deverest hand over an envelope to Patsy and then leave. Simon follows Patsy to a room where she hands over the money to her boyfriend Eddy. Simon enters the room and after a brief struggle Eddy escapes on his motorbike. Simon returns to his flat to find Long Harry murdered. He calls in Inspector Teal of the Yard, who tells him that the Scorpion is wanted in connection with several crimes. Simon visits Patsy at her home and questions her about the Scorpion, then he returns to see Mark Deverest who finally confesses that he is being blackmailed over an earlier indiscretion. Patsy is savagely attacked by Eddy on instructions from the Scorpion and is hospitalised. The Saint returns home with Karen and finds a small package has been left. Karen opens the package and a large Scorpion crawls onto her hand, but Simon manages to knock it off before it stings Karen. While Simon is out Karen takes a message from the hospital that Patsy wants to see him urgently. Patsy tells Karen that the only clue she has to the Scorpion's identity is a telephone number, then, while leaving the hospital, she is kidnapped by the Scorpion. Simon returns to the Bird's Nest to question Bird, the club's owner. Eddy appears and attacks Simon, but The Saint knocks him out. Can Simon rescue Karen in time before the deadly Scorpion strikes again?

Based on the 1932 novella, *The Inland Revenue*, originally Published in *The Thriller* as *The Masked Menace*.

THE REVOLUTION RACKET (1964)

Simon Templar	Roger Moore
Doris Inkler	Suzanne Lloyd
Carlos Xavier	Eric Pohlmann
Pablo Enriquez	Peter Arne
Sherm Inkler	Edward Bishop
Manuel Enriquez	Michael Godfrey
Vincente	Hal Gallili
Jose Jalisco	Alec Mango
Esteban	Clive Cazes
Rainer	Michael Lynch
Francisco	Reginald Jessup
Juan	Walter Randall
Immigration Officer	Richard Montez
Screenplay by	Terry Nation
Directed by	Pat Jackson

THE SAINT IS IN South America, at a sports arena, watching a game of Hi-Li when a man approaches him. A gun is stuck in his back, and the man takes Simon to a nearby restaurant where he is shown to a table. Waiting for him is the local Police Inspector Carlos Xavier. The Inspector tells Simon that the man with the gun was his little joke, as he knows that The Saint thrives on danger. Carlos points out to Simon the other people in the restaurant: there is Doris Inkler, an attractive American girl, and the Enriquez brothers, who according to Carlos, are very bad men. Carlos tells Simon that the brothers have been making millions out of the country and that they are under investigation by the Government. He also tells Simon that the brothers are about to finance a revolution that would put the Government out of office. The Inspector knows Simon's reputation and asks him for his help. As Simon leaves the restaurant he sees Doris being forced into a car by Manuel Enriquez and a man called Francisco. Manuel drives off, and Simon follows Francisco down a side street. He corners him and forces him to tell him where they have taken her. Doris has been taken by Manuel to a cellar where she is reunited with he partner, Sherm. The two of them are gun runners. The Enriquez brothers know this and need the guns to start their revolution. They make a deal and the brothers release them, and Sherm goes off to arrange delivery of the guns. Simon confronts Doris, and tells her that by providing guns for the revolution, a lot of innocent people will be killed. Doris tells him that there are no guns, and that the boxes contain only bars of lead. They plan to trick the Enriquez brothers, and in return for Simon's help she offers him a third of the money. There are a few real guns in the cases just in case the brothers want to examine them. The guns are to be transported to a small village 100 miles away. The brothers examine one of the cases before they leave and Doris makes sure the right one is opened. The trucks leave and a dangerous and hazardous journey lies ahead with several mishaps before it's over. Will the Police Captain be able to help Simon? Can Doris and her partner be trusted completely? Will Simon uncover the truth behind the revolution racket?

Based on the 1958 novella.

THE SAINT STEPS IN (1964)

Simon Templar	Roger Moore
Andrea Quennel	Justine Lord
Hobart Quennel	Geoffrey Keen
Walter Devan	Peter Vaughan
Calvin Gray	Moultrie Kelsall
Madeline Gray	Annette Andre
Morgan	Neil McCarthy
Smith	Michael Robbins
Cy Imberline	Edward Bishop
Detective Inspector	
Malloy	Robert Bruce
Undergraduates	Nicholas Pennell
	David Jackson
Screenplay by	John Kruse
Directed by	John Gilling

SIMON IS IN London, staying at the Savoy Plaza hotel while his flat is being decorated. He is at the hotel bar when he is approached by a pretty girl who asks him for help, and shows him a letter warning her to stay away from a man called Quennel. Simon refuses to help, thinking it has been arranged as a joke by the two young men at the bar. The girl, Madeline Gray, leaves in a taxi and is followed by two men in a car. Simon goes over to question the two young men at the bar about the girl, but they tell him that they have never seen her before, and so realising his mistake, Simon questions the doorman and chases after her. Simon catches up with her just as she is about to be taken away by the two men. He tackles them and they run off. He takes her home after they have tried to visit a business associate of her father's, Hobart Quennel. Madeline tells Simon that her father has

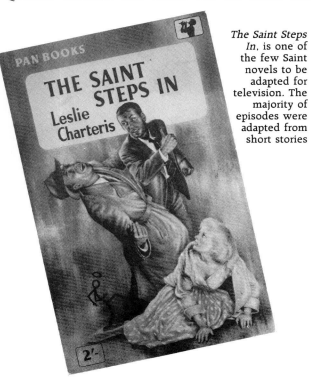

The Saint Steps In, is one of the few Saint novels to be adapted for television. The majority of episodes were adapted from short stories

perfected a new chemical called 'process G' which Quennel is interested in. Simon calls on Quennel again and is greeted by his daughter Andrea. He then meets Quennel and questions him about Calvin Gray's new discovery, but Quennel tells Simon that it is worthless. The Saint believes that someone is out to steal Gray's formula. He returns to his hotel where he finds Andrea waiting for him, but before he can discover why she is there Madeline rushes into the room, telling him she has tried to telephone her father and there is no reply. They drive down to Gray's country house, and search the place but he is nowhere to be found. Simon sees a light coming from the Gray's laboratory: he goes in and finds Morgan, one of the men who attacked Madeline, searching the place. Simon questions him and as he is about to reveal where Gray is, Smith (another hood) appears, fires at Simon, but shoots Morgan instead. Simon calls in the police and Inspector Malloy takes charge. Quennel pays a visit on Madeline and tells her that his right-hand man Walter Devan has disappeared. Simon returns to London to pay a call on Cy Imberline, the man who has offered Gray $1,000,000 for process G. Simon leaves and returns to his hotel room to find Andrea waiting for him again. He asks her to help him find Walter Devan and she agrees. Back at the Gray house, Madeline is under police guard. Suddenly there is an explosion in Gray's lab, the police go off to investigate and Madeline is kidnapped by Smith. Simon drives Andrea back to the Quennel house, where he finds Quennel talking with Devan. Quennel tells Simon that he arranged the kidnapping of Gray. Simon holds them at gunpoint, while he questions them about process G. Quennel tells Simon that if the process is manufactured it will put him out of business. Smith sneaks up behind Simon and knocks him out. Andrea questions her father about Simon, but he strikes her and tells her to stay out of his business. Simon recovers to find he is a prisoner in Quennel's cellar, and is told that he must persuade Gray to sign over the formula to Quennel or they will all be killed. Can the Saint come up with an electrifying plan to free them, or is it the last time, the Saint steps in to a case?

Based on the 1944 novel.

THE LOVING BROTHERS (1964)

Simon Templar	Roger Moore
Pop Kinsall	Reg Lye
Willie Kinsall	Ray Barrett
Wally Kinsall	Ed Devereaux
Edna Kinsall	Betty McDowall
Charley O'Shea	Dick Bentley
Pete Grove	Grant Taylor
Joe Casey	Noel Trevarthen
Assayer	John Tate
Linda Henderson	Annette Andre

Screenplay by	John Graeme
Directed by	Leslie Norman

THE SAINT IS in Australia, driving through the bush, when his Land Rover breaks down. His search for the nearest town takes him to Stoney Creek and to Pop Kinsall, a rugged old man who greets him with a rifle. Pop's unfriendly greeting changes when Linda Henderson comes out of the house. She is Pop's district nurse. Pop is quite a character. – twice he has struck a fortune, and then lost it all. However, in between the two strikes he has been able to stake his two sons Willie and Wally, who are now wealthy men living in Sydney. Pop now has an option on a mine which he believes contains silver and will be his richest strike yet. The only thing that is holding him up is capital – he needs £3,000 to take up the option on the mine. Pop tells Simon that his boys will finance him, but Simon later finds out from Linda that there is little hope of that. Pop hasn't seen his boys for over 15 years – they just don't want to know him. Back in Sydney the two brothers are quarrelling as usual, and refuse to accept telephone calls from their father. Pop tells Simon that they are going to help, but Simon can see through his bluff. Simon suggests to Pop that they go to Sydney. Pop goes to see the boys while Simon arranges for an assayer's report on the mine. The boys refuse to see Pop and he returns to Stoney Creek with Simon. The boys later learn that Pop has struck it rich, and they rush back to see him, only to learn that Simon has gone into partnership with him. Willie and Wally want part of the action, and it's up to The Saint to teach a lesson to the loving brothers.

Based on the 1934 short story.

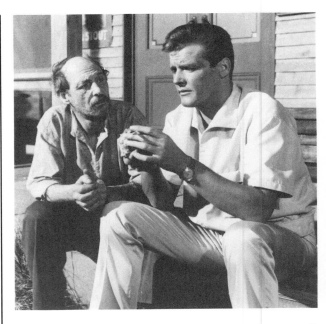

In the Australian outback, Simon meets up with Pop Kisall, played by Reg Lye

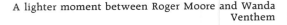

A lighter moment between Roger Moore and Wanda Venthem

THE MAN WHO LIKED TOYS (1964)

Simon Templar	**Roger Moore**
Inspector Teal	**Ivor Dean**
Lewis Enstone	**John Baskcomb**
Marjorie Enstone	**Jeanne Moody**
John Hammel	**John Paul**
George Fowler	**Maurice Kaufmann**
Claire Wheeler	**Rosemary Reede**
Harry Duggan	**David Lodge**
Albert Costello	**Inigo Jackson**
Screenplay by	**Basil Dawson**
Directed by	**John Gilling**

SIMON MEETS Lewis Enstone, a portly man with a love of toys. Enstone's secretary, Claire Wheeler, believes that he is being blackmailed and asks Simon to investigate. Simon follows Enstone's assistant and discovers that Enstone is not being blackmailed, but that he is paying off a man called Duggan, a union man who is behind the strikes at a rival firm to Enstone's, a firm which Enstone wishes to buy. Simon questions Duggan and after a fight with The Saint, Duggan sees the error of his ways and agrees to end the strike. Enstone discovers that his wife Marjorie is having an affair with his personal assistant, George Fowler. That evening Simon pays a visit to Enstone just after he has had a meeting with Hammel and Costello, the directors of the company he plans to take over. Simon hears a shot and finds Enstone dead, shot in the head. Simon calls in his old adversary, Inspector Teal, who believes it to be a case of suicide, but Simon calls it murder. Simon questions Mrs Enstone who confesses to having an affair with Fowler, but Simon is convinced that the guilty parties who murdered Enstone are Hammel and Costello, the two men Enstone tried to put out of business. But how did they persuade Enstone to take his own life? Simon breaks into their business offices to search for clues, and a few more bullets are fired before the case of 'the man who liked toys' is closed.

Based on the 1934 short story.

THE DEATH PENALTY (1964)

Simon Templar	**Roger Moore**
Abdul Osman	**Paul Stassino**
Galbraith Stride	**Brewster Mason**
Laura Stride	**Wanda Venthem**
Toby Haildon	**Scot Finch**
Colonel Latignant	**Arnold Diamond**
Clements	**Rory MacDermot**
Smith	**William Marlowe**
Trape	**Alan Curtis**
Dali	**Arthur Gomez**
Suzu	**Philo Hauser**
Screenplay by	**Ian Stuart Black**
Directed by	**Jeremy Summers**

TRAVELLING THROUGH Marseilles late at night Simon narrowly misses hitting a man on the road, and on stopping his car he discovers that the man has been shot in the back. The following day while driving through the mountains Simon offers a lift to a young woman, Laura Stride, who has just had a row with her boyfriend. Laura invites Simon in to meet her father Galbraith Stride. Laura asks Simon if he will take her to dinner that evening, as she had already booked reservations. Simon agrees and leaves to check into his hotel, where he is visited by Colonel Latignant of the local police who warns Simon to stay out of trouble. That evening during dinner Laura's boyfriend Toby arrives. Simon invites him to join them and suggests that he take Laura for a dance while he visits the owner of the club, an old friend. Simon enters the manager's office and finds him being threatened by two men who plan to take over the nightclub. Simon recognises one of the men, Osman, from the previous evening when the man was killed. Osman is trying to take over the local branch of a crime syndicate known as the Latini. After threatening Simon to stay out of his way, Osman leaves. Laura returns home to find her father and Osman discussing business plans, but she is unaware that her father is the present head of the Latini. Returning from the nightclub, Simon is attacked by two of Osman's men, but he chases them off. The next day Osman visits Laura and invites her to visit him on his yacht. Osman begins to woo Laura as part of his plan to oust Stride from the organisation. Simon visits Stride and reveals that he knows of his involvement with Osman. He warns Stride that he is out to get him and Osman, and break up the Latini. Stride goes to see Osman and warns him to stay away from his daughter, in return for which he will give up part control of the organisation, but Osman wants complete control. Laura returns to see Osman on his yacht. Later, when she tries to leave she finds she is a prisoner. Simon and Toby set out to rescue her, but before the case is closed both Stride and Osman will have paid the 'death penalty'.

Based on the 1933 novella.

THE IMPRUDENT POLITICIAN (1964)

Simon Templar	Roger Moore
Christopher Waites	Anthony Bate
Janet Waites	Jennifer Wright
Denise Grant	Justine Lord
Colin Phillips	Michael Gough
Spencer Vallance	Maxwell Shaw
Tim Burton	Jeremy Burnham
Alex Morgan	Mike Pratt
Helen Phillips	Jean Marsh
Mister Anthony	John Bryans
Ken Shield	Moray Watson
Mechanic	Jimmy Gardner
Screenplay by	Norman Hudis
Directed by	John Moxey

SIMON TEMPLAR visits an old friend, Christopher Waites, MP and his wife, at the Houses of Parliament. During tea with Simon, Waites is called away by an urgent message. Waites is handed a note by a messenger, a man with blackmail on his mind. Waites makes his excuses to his wife and Simon and invites Simon down to his country house for the weekend. He then leaves and heads to the flat of his mistress, Denise Grant. A copy of a letter he had written to Denise was shown to him by the blackmailer, but Denise denies giving the letter to anyone. Waites leaves the flat and is confronted by two men who demand money in return for the original letter. Waites refuses and heads home to the country house, where a weekend party awaits him. A messenger from the Prime Minister bearing a copy of an important speech for Waites to be read in Parliament on Monday is ambushed by two men, but before they can snatch the security bag Simon drives up and the men run off. Simon realises that Waites is being blackmailed, and at the request of Janet Waites he agrees to help flush out the blackmailers. The next day he travels to London to Fleet Street, to see Ken Shield, a 'society' reporter. He questions Ken about various guests at the party, as they all seemed to be likely blackmail suspects. Simon then decides to visit Denise, Waites's mistress, and while questioning her he is confronted by two men, Burton and Morgan, the blackmailers, and after a brief struggle Simon is knocked out and the men escape. The next day Janet Waites receives a message from the blackmailers to meet her on a boat moored on the Thames. She is made the same offer that was made to her husband, a look at the ministry report before it is made public. Janet leaves to fetch the report. Shortly afterwards Simon arrives at the boat and is attacked by Morgan, but this time The Saint gets the upper hand. Janet delivers the vital document, but Simon prevents the papers from changing hands and recovers the blackmail note. Simon and Janet return to the Waites's house and leave the papers in Waites's safe in a final attempt to flush out the mastermind behind the blackmail plot. Can Simon discover the identity of the blackmailer, before the imprudent politician goes to Parliament the next day.

Based on the 1933 short story, *The Appalling Politician*.

THE HI-JACKERS (1964)

Simon Templar	Roger Moore
Mathilde Baum	Ingred Schoeller
Robert Pargo	Robert Nichols
Ed Jopley	Neil McCallum
Hans Lasser	Walter Gotell
Sergeant Henry Johns	Kevin Scott
Borieff	Michael Collins
Schultz	Richard Shaw
Major Smith	Shane Rimmer
P.F.C. Kirk	Roy Stephens
Screenplay by	Paul Erickson
Directed by	David Eady

THE SAINT IS IN Munich at the time of the famous October Festival. As he watches the parade go by he spots an old friend, Sergeant Henry Johns, in the crowd. The meeting is fortunate for Henry as he is with his girlfriend, Mathilde Baum. The Sergeant had promised to take Mathilde out, but he has drawn guard duty for the evening. He asks Simon if he will help out and look after Mathilde until he comes off duty at midnight. Sergeant Johns never keeps his appointment as he is murdered while trying to stop a robbery at the base. It was a well-planned crime in which Mathilde was involved, along with three men, Jopley, Borieff and Schultz. The gang received their orders from the mysterious Mr Lasser. The stolen Army goods are taken away in a hi-jacked US truck. A friend is dead and Simon takes a personal interest in the case. He soon discovers that Mathilde is involved in the crime when he talks to Master Sergeant Robert Pargo, who also thinks that Mathilde is his girlfriend. He was tricked into letting her steal the key to the storeroom.

Simon and the Sergeant team up to get the goods back, and the gang nearly get caught when they switch the stolen goods from one truck to another. Simon manages to recapture the goods when the truck crashes trying to run Simon off the road.

The Saint still has to capture the gang and their leader, not forgetting Mathilde. The Saint will make sure that the hi-jackers pay.

Based on the 1937 novella, *The Unlicensed Victuallers*.

THE UNKIND PHILANTHROPIST (1964)

Simon Templar	Roger Moore
Elmer Quire	Charles Farrell
Dolores Gamma	Pat Michon
Juan Gamma	David Graham
Tristan Brown	Sarah Brackett
Victor Gamma	Garry Fulsham
Twinewright	John Bloomfield
Maria Gamma	Dawn Davies
Portagee	Anthony Morton
Alicron	Larry Taylor
Mrs. Hendricks	Joan Ingram
Chic Woman	Olive Lucius
Screenplay by	Marcus Demain
Directed by	Jeremy Summers

SIMON TEMPLAR is in Puerto Rico, where he goes to the aid of an attractive young girl whose car has broken down. She reluctantly accepts his help, and she later tells him that she is not the least bit interested in the famous Simon Templar. The girl, with an unusual name, Tristan Brown, is in Puerto Rico on behalf of an American charity organisation. She is there to find someone who can be left in charge of the organisation's money to be distributed among the poor and needy. Tristan thinks that Elmer Quire is the man she's looking for. He's a local man with a good reputation, but unknown to her, Quire is really a ruthless trickster. Simon discovers the truth about Quire when he learns that he is about to foreclose on a mortgage taken out by a local farmer, Juan Gamma. Quire plans to sell the land to a wealthy American for a large profit. Simon goes to Juan's aid when he is threatened by Quire's men. He chases them off; legally there is nothing he can do, but The Saint is known for bending the law. Elmer Quire has heard of Tristan Brown, but does not know she's a girl. Simon borrows the name, and posing as Brown, he goes to see Quire. He fools him into thinking that he is going to be put in charge of the organisation's funds, and he then tricks Quire into putting down a deposit as a sign of good faith. Simon hands the money over to Juan who uses it to pay off the mortgage. Quire then discovers who the real Tristan Brown is. Can The Saint complete his plan and teach a lesson to the unkind philanthropist?

Based on the 1955 short story.

THE DAMSEL IN DISTRESS (1965)

Simon Templar	Roger Moore
Allessandro Naccaro	Richard Wyler
Barbara Astral	Catherine Woodville
Domenick Naccaro	Paul Whitsun-Jones
Guiseppe Rolfieri	Harold Kasket
Inspector Teal	Ivor Dean
Arthur	Ray Austin
Guido Naccaro	John Bluthal
Maria Naccaro	Camilla Hasse
Jennifer	Gwynneth Tighe
Screenplay by	Paul Erickson
Directed by	Peter Yates

SIMON RELAXES AT home with his friend Jennifer. Suddenly the door bell rings and they are interrupted by restaurant owner Domenick Naccaro, and his daughter Maria, who is holding a small baby. He tells Simon that he is the only one who can help. Domenick takes Simon back to his restaurant and there he tells him that the father of Maria's child is Guiseppe Rolfieri, and that he disappeared before he could marry Maria. The next day Simon goes to Rolfieri's offices to enquire about him. He finds Inspector Teal there investigating Rolfieri's disappearance and the embezzlement of £1,000,000.

Simon and Barbara Astral (Catherine Woodville) are about to aid *The Damsel in Distress*

Simon returns to the restaurant where Domenick tells him that Rolfieri has been traced to Florence, and he asks Simon to fly out with his son Allessandro to bring him back. Simon and Allessandro go to see Guido, a relative of Domenick's, and he tells them that Rolfieri and his secretary, Barbara are staying at a villa nearby. Simon calls at the villa in answer to an advert in the local paper for a chauffeur. Barbara likes him and he is hired. That evening Simon searches Rolfieri's study for clues to the hiding place of the money. Later he returns to see Guido and tells him to have a small plane standing by, and he also wants something to drug Rolfieri with. The next day Simon drives Barbara into town, and while she is off shopping he meets Allessandro who gives him the drug. He leaves unaware that he is being followed by Rolfieri's man Arthur, who then follows Allessandro. He attacks him in an alleyway and steals his passport. Arthur reports to Rolfieri who checks up on Simon's references, and Simon returns to the villa unaware that his cover has been broken. That evening Simon plans to slip the drug into Rolfieri's wine in the study, but he is interrupted by Arthur and Rolfieri. They attack him and after a savage fight with Arthur, Simon is stopped when Arthur pulls a gun on him and he is knocked out. They drive the unconscious Simon to a lonely wooded area, where they drag him onto the driving seat and release the car's brakes. The car rushes down the hill through the woods heading for the lake. If Simon is not around, who will see that Maria's honour is protected? Who will bring Rolfieri to justice and rescue the damsel in distress?

Based on the 1934 short story.

THE CONTRACT (1965)

Simon Templar	**Roger Moore**
Dunstan	**Dick Haymes**
Farnberg	**Robert Hutton**
Eileen Ballinger	**Elizabeth Weaver**
Inspector Teal	**Ivor Dean**
Ardossi	**John Bennett**
Friste	**Michael Peake**
Chuck Powers	**Richard Easton**
Doctor Jerome	**Douglas Muir**
Mrs Evans	**Mary Jones**
Screenplay by	**Terry Nation**
Directed by	**Roger Moore**

SEVERAL YEARS ago an American airman named Farnberg, was involved in a robbery on his airbase. He was eventually caught and sent to prison, but the money was never recovered. It was partly The Saint's evidence that helped convict him. Now Farnberg is back, he's out to recover the stolen money, and get even with The Saint. The first indication that Simon has that Farnberg is back, is when he is nearly run over by him. Simon is saved just in time by an American Airforce man, Dunstan, who was the security chief at the base at the time of the robbery. Dunstan explains to Simon that he has been following Farnberg ever since his release from prison. A clue leads Simon and Dunstan to a woman called *Ballinger*, who is the widow of an American airman killed in a plane crash just after the robbery. Simon warns her that he believes her husband was involved in the robbery, and that he hid the stolen money for Farnberg while he was in prison. Mrs *Ballinger* insists that her husband did not leave the money with her, but Simon warns her that now Farnberg is back, her life is in danger. Simon and Dunstan continue with their investigations, and then another attempt is made on Simon's life. Slowly it becomes clear what happened the night of the robbery. Simon discovers that an Airforce man, Chuck Powers, who flew with *Ballinger* the night of the crash, is alive but an invalid. Simon visits him and he gives the Saint vital information about the events leading up to the crash. The race is on for the money. Who will find it first — Simon or Farnberg? The case builds up to a climax, a case that began when three men signed a contract that led to murder.

Based on the 1931 novella, *The Impossible Crime*.

Simon and Dunston confer with Inspector Teal

Teal questions Simon and the lovely Oonagh O'Grady as to their involvement in a casino robbery

THE SET-UP

Simon Templar	Roger Moore
Oonagh O'Grady	Penelope Horner
Ted Orping	John Stone
Tex Goldman	Henry Gilbert
Chief Inspector Teal	Ivor Dean
Jack Laurie	Edward Underdown
Nilder	Redmond Phillips
Clem Enright	Norman Florence
Corrigan	Anthony Waser
Mrs Donaldson	Faith Kent
Screenplay by	Paddy Manning O'Brine
Directed by	Roy Baker

THE SAINT is a seasoned traveller, and you can be certain that wherever he goes he is sure to know somebody. So it is not surprising that in a London gambling club he runs into Oonagh O'Grady, an attractive young actress whom he has known for some time. Oonagh introduces Simon to her agent, Tex Goldman, the man who has launched her on her screen career. Little does Simon know that his meeting with the lovely Oonagh will lead him into another exciting adventure and put him in a sniper's gunsight. A skilfully planned robbery is about to be undertaken by three men, Orpin, Corrigan and Enright. They cosh the club owner, Jack Laurie, and are about to get away with a large sum of money, when they are stopped by the doorman, Charley Baker. He makes a grab at Corrigan, and Orping shoots him. Orping and Enright make their getaway, leaving Corrigan to struggle with the dying man. He eventually escapes, but is pursued by Simon. He returns to his home with Simon close behind him. Orping realises that Corrigan is a potential danger to the gang and waits in hiding at the flat. Simon catches up with Corrigan and starts to question him, but before he can reveal the names of the other gang members, Orping shoots him and escapes. Chief Inspector Teal takes charge of the case and he is not at all pleased that Simon is involved. Orping reports back to the gang's boss about Simon's involvment in the case, and the boss issues the order to kill The Saint. Chief Inspector Teal believes that the robbery is the latest in a long series of crimes which are building up to one big final job. Teal is correct, the gang is planning its biggest job, the hold-up of a mail van. The operation is very carefully planned, but first, The Saint must be removed. Once again Orping is given the role of assassin. He takes a room opposite Simon's house and sits waiting, ready with a telescopic rifle, waiting for the right moment to kill. Later that evening Oonagh calls on Simon, and as they settle down for a drink, Simon makes the perfect target in the window. Orping fires. Is this the bullet with Simon's name on it or has The Saint outwitted the gang with the set-up?

Based on the 1933 novella, *The Man from St.Louis.*

THE INESCAPABLE WORD (1965)

Simon Templar	Roger Moore
Marjorie North	Ann Bell
Jock Ingram	James Maxwell
Ivor North	Maurice Hedley
Professor Soren	Robert Dean
Professor Oakridge	Robert McLeod
Professor Walter Rand	Ronald Ibbs
Simms	Donald Bisset
Dr Carey	James Copeland
Thompson	Russell Waters
Screenplay by	Terry Nation
Directed by	Roy Baker

SIMON TEMPLAR is with a hunting party, grouse shooting in the Scottish highlands At the end of the day, walking back through the woods, Simon hears a high pitched noise and discovers a small dead animal. Simon then sees what appears to be a man in a spacesuit with some kind of laser gun. He is then hit on the back of the head by an unseen assailant. Simon returns to the hotel and is introduced by Ivor North, the owner and part-time constable, to Professor Oakridge and Jock Ingram, a scientist, and a security officer working at the top level research station nearby. Simon offers to help North search for one of his men who has not returned from the grouse

shoot, and for one of the hounds which is also missing. They go out onto the fog-shrouded moor where they find the dog standing guard over the man's dead body; all of the man's bones have become brittle. The next day Simon is asked by North to accompany him to the research station where there has been a murder. The dead man is scientist Professor Oakridge. Simon and North question the remaining members of the research team but no clue to the murder is found, although Professor Soren and Professor Rand seem to be hiding something. Simon, North and Ingram, the security chief leave but Simon sneaks back inside the centre to search one of the rooms to which he was refused entry by Professor Soren. He finds a secret door leading to the cellar where he finds the laser gun and costume. The next day Ingram arrives with background information on all of the scientists and a warrant to search the laboratory. Simon and North return to the station with Ingram. Simon arranges with North's daughter, Marjorie to go into town to bring back vital information that will reveal the killer. Someone overhears the call and tampers with Simon's car. Marjorie, driving through the fog to the centre, is stopped and attacked by a masked man who tries to kill her, but The Saint arrives just in time to save her and the killer escapes into the fog. They return to the lab with a clue to the killer's identity. If Simon is to unmask the killer, he must ignore the inescapable word!

Based on the 1957 short story.

The Saint and Marjorie North have a mystery to solve. A man is accused of murder – his accuser, a word written in blood

THE RHINE MAIDEN (1965)

Simon Templar	**Roger Moore**
Charles Voyson	**Nigel Davenport**
Dr Schreiber	**Victor Beaumont**
Julia Harrison	**Stephanie Randall**
Hans	**Anthony Booth**
Inspector Glesson	**George Pravda**
Helga	**Adline Mandlova**
Otto	**Frederick Schiller**
Train Steward	**Ernst Walder**
Barman	**Michael Wolf**
English Man	**Ernest Hare**
English Woman	**Totti Truman Taylor**
Screenplay by	**Brian Degas**
Directed by	**James Hill**

SIMON TEMPLAR is staying at the Hotel Europa in Baden Baden, Germany, relaxing at the hotel's outdoor bar. He orders a drink; at that moment an attractive girl enters and sits down at one of the tables nearby. She is waiting to see a man called Voyson. Simon rescues the girl when a huge slab of masonry falls and crashes onto the table. The man who pushed the slab was Charles Voyson, the partner of the girl's father. Voyson has an elaborate plan to run off with £250,000 and change his identity. Simon takes the girl, Julia, up to see Voyson, and while he waits outside the room Julia questions Voyson about the money which has been taken from the business account. Voyson tells Julia that he is dying and then apparently collapses. Simon rushes into the room, and a few seconds later Dr Schreiber appears and takes Voyson off to his clinic, which is all part of Voyson's plan. Simon and Julia search the apartment but fail to find the money, and Simon realises that Schreiber is in the plot to help Voyson escape. That evening Simon and Julia visit the Schreiber clinic to see Voyson, and Schreiber tells them that Voyson died earlier that evening. Simon upsets Dr Schreiber when he asks to see the body, but they are taken and Julia identifies the body. Simon and Julia pretend to leave, but Simon sneaks back to search the clinic giving Julia instructions to go to the police if he does not return. Simon is caught by a man with a gun, but he overpowers him. Dr Schreiber enters his office and sees Simon's reflection in the glass and sends his nurse Helga to fetch his man Hans. Meanwhile, Julia, fearing Simon is in trouble, goes to see the local police chief Inspector Glessen. Simon is suddenly confronted by Dr Schreiber, Hans and Voyson. Julia returns to the clinic with Inspector Glessen to look for Simon. Meanwhile Voyson holds a gun on The Saint while Schreiber is questioned by the police. Schreiber convinces the Inspector that Julia is a former patient and cannot be trusted. They leave and Julia drives the Inspector back to the police station. Simon makes a desperate bid to escape before Schreiber returns to the room, but is knocked out by Voyson. Julia returns from the police station to keep a watch for Simon. Voyson leaves with Hans to take the next train to Switzerland, leaving Schreiber to kill The Saint. Schreiber prepares a hypodermic to kill him but is knocked out by Simon before he can use it. Voyson and Hans board the train with Simon and Julia racing to catch up at the next station. With seconds to spare they make the train. Simon and

Julia separate and begin to search the train. Hans goes to fetch Voyson some cigarettes and spots Julia, captures her and takes her back to Voyson. Hans then sets out to look for Simon: he attacks him with a knife, but The Saint gets the better of him and knocks him out. Simon climbs outside the train and works his way along to Voyson's carriage where Voyson is holding Julia at gunpoint. A man must die before the case of the Rhine maiden is closed.

Based on a 1954 short story.

THE GOLDEN FROG (1965)

Simon Templar	Roger Moore
Alice Nestor	Jacqueline Ellis
Nestor	Hugh McDermott
Captain Quintana	Alan Tilvern
General Cuevas	Walter Brown
Fergus Maclish	Alex McCrindle
Loro	Inia Te Wiata
Julio	Alvaro Fontana
Paco	Barry Shawzin
Vargos	Alan Curtis
Screenplay by	Michael Cramoy
Directed by	John Moxey

THE SAINT IS in Latin America. He has been called there by a friend, Fergus Maclish, a rugged old Scot, who has spent his last few years running an English-style inn. He had been saving up his money so that he could return to England to retire. Fergus's plans had been upset when he had been swindled out of his savings by a 'Prof' Humphrey Nestor and his daughter. He warns Simon that the very attractive, Alice Nestor, is just as scheming as her father. Simon discovers that besides the Nestors he has another problem on his hands, that of General Cuevas, who is plotting a revolution. The General puts his man Julio on Simon's tail. The 'Prof' and his daughter think that they have found another sucker in Simon, and they show him a gold statue carved in the shape of a frog. They tell him that it is one of the sacred frogs of the Incas, and that there are lots more of them if they can raise the money to fund an expedition. Simon (knowing that it's a trick) goes along with the plan. The only problem is that Julio is keeping an eye on him constantly, and now Captain Quintana of the Security Police has also taken an interest in him. The expedition leaves – the Nestors have a few things planned along the route, but they are unaware that Simon has a few things planned for them. Suddenly, they are attacked by the Aztecs. It's all part of the Nestors' plan – the Indians are fought off and the party continues up river. Simon slips off and plants some phoney gold, well aware that when he 'finds' it later the Nestors will take an interest in it. Later Simon discovers an additional problem – the Nestors have been forced to take a cargo of arms along with them for the revolutionaries. Simon has a lot on his hands. He must prevent the guns from falling into the wrong hands, and at the same time teach a lesson to the Nestors over the affair of the Golden Frog.

Based on the 1958 novella.

Jacqueline Ellis and Hugh McDermott try their best to trick Roger Moore as The Saint, over the affair of *The Golden Frog*

THE SIGN OF THE CLAW

Simon Templar	Roger Moore
Jean Morland	Suzan Farmer
Don Morland	Peter Copely
Max Valmon	Godfrey Quigley
Major Rowney	Geoffrey Frederick
Dr Julias	Leo Leyden
Angkor	Kenjin Takari
Tawau	Burt Kwouk
Gale	John Rees
Harlun	Kristopher Kum
Rawach	Michael Chow
Screenplay by	Terry Nation
Directed by	Leslie Norman

THE SAINT IS in the jungles of South-East Asia. It's a different world from the usual, more sophisticated one he can usually be found in. The reason he is there is to help an old friend, Jean Morland, an attractive young girl, who has sent for him. Besides helping Jean, Simon has another purpose for being there, as he is on an undercover assignment for the British Government. His task is to find, and stop a terrorist who has been stirring up a lot of trouble recently, and has caused the death of one of Simon's friends. Jean's father, Donald Morland, has recently inherited a farm from his brother, but he is already facing demands from a neighbour, Max Valmon, to sell up, and move out. Valmon wants the property, one way or another. Simon has been staying with the Morlands for only a couple of days when the house is attacked by terrorists. Donald Morland is injured, and one of the servants killed. The attack is called off only when Simon succeeds in getting a message through to the Army. He realises that something strange is happening at Valmon's farm, and several incidents lead up to the kidnapping of Morland. Valmon admits to Simon that he and his partner, Dr Julias, are behind the campaign to overthrow the government, and later Jean is also kidnapped and held as a hostage. Can Simon rescue Jean and her father? There's a deadly time ahead for The Saint when he goes up against the sign of the claw.

Based on the 1942 novella, *Arizona*.

Peter Copely, Susan Farmer and Roger Moore

THE FRIGHTENED INN-KEEPER

Simon Templar	Roger Moore
Martin Jeffroll	Michael Gwynn
Julia Jeffroll	Suzanne Neve
Tom Kane	Percy Herbert
Portmore	Howard Marion Crawford
Weems	Norman Bird
Yesterman	John Gabriel
Bellamy	Edward Cast

Screenplay by	Norman Hudis
Directed by	Roy Baker

THE SAINT receives an urgent request from a young girl called Julia Jeffroll, who tells The Saint that she needs his help and asks him to come to a remote inn in Cornwall. Her letter says that there are strange and frightening things happening there. The Saint responds to her plea for help, but on his arrival at the inn he receives a cool reception from Julia's father, the inn-keeper, Martin Jeffroll. He makes it obvious that he does not want The Saint there, and it's obvious to Simon that he is very frightened. Julia tells Simon that at night there are strange noises, and that her father is afraid of the three men who are staying at the inn. They have been there for the last six weeks, and like Jeffroll, they are all former members of the Royal Engineers' Corps. Later that day Simon almost comes to blows with one of the men, Tom Kane, and after the incident Simon is convinced more than ever that Julia needs his help. That night, as Martin Jeffroll and the three men go off in a truck, Simon decides to have a look around. At first he can find nothing wrong, but as he examines the cellar, he finds a tunnel with a purpose-built railway. The next day, Julia, overhears a conversation between the three men in which they talk about coming into a large sum of money. What kind of mystery has The Saint stumbled on to? What kind of hold do the three men have over the frightened inn-keeper?

Based on the 1934 novella, *The Case of the Frightened Inn-Keeper.*

Simon Templar seeks the answer in a mysterious underground tunnel to the mystery of *The Frightened Inn-Keeper*

SIBAO (1965)

Simon Templar	Roger Moore
Theron Netlord	John Carson
Sibao	Jeanne Roland
Tony Kreiger	Jerry Stovin
Atherton Lee	Nicholas Stuart
Dr Farrere	Kevin Stoney
Manon	Christopher Carlos
Tamo	Tracey Connell
Hamilton	Bruce Boa
Brinkley	John McLauren
Voodoo Dancer	Boscoe Holder

Screenplay by	Terry Nation
Directed by	Peter Yates

THE SAINT is on the island of Haiti, an island known to be the haven of voodoo and black magic. Atherton Lee, the owner of the hotel where Simon is staying, discusses the power of voodoo with him and Tony Kreiger, a sceptical American. They arrange to visit one of the local nightclubs that evening where black magic is practised. At the club Simon meets Sibao, a mystical young lady who performs tricks in the club. She is called away by Theron Netlord, an Englishman who tells her that she should not use her powers for simple parlour tricks. Kreiger becomes drunk and abusive and Simon tells him to leave. Driving away, Kreiger is unaware that his brakes have been tampered with; the car goes out of control and he accidentally runs into Sibao and her brother walking home. Her brother is knocked down and killed. As they are driving back to the hotel Simon and Lee come across the accident. Lee takes Kreiger back to the hotel while Simon returns Sibao to her village, where she is examined by the local doctor and found to a have only a few bruises. Simon leaves and passes by a voodoo ritual of the body of her dead brother. As he is driving back to the hotel, his car stops and refuses to start. Meanwhile back at the ceremony, Sibao's brother's body has mysteriously disappeared. Suddenly Simon's car starts up again and upon returning to the hotel he finds Kreiger dead from a broken back. Simon goes through Kreiger's belongings and finds a security card with the name David Grant, Kreiger's real identity, and so he telephones Hamilton a US security chief in Washington, who sends down another agent Brinkley, to replace Grant. Brinkley tells Simon that Grant had been sent by Washington to keep an eye on Netlord. Later that day Simon receives a visit from Netlord who invites him to his house for supper that evening. The meal will be cooked by Netlord's fiancée, Sibao. Before he leaves the hotel Simon receives a package, inside which he finds a strange talisman, sent by Sibao to protect him. He arrives at Netlord's house to discover that the wedding ceremony is to be later that evening. He also discovers that the only reason Netlord is marrying Sibao is that he will then be trained in all the secrets of voodoo. After the meal Simon discovers that he has been drugged by Netlord. Simon pulls a gun and after the brief struggle Netlord shoots him and leaves for the ceremony. Can Sibao save Simon in time to stop Netlord before the ceremony has been completed?

Based on the 1955 short story, *The Questing Tycoon*.

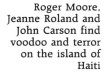
Roger Moore, Jeanne Roland and John Carson find voodoo and terror on the island of Haiti

THE CRIME OF THE CENTURY
(1965)

Simon Templar	Roger Moore
Bernhard Raxel	Andre Morell
Betty Tregarth	Sarah Lawson
Crantor	William Lucas
Inspector Teal	Ivor Dean
Gregory Marring	Peter Jeffrey
David Tregarth	David Saire
Phillip Gray	John Forbes-Robertson
Gloria Mancini	Carol Cleveland
Joan Vendel	Alexandra Bastedo
Flavel	Cyril Chamberlain
Madeline	Maggie Wright

Screenplay by	Terry Nation
Directed by	John Gilling

SIMON TEMPLAR is in London, and at the invitation of Inspector Teal he joins him at a piano recital. Teal's real reason for inviting The Saint is to point out to him Bernhard Raxel, the man, who according to Teal, was about to commit the crime of the century. The next day Raxel orders the murder of one of his men, whom he has discovered was really an undercover policeman. Simon agrees to help the police, and accompanies Teal to London Airport where he will assume the identity of an American safecracker, called Munster. Simon is briefed by Teal on Munster's background, and on leaving the plane Munster is arrested by Teal's men. Betty Tregarth is also at the airport about to go off on holiday. She is stopped from boarding the plane by phoney police officers, on the pretext that her brother has been in a car accident. Betty is taken by the men to a large country house, owned by Raxel, and she is told by him that unless she co-operates her brother will be killed. Betty is the head of a government research team working on top secret experiments with a new nerve gas. Simon, as Munster, is paged at the airport and picks up instructions to go to a London nightclub. There he meets Madeline, a hostess, who pushes him into a lift. As he leaves the lift he is attacked by Marring, one of Raxel's men. Simon overpowers him, but a second man appears with a gun, who then handcuffs Simon to a safe and gives him three minutes to open the safe to prove he is Munster. If he fails to open it in time he will be killed by a small phial of nerve gas. With only seconds to spare Simon opens the safe. Simon is then taken to meet Raxel. Marring is still not sure that Simon is Munster, so Raxel sends to New York for Munster's girlfriend, Gloria. The next day Raxel instructs an assembled group of criminals on the details of the crime. The plan is to steal the plates and paper from the Bank of England's printing house. A commando-style assault force goes through a test run. Simon is shown a mock-up of the master safe he is to crack, then they rehearse the plan over and over until Raxel is convinced it will work. Betty is forced to perfect the nerve gas under threat of her brother's life. The gas will be used to subdue all the security guards. Simon signals the Yard, and arranges to meet his contact the next evening in the grounds of the house. Simon arrives in the grounds the next night to find the police officer dead, killed by Marring who accuses Simon of being a spy. He takes him to see Raxel just as Munster's girlfriend arrives from the airport, but she greets Simon as if he were Munster. Raxel informs Simon that the robbery will take place that evening, and the gang proceeds to attack military style. Can Simon rescue Betty and her brother in time. Can he stop Raxel from getting away with the plates and prevent him from committing the crime of the century?

Based on the 1931 novella, *The National Debt.*

Ivor Dean as Inspector Claude Eustace Teal ponders how he can keep The Saint from getting involved in another murder case

THE HAPPY SUICIDE (1965)

Simon Templar	Roger Moore
Lois Morray	Jane Merrow
Ziggy Zaglan	John Bluthal
Ralph Damian	William Sylvester
Ted Coblin	Jerry Stovin
Paul Zaglan	William Dexter
James McCleary	Donald Sutherland
Captain Williams	Fred Sadoff
Texas Mother	Mavis Villiers
Jack Gill	Kevin Brennan
Screenplay by	Brian Degas
Directed by	Robert Tronson

SIMON IS IN New York, and late at night he watches Ziggy Zaglan, the current TV favourite, host his chat show. Shortly after the show Simon receives a visit from Ziggy's manager, Ralph Damian, who wants Simon to be a guest on Ziggy's show, but Simon refuses. On screen Ziggy is a warm pleasant person, off screen he is a nasty, unpleasant man. He fires one of the stage hands over a trivial matter and then threatens to fire his personal assistant, Lois Morray, unless she persuades Simon to change his mind. Lois goes to see Simon and tries to convince him to change his mind. Meanwhile Ziggy returns home to find his half brother, Paul, about to quit the show. Paul is Ziggy's scriptwriter and one of the reasons the show is a success. He is leaving to write a book about the real Ziggy Zaglan. Simon agrees, for Lois's sake, to meet Ziggy the next day. Later that evening Paul receives a visit from James McCleary, the brother of a young girl called Arlene who was involved with Ziggy. She died in a swimming accident. McCleary threatens Paul. The next day Lois and Simon arrive to find Paul dead. He has hanged himself – it was suicide. Simon finds a spool of tape still running in the recorder; he plays it back and then calls the police in. Ralph Damien, and Ziggy's press agent, Ted Coblin, arrive. Simon questions them about Paul's state of mind. They say he was very happy. Simon leaves and goes to Ziggy's boat, where he finds some rope, the same kind that was used in Paul's suicide. Ziggy prepares the script for his next show. He's rehearsing and overacting when Simon appears and tells him that he will reveal the identity of Paul's killer on the next show. Lois finds a tape in Ziggy's apartment and takes it to Simon. It's the sound of someone typing. The Saint goes to see McCleary at his flat; he is out, so he searches the place looking for clues. McCleary suddenly appears, and tells Simon about his sister's involvement with Ziggy. She was found dead after a swimming accident, but she was a perfect swimmer. McCleary also tells Simon about his visit to Paul's house, and that he struck him but did not kill him. Just then Captain Williams of the police department arrives and arrests McCleary for the murder of Paul. Lois telephones Ziggy and tells him that Simon knows who the killer is. On his way over to Ziggy's place, Simon's car has a burst tyre caused by some wood and nails being placed on the road, and then someone fires a shot at him. Does Simon know the real identity of the killer? What is the true story behind McCleary's sister's drowning? Could Paul Zaglan have possibly been a happy suicide?

Based on the 1957 short story.

THE CHEQUERED FLAG (1965)

Simon Templar	Roger Moore
Oscar Newley	Eddie Byrne
Mandy Ellington	Justine Lord
Beau Ellington	Edward De Souza
Catherine Marshall	Pamela Conway
Lee Leonard	Tim Barrett
Alec Hunter	Neil McCarthy
Bateman	John Kidd
Hunter's Landlady	Dorothy Frere
Bank Clerk	Eliza Buckingham
Screenplay by	**Norman Hudis**
Directed by	**Leslie Norman**

SIMON IS AT A motor racing track, where he is approached by a beautiful girl, Catherine Marshall, who asks Simon for his help. She points out to him Oscar Newley, one of the car owners. She tells Simon that Oscar was planning to go into partnership with her father who, before he died, had invented a new fuel injection system. Oscar borrowed the blueprints and then patented them under his own company's name. Simon knows a little about Oscar – he knows that he is permanently in financial difficulty. The Saint is not completely convinced by Catherine's story but he feels that the case is worth investigating. Simon approaches Oscar as a financial backer and wins his friendship. Bad luck seems to have dogged Oscar for some time now, and the only support he has is from his mechanic, Alec Hunter and his driver, Lee Leonard. Oscar is convinced that the man behind his troubles is the wealthy owner-driver Beau Ellington. Simon promises to invest money in Oscar's car if it wins the race, which is to be held the next day, but the car breaks down before the end of the race. Simon is convinced that someone is out to sabotage Newley. The next day Simon meets Beau's sister, Mandy, who makes it quite clear that she is attracted to Simon, and to complicate matters. Catherine is strongly attracted to Beau. Later that day there is a fire at Oscar's garage and Oscar is saved just in time from being killed when Simon manages to drag him out. Simon then takes Oscar's car out for a trial run, but unknown to The Saint the car has been tampered with and it crashes. The evidence points to Alec Hunter being involved, but the situation changes when Hunter is murdered. Simon has several suspects for the murder of Hunter, and it's a while before the chequered flag is brought down on the killer.

Based on the 1934 short story, *The Newdick Helicopter*.

Eddie Byrne, Roger Moore and Pamela Conway discuss the possibilities of sabotage

THE CROOKED RING (1965)

Simon Templar	**Roger Moore**
'Doc' Spangler	**Walter Brown**
Steve Nelson	**Tony Wright**
Whitey Mullins	**Meredith Edwards**
Connie Grady	**Jean Aubrey**
The Angel	**Nosher Powell**
Dave Saunders	**John Tate**
Max	**Barry Linehan**
Torpedo Smith	**Irvin Allen**
Mrs Barlow	**Doris Hare**
Radio Commentator	**McDonald Hobley**
Screenplay by	Harry W. Junkin
Directed by	Leslie Norman

SIMON RECEIVES a note asking him to visit Grady's Gymnasium. When he arrives he discovers that it was Grady's daughter, Connie, who sent for him. She is engaged to a boxer, Steve Nelson, a young man Simon knows well. Connie is scared. Steve's next fight is against an Australian boxer, known as the Masked Angel, and she is terrified that the men behind the 'Angel' are vicious syndicate crooks, and that they will do anything to protect their investment. Simon watches the 'Angel' working out with his sparring partner, Torpedo Smith. He then meets his trainer, Whitey Mullins, and his manager, 'Doc' Spangler. Simon is puzzled, as he watches the two men working out in the ring, for he can see that Torpedo is the better of the two men. Suddenly, Torpedo is floored by a blow that kills him. There are no signs of foul play, but Simon is sure that Torpedo did not throw the fight. He starts to question the people in the gym, in particular, 'Doc' Spangler, who is not pleased with Simon's interference. The next day Simon's flat is broken into, and he is attacked by one of Spangler's men, Max. Dave Snyder, the Torpedo's second, says there was nothing unusual about the fight between the two men. He tells Simon that for £500 he will snoop around for him. Simon leaves, and Dave goes straight to 'Doc' Spangler, and tells him that for £500, he will keep quiet. It's a fatal mistake for Dave, one that will cost him his life. When Simon returns to the gym he finds Dave dead, and then someone takes a shot at him. The next victim is Whitey Mullins, Steve's trainer, but it's not a serious wound. Things are starting to hot up. When Steve is out training he is deliberately run down and injured. Simon decides that with Steve out of the fight he must take his place, and so it is Saint vs. the Masked Angel. Can Simon discover close up how the 'Angel' wins his fights in the crooked ring?

Based on the 1948 novella, *The Masked Angel*.

Roger Moore, aided by Tony Wright, enters *The Crooked Ring* to solve a murder

THE ABDUCTORS (1965)

Simon Templar	Roger Moore
Jones	Dudley Foster
Brian Quell	Robert Urquhart
Madeline	Annette Andre
Olga	Jennifer Jayne
Sergeant Luduc	Robert Cawdron
Inspector Quercy	John Serrett
Alain	Nicholas Courtney
Professor Quell	Ronald Ibbs
Hotel Clerk	Sandor Eles
Peter	David Garfield
Mr Marson	Martin Wyldeck
Screenplay by	**Brian Degas**
Directed by	**Jeremy Summers**

AN ENGLISH GIRL Madeline Dawson, wins a weekend in Paris as a prize, and on arrival she finds it's far less glamorous and exciting than she had hoped, that is, until she meets The Saint. Something always happens when the Saint visits Paris. He is having a quiet drink in a nightclub, when he meets a fellow Englishman, Brian Quell, and an attractive hostess, Olga. Simon notices that Quell is agitated, and he tells The Saint that he is being watched by two men, Alain and Peter. Unknown to Simon, Olga is also agitated because she has failed so far to deliver Quell over to the two men. The Saint's unexpected appearance is interfering with their plan to kidnap Quell. Alain and Peter are working for a man called Jones, who plans to use Brian Quell as a decoy to lure his brother, Professor Quell to Paris so that he can be handed over to foreign agents. Jones eventually corners Brian in his hotel room, but Brian refuses to help them, and so Jones shoots him. Jones will now put his alternative plan into action, and posing as a friend of Brian's he will arrange to have the Professor flown to Paris to attend Brian's funeral. Simon is worried about Quell after their conversation in the nightclub so he goes to visit him at his hotel. He finds him dead in his room and, as he is leaving the room he spots two gendarmes approaching. He ducks quickly into the nearest room, which happens to be Madeline's. Suddenly the English girl has all the excitement she needs, but in trying to help Simon she is arrested as his accomplice, and once again, Simon comes under the suspicious eye of Inspector Quercy. Before the case is closed there are two more killings, one of them a policeman, and then Madeline is kidnapped by Jones. Simon must now not only rescue the Professor but also Madeline, and then deal out justice to the abductors.

Based on the 1933 novella, *The Gold Standard*.

A quiet weekend in Paris turns into an exciting adventure for Madeline (Annette André) when she meets The Saint

THE SMART DETECTIVE (1965)

Simon Templar	**Roger Moore**
Peter Corrio	**Brian Worth**
Janice Dixon	**Anna Lawson**
Aunt Prudence	**Fabia Drake**
Inspector Teal	**Ivor Dean**
Nick Nigkoma	**Barry Shawzin**
Mr Justin	**Martin Miller**
George	**Reg Lye**
Swann	**Larry Taylor**
Miller	**Dennis Blake**
Garage Mechanic	**Ron Welling**
Screenplay by	**Michael Cramoy**
Directed by	**John Moxey**

SIMON TEMPLAR is at a London jewellery exhibition where he meets a private detective, Pete Corrio who has built up quite a reputation for himself over the last few months. He is known as 'the Gem Detective', because he has recovered the jewels from seven robberies, in the last eight months. Corrio boasts to Simon and Chief Inspector Teal that his security precautions for the famous Oppenheim emerald are foolproof. Simon leaves the exhibition and returns home. Later that evening he hears screams outside his front door, and he finds an attractive girl, Janice Dixon, struggling with two men, Swann and Miller. Simon tackles them and the two men run off.

Simon Templar tries to help Janice Dixon prove her brother was framed by *The Smart Detective*

Simon discovers that Janice's brother was Roy Dixon, a jewellery designer accused of stealing diamonds who was killed while trying to escape from the police. Janice tells him that the jewels were planted on her brother so that they could be recovered by Pete Corrio, but not all the jewels were recovered. Janice tells Simon that she believes Corrio's men are watching her, because Corrio believes Roy may have left some of the jewels with her. She is convinced that Corrio planned the last seven robberies, and then recovered the stolen goods for the reward money. Simon pays a visit to Chief Inspector Teal and tells him about Janice's theory. Teal is dubious, and not pleased when Simon points out that the police have failed to recover any of the stolen loot. Simon discovers that Corrio is a judo expert, and that he trains a couple of times a week in a local gym. Simon goes along there to watch Corrio training, but ends up in a bout with him. Simon discovers that Corrio is a ruthless and deadly opponent. The next day Simon is out with Janice, and when they return to her flat they find it has been ransacked by someone looking for the missing jewels. Janice later shows Simon Roy's address book, and one name interests The Saint, Miss Dallas. Simon takes Janice to a character known as 'Aunt Prudence' – according to Simon she is the sort of person who could cope with any emergency. Simon leaves Janice, and sets out to look up Miss Dallas. He discovers that the name belongs to a boat owned by Pete Corrio.

Simon returns to 'Aunt Prudence' to discover that Janice has been kidnapped, and Prudence tells him that she overheard the men say that they were taking her to 'Dallas'. Simon sets out to rescue Janice, and to steal the Oppenheim emerald from under Corrio's foolproof security system. Can The Saint rescue Janice? Was her brother really innocent? Can Simon outwit the smart detective?

Based on the 1939 short story.

Michael Cramoy was the only writer to work on the radio series as well as the TV version.

THE PERSISTENT PARASITE (1965)

Simon Templar	**Roger Moore**
Waldo Oddington	**Cec Linder**
Vera	**Jan Holden**
Wilma	**Ann Gillis**
Katerina	**Annette Carell**
Nadine	**Sonia Fox**
Colonel Latignant	**Arnold Diamond**
Pierre	**Brian MacDermott**
George McGeorge	**Jeremy Longhurst**
Howard Mitchell	**Donald Hewlett**
Monsieur Phillippe	**David Garth**
Latignant's Assistant	**Keith Smith**
Screenplay by	**Norman Hudis**
Directed by	**Robert Tronson**

SIMON TAKES A ferry boat to a small island off the French Riviera. He is on his way to the wedding of an acquaintance, Waldo Oddington, a very wealthy man. Simon's companions on the boat are Waldo's three ex-wives, who have also been invited to the wedding. They are met at the dock by Waldo and his young fiancée, Nadine. They stop off for a drink while the boat is being unloaded and as they are talking a young man passes by and Nadine gives him a furtive glance, which Simon notices. Waldo goes off to pick up something for Nadine. Suddenly, a young girl screams that a man has been stabbed in the back and killed. Is it Waldo? No, but the dead man is wearing a shirt identical to his. The party returns to Waldo's villa. Simon questions the ladies as to who might have a reason to kill him, but they all receive a large alimony cheque each month. Simon questions Nadine about the young man at the café, but she refuses to answer and leaves for town. Simon follows her into town where she meets the young man, Pierre. She has come to see him to break off the affair. Pierre slaps her and she rushes off, he tries to follow but is stopped by Simon. That evening one of Waldo's relatives arrives, his nephew George, and also his lawyer, Howard Mitchell. They are both convinced that Waldo is dead – they say that they heard the news on the mainland. That evening Waldo questions his ex-wives, Nadine and his nephew as to why they love him. They all have different reasons. He tells them that he has a big surprise for them all, which he will reveal the next day. George tries to tell Waldo something about Nadine's past, but Waldo refuses to listen. George goes into town to see Pierre, whom he has hired to break up the forthcoming marriage. Later that evening Waldo signs a document prepared by his lawyer, Howard, and then retires for the evening. Simon keeps watch convinced that another attempt will be made on Waldo's life. Simon sees a man sneaking around the grounds and then enter the house. It's Pierre. Simon tackles him and the household is awakened. He questions Pierre as to why he is sneaking around the house in the early hours of the morning. He is there, according to Pierre, at George's request. George wants Pierre to tell Waldo all about Nadine, and Waldo agrees to listen to him alone. Simon sends everyone else to bed while he stands guard at the top of the stairs. Pierre tells Waldo that he was hired by George to break up the affair between Nadine and Waldo. Suddenly a shot is fired through the window from outside, and Waldo falls to the ground. Simon races into the room to find Waldo dead. The rest of the household is woken up. Simon searches through Waldo's private papers before the police arrive to investigate and he finds Waldo's insurance policy on his life for £200,000. Simon has seven possible suspects for murder. Can he trace which of Waldo's guests is the persistent parasite?

The original 1957 short story, *The Reluctant Nudist*, was set in and around a nudist colony. The plot was 'dressed up' for TV.

THE MAN WHO COULD NOT DIE (1965)

Simon Templar	**Roger Moore**
Miles Hallin	**Patrick Allen**
Moyna Stanford	**Jeannie Linden**
Nigel Perry	**Robin Phillips**
Roddy Morton	**Richard Wyler**
Inspector Teal	**Ivor Dean**
Emrys Pugh	**Meredith Edwards**
Mrs Pugh	**Mary Jones**
Screenplay by	**Terry Nation**
Directed by	**Roger Moore**

POLO IS THE sport of the English upper classes, and Simon is invited to watch a polo match by Nigel Perry, a young friend who is about to get married to the lovely Moyna. Nigel has recently taken over his father's business after his father was killed while working in the Australian outback. Nigel's partner is Miles Hallin, an all-round sportsman who often defies death, and has been nicknamed by the press, 'the man who could not die'.

A tense moment for Jeannie Linden and Roger Moore

Nigel tells Simon that Miles has been drawing large sums of money out of the business account recently. He tells him that Miles was with his father when he died, and that he's not interested in the money, he just wants to help him. Nigel thinks that Miles is being blackmailed. Simon meets Miles and takes a dislike to him, but reluctantly agrees to help as a favour to Nigel. That evening after another sum of money has been withdrawn from the bank, they follow Miles to a deserted house where he drops off a package. Simon goes to the house to investigate and he finds that the package contains several thousand pounds. Suddenly a man appears looking for the money; the man sees Simon and rushes off, jumps on a motorbike and drives away, followed by Nigel, who he loses in the traffic. Simon drops off the money secretly to Hallin, who then receives a call from the blackmailer, Roddy Morton. He arranges to meet him the next evening. Hallin visits Morton on a houseboat on the Thames, and pays him the money, but Morton wants more. Hallin says he can have it when he returns from a shooting holiday with Nigel, when Hallin will own the business completely. Hallin starts to leave but then suddenly turns and jumps Morton. He points a gun at him and kills him in cold blood. The next day Miles and Nigel leave on their shooting holiday. Simon and Moyna see them off at the station. Simon traces Morton's houseboat, and arrives to find Chief Inspector Teal investigating the murder. Simon drives Moyna home and on the way she tells him the story of how Nigel's father died. She believes it was murder, and now so does The Saint. Simon decides to drive to Wales with Moyna to keep an eye on Hallin. They check into the hotel to discover that Miles has changed his mind and they have decided to go pot-holing instead, in an area known as the Dragon's Cave. Simon and Moyna decide to go after them with the aid of Emrys Pugh, a local man who knows the caves. Miles and Nigel go deeper and deeper. While Simon and Emrys look for their trail, Moyna finds a fresh cigarette stub and suddenly they are hot on the trail. Moyna sprains her ankle and is unable to continue. Simon reluctantly leaves her and continues on with Emrys. Miles and Nigel continue to climb deeper, and suddenly Miles lets go of the rope and Nigel falls onto a ledge 20 ft below. Moyna comes across a skull and screams out, and Simon sends Emrys back to look after her. Simon runs into Miles who pretends that he was going for help. He makes him return to where Nigel fell. Simon climbs down to fetch Nigel up, warning Miles that two accidents would be hard to explain. Simon is nearing the top of the ledge just as Emrys arrives. Simon sends Emrys for a doctor, but as he makes it to the top a rock slide seals the entrance to the cavern. Simon and Miles look for another way out, which they find via a narrow cliff edge. Simon slips and Miles stands over him laughing. Is it the end of the road for The Saint, coming up against the man who could not die?

Based on the 1931 novella.

THE SAINT BIDS DIAMONDS (1965)

Simon Templar	Roger Moore
Christine Graner	Eunice Gayson
Abdul Graner	George Murcell
Madame Calliope	Jean St Clair
Joris Vanlinden	Gerard Heinz
Captain Garcia	Peter Illing
George Felson	Edward Bishop
Palerno	Neville Becker
Lauber	Laurence Herder
Policeman	Richard Montez
Screenplay by	Pat and Jesse Lasky Jr
Directed by	Leslie Norman

THE SAINT IS IN the Canary Islands, on the Island of Tenerife, where he visits a famous astrologer called Madame Calliope, who is also an old friend. She warns Simon that danger is just around the corner, and to be careful. Simon is in Tenerife to retrieve a fabulous diamond that was stolen from the Louvre museum in Paris, by a man called Abdul Graner, who plans to have the diamond cut up. Graner employs a man called Vanlinden to cut the stone, but Vanlinden is a drunk and cannot be trusted to do the job properly so Graner sends to New York for another expert, George Felson. Simon waits at the airport for Felson, and while he is waiting he is approached by Captain Garcia of the local police, who warns him to stay out of trouble, and report in every day. Simon meets Felson off the plane posing as one of Graner's associates. With Madame Calliope's help he takes him to her cellar where he plans to assume his identity, after a crash course in diamond cutting from Felson. Graner's wife Christine realises that Vanlinden is to be killed as he has become a liability to them; she helps him escape and he hides out in the woods. Graner discovers that he has escaped with his wife's help and he is just about to deal with her when he receives a call from Simon posing as Felson. Just as Graner's men find Vanlinden, Simon and Madame Calliope drive up. Simon tackles the men and chases them off. Madame Calliope takes Vanlinden to her home, while Simon continues up to the house. Simon arrives at the house and is greeted by Graner. Simon plays the heavy – Christine is impressed and Graner is convinced that Simon is Felson. The next day Simon tells Felson that he must go into town to fetch some special equipment to cut the stone. Christine offers to drive him and on the way to town they stop off for a drink, and she tells him that she lives in terror of her husband. Christine tries to persuade Simon to steal the diamond from her husband. She drops Simon off and returns to the house, while Simon reports to Captain Garcia, who questions him about the diamond and the disappearance of Felson. Simon denies any knowledge of either. Simon returns to the house and opens Felson's safe, but he is interrupted by one of Felson's men. Simon deals with him and takes the diamond. Felson returns to the house after collecting a consignment of diamonds. Simon leaves the diamond with Christine while he returns to Madame Calliope. Graner discovers the diamond is missing and questions Christine, then sets out to look for Simon. Simon returns to see Vanlinden and tells him that the diamond in the safe is a fake and that he has the real one. Vanlinden confesses and hands over the real diamond. Graner and his men arrive and take the real diamond, still believing Simon to be Felson. Graner forces him at gunpoint to cut the stone, while his men hold Vanlinden and Christine prisoner. Will Simon cut and destroy the fabulous regency diamond, or will The Saint's bid for diamonds triumph?

Based on the 1937 novel.

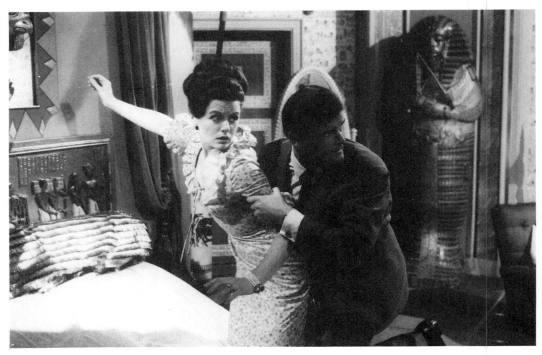

Eunice Gayson and Roger Moore attempt to recover stolen diamonds

THE SPANISH COW (1965)

Simon Templar	Roger Moore
Gilberto Arroya	Gary Raymond
Consuela Flores	Viviane Ventura
Dona Luisa Arroya	Nancy Nevinson
Colonel Latignant	Arnold Diamond
Deigo Ramirez	Leonard Sachs
Rene	Michael Wynne
Chico	David Jackson
Jean	Nicholas Donnelly
Sancho	Terry York

Screenplay by   Michael Cramoy
Directed by   John Gilling

SIMON IS DRIVING through the South of France along quiet country roads. Suddenly ahead he sees two women, who passed him on the road earlier, being held up by two men at gunpoint. Simon stops to offer assistance to the ladies, and after a brief struggle with the men he disarms them and chases them off. He then escorts the two ladies, Dona Luisa and her companion, Consuela, back to their home. The reason for the hold-up was Dona Luisa's jewellery, which is worth a small fortune. Simon checks into a hotel and is greeted by his old friend Colonel Latignant of the police department. He asks Simon about ' the Spanish Cow', the nickname given to Dona Luisa. Colonel Latignant explains that the French use the term 'Spanish Cow' for someone who is clumsy and absurd. He mentions her diamonds and warns Simon to 'back off'. Simon cannot comply with his wishes as he has been invited to have dinner with the two ladies that evening. After dinner, Dona Luisa tells Simon about her husband. Their talk is interrupted by the arrival of Gilberto Arroya, Dona Luisa's brother-in-law, who tells Simon that the Arroya family, exiled from the island of Santa Cruz, plan to return to power using the money that the jewels will bring when they are sold. As Simon leaves Dona Luisa gives him a gold cigarette lighter for his kindness in helping them on the road. Back at the police station the Colonel briefs his men on the possibility of the jewels being stolen – one man is assigned to watch the jewels and the other to keep watch on Simon. Simon takes Consuela out dancing, but their evening is interrupted by Gilberto who offers Simon 100,000 francs

to stay away from the ladies. He refuses and and Gilberto storms off. Simon returns to his hotel to be greeted at gunpoint by Diego Ramirez, a representative of the Santa Cruz government. Diego says he will kill Simon if he tries to steal the diamonds, but Simon says he has no intention of taking them. Diego then tells Simon that he must steal them and return them to the people of Santa Cruz. Later that evening one of Gilberto's men breaks into Simon's room to kill him. Simon awakens just in time and tackles him, but just as he is about to talk he is shot by Gilberto. Simon calls in the police and Colonel Latignant questions him. Once again he insists that Simon stay away from Dona Luisa, but when she telephones Simon, and invites him to tea, the Colonel gives in. During tea Dona Luisa goes to her safe to put her jewellery away. She makes a clumsy display of letting Simon know where the jewels are kept, and the safe's combination. The Colonel visits Dona Luisa and says he will surround the house with police officers to protect her, but she refuses his help and tells him to leave. That evening Simon drives to the Arroya house, in the grounds of which he finds hidden microphones left by the Colonel to record any sound, but Simon is prepared for this with a plan of his own. Simon sneaks into the house and opens the safe, but while he is removing the jewels he is confronted by Consuela. He realises that it was a put-up job, and that the diamonds are a fake. What is Dona Luisa's real reason for getting Simon involved, and where do her sympathies lie? Simon gets to find the truth behind the reasoning of the Spanish Cow.

Based on the 1954 short story.

THE OLD TREASURE STORY (1965)

Simon Templar	Roger Moore
Duncan Rawl	Jack Hedley
Jack Forrest	Robert Hutton
April Mallory	Erica Rogers
Captain Bill Williams	Reg Lye
Jim Reston	Frank Wolff
Maria Cavallini	Jill Curzon
Big Tom	Roy Patrick
Sailors	Joby Blanshard
	Timmy Gardner
Screenplay by	Ronald Duncan
Directed by	Roger Moore

THE SAINTS HAS friends all over the world and in all walks of life, and so when he visits a pub in Cornwall owned by an ex-sailor, Captain Bill Williams, he receives a warm welcome. The Captain runs the pub along with his attractive ward, April Mallory, who has been brought up by the Captain ever since the death of her parents. Simon's visit is in answer to a letter from the Captain, who has written a book under a pseudonym. The Captain reveals to Simon that three men each have a part of a treasure map that reveals the hiding place of a fabulous treasure somewhere in the West Indies. The Captain hopes that the publication of the book will bring the three men together. The first person to turn up at the inn is Jim Reston, who served with the Captain. He is the only one who knows the Captain's secret which was that he was responsible for the death of April's father, when they quarrelled over the treasure map. Before long Reston and the Captain quarrel and in a fight, the Captain is killed over his part of the map. As he is dying he tells the truth to April about her father's death, and then gives her his piece of the map. Shortly after the Captain's death, Duncan Rawl turns up at the inn. He has the second piece of the map, and he tells Simon that film producer, Jack Forrest, will be along in a couple of days, with his friend, Maria. He has the third part of the map. Forrest arrives and the treasure hunters are gathered. They prepare to go off to the West Indies. Does the treasure really exist and, if so, will greed take over? Simon finds out the answers in the old treasure story.

Based on the 1955 short story.

Erica Rogers and Roger Moore travel from Cornwall to the Bahamas to uncover the truth behind *The Old Treasure Story*

QUEEN'S RANSOM (1966)

Simon Templar	Roger Moore
Queen Adana	Dawn Adams
King Fallouda	George Pastell
Hortense	Nora Nicholson
Michele	Catherine Feller
Georges	Stanley Meadows
Major Aboukir	Gary Hope
Saleb	Patrick Westwood
Faied	Peter Madden
Mahmoud	Neville Becker
Pilot	John Woodvine
Mustafa	Larry Taylor
Claude	John Forbes Robertson
Bank Manager	Jean Serret
Gendarme	Andre Charise
Arab Servant	Ernst Ulman

Original Screenplay by	Leigh Vance
Directed by	Roy Baker

THE SAINT IS IN Monte Carlo. He observes the ex-King of Fedyra, as he plays cards at one of the tables. Simon stands behind King Fallouda and watches the game. Suddenly, a man with a walking stick enters the room – he twists the stick into a sword stick and lunges at the King. Simon pulls the King out of the way just in time. Fallouda thanks Simon, and tells him that he plans to return to power in his country by selling his wife's jewellery, worth over $5m. The diamonds must be collected from a Swiss bank. Fallouda asks Simon if he will accompany the Queen and guard the jewels and he reluctantly agrees. One of the King's aides has been listening at the door and reports back to his chief Farid. Simon and the Queen leave for Zurich on the King's private plane. The Queen is the daughter of a London bus driver and she takes an instant dislike to Simon, who amuses himself by gently mocking her. The limousine, on its way to pick up Simon and the Queen, is stopped and the driver attacked and replaced by Farid's man. The phoney driver collects them at the airport and takes them to the bank, where they collect the jewellery, and then make their way back to the plane. The driver makes a diversion down a quiet country road and they are followed by two men in a car. The Saint's driver stops the car, and the three men tackle The Saint. He is prepared for them and after a brief struggle Simon and the Queen make their getaway and head for the airport. On the flight back to Monte Carlo the pilot pulls a gun on them and the plane lands at a remote airstrip 100 miles from Nice. As they are taken from the plane at gunpoint, Simon and the Queen make a break for it and they escape by car, though the pilot fires several shots at them and one hits the gas tank. After they have travelled some distance the car breaks down and they have to walk to the nearest garage, where the owner offers to put them up for the night. Simon goes off to collect their things from the car and the Queen telephones the King. Once again his aide listens in on the conversation and then calls Farid, who sends one of his men after Simon. The next day Simon comes across Mustafa, Farid's man, in the garage, tackles him and after a short fight he knocks him out and puts him in the car. While they are waiting for a taxi an elderly British lady arrives at the garage, and she offers to give them a lift into the nearest town. As they proceed along the road they are followed by Mustafa in another car. They manage to lose him, and then the lady, Hortense, offers to give them shelter until it's time to catch the train to Nice. Hortense prepares them some tea and slips something into it. Will Simon recognise the drug in time, and if so, how many more traps will Farid and his men have waiting for The Saint, on the road to returning the Queen's jewels?

THE HOUSE ON DRAGON ROCK (1966)

Simon Templar	Roger Moore
Dr Sardon	Anthony Bate
Carmen	Annette Andre
Dr Davis	Mervy Johns
Dr Armstrong	Alex Scott
Dylan Williams	Glyn Houston
Shoni Morgan	Richard Owens
Owen Thomas	Talfryn Thomas
Mary	Heather Seymour
The Guard	Anthony Blackshaw
Locals	David Garfield
	Dafydd Havard
	Peter Lawrence
Screenplay by	Harry W Junkin
Directed by	Roger Moore

SIMON IS DRIVING through the Welsh mountains late at night and he stops off at the local inn, only to find it deserted except for a young child. Simon questions the little girl as to where everybody has gone, but just then a man with a shotgun arrives, the publican, Dylan Williams. The villagers are out on the moor looking for a lost shepherd. Simon tells Williams that he has come to the village at the request of Dr Davis. He then joins Williams in the search for Owen Thomas on the moor, and they team up with Dr Davis and the rest of the party. Suddenly, Owen stumbles out of the mist, terrified and unable to speak. Dr Davis takes Owen back to the surgery to examine him, where he finds strange lash marks on Owen's back. Dr Davis and Simon try to question him, but all he is able to do is write the words, 'a big . . .' Davis tells Simon of several strange incidents that have happened lately. Simon stops off at Dylan's inn for a drink and listens to the villagers speculate on what happened to Owen. A young girl arrives to enquire about Owen, but she is given a hostile reception by the locals. Simon discovers that Carmen is from the research centre on Dragon Rock. He escorts her back to her car, and she returns to the house to question her uncle about the incident, who refuses to give her an explanation. The next day Simon drives to the centre to see Dr Sardon and his associate Dr Armstrong. Sardon shows him round, and Simon mentions the recent incidents but Sardon denies any knowledge of them. Simon leaves, but he is not convinced that Sardon is as innocent as he makes out. Sardon and Armstrong go through a secret panel in the wall to another laboratory to continue with their secret experiment. Carmen telephones Simon and asks him to meet her at Devil's Gorge later that evening. Simon goes along taking Dylan's shotgun with him. Carmen arrives first and while waiting for Simon she is attacked suddenly by a giant creature, who disappears just before Simon arrives. Together they follow a trail of prints that leads them to a large cavern. Dr Sardon continues to experiment with controlling the creature. Meanwhile, Simon and Carment follow the trail which leads up to the house. Dr Armstrong realises that the experiment is getting out of hand, and tries to stop but Dr Sardon shoots him. Simon and Carmen return to the house where Carmen tries to distract her uncle while Simon searches for the hidden room. He finds it and discovers Armstrong. He unknowingly sets off an alarm which brings Dr Sardon down on him. Sardon holds The Saint at gunpoint while he explains his plan for the future. Carmen sneaks into the laboratory and tampers with the dials that control the creature. This distracts Sardon and Simon jumps him, knocking him out. Simon must follow the creature back to where it has laid its eggs, and another man must die before the house on Dragon Rock finds tranquillity.

Based on the 1933 story, *The Man Who Liked Ants*.

THE RUSSIAN PRISONER (1966)

Simon Templar	Roger Moore
Irma Jorovitch	Penelope Horner
Professor Karel Jorovitch	Joseph Furst
Inspector Oscar Kleinhaus	Guy Deghy
Milanov	Yootha Joyce
Kirill	Godfrey Quigley
Pyotr	Anthony Booth
Mikhail Zhukov	Robert Crewdson
Andre	Sandor Eles
Guard at Villa	Raymond Adamson
Aristov	Alexis Chesnakov
Clerk	William Buck
Screenplay by	Harry W Junkin
Directed by	John Moxey

THE SAINT flies to Geneva, Switzerland, and as he is leaving the airport lounge he sees several foreign delegates arriving for an international disarmament conference. Simon checks into a local hotel and on entering his room he finds the local police inspector waiting for him, who warns Simon to stay out of trouble. The Russian delegates prepare for the meeting. One of the Russians is Professor Karel Jorovitch, a scientist who has not seen his daughter in over 20 years. He is planning to defect to the West to join his daughter. The Russian security chief Milanov is keeping a close watch on Jorovitch. She knows that Jorovitch is planning to defect, and has her men follow him when he leaves the Embassy. Simon is at the hotel reception desk when Jorovitch calls to collect a letter from his daughter. Kirill and Pyotr, Milanov's men try to make Jorovitch leave with them, but Simon helps Jorovitch escape by starting a fight with the two men. Jorovitch telephones his daughter, but is taken away by Milanov's men before she arrives. The police arrive and arrest Simon for starting the fight. They take him to see Inspector Kleinhaus, but after another warning from the Inspector, Simon is released. Simon returns to his hotel and in the lobby he is stopped by a beautiful young woman who asks The Saint for help. She is Irma Jorovitch, the Professor's daughter, and she tells Simon that she has been in touch with her father during the last couple of years by mail. Simon tells Irma to wait in his hotel room while he goes off to the Russian Embassy to a reception, where he bumps into Inspector Kleinhaus. Simon then meets Milanov who asks him about Irma, and she suggests a meeting between Irma and her father. Simon searches the Embassy looking for a clue to the Professor's hideout, but suddenly he is surprised by Milanov and Kirill. They plan to take Simon out at gunpoint, but as they leave he spots Inspector Kleinhaus and uses him to make his escape. Simon returns to the hotel, unaware that he has been followed by Kirill and Pyotr. Fortunately Simon is warned of their approach by the hotel receptionist, and he hides Irma and waits for the two men. The men pull a gun on Simon and search for Irma, and with a gun at his head they threaten to kill him unless Irma comes out of hiding. Irma appears just in time, but the two men let slip where the Professor is being held. They still plan to kill Simon but he manages to make his escape with Irma. Milanov warns her men that unless Simon and the girl are caught, she will give them no mercy. Simon and Irma drive to where the professor is being held, they check into a hotel and wait until dark. Simon plans to sneak into the house using Irma as a distraction. Irma drives up to the house where the Professor is being held while Simon approaches via the river. He sneaks into the house, while Irma calls pretending her car has broken down. Simon knocks out the guard and then they find the Professor's room. A shot is fired and The Saint is left for dead. Several more twists occur before the case of the Russian prisoner is closed.

Based on the 1963 short story.

THE RELUCTANT REVOLUTION
(1966)

Simon Templar	**Roger Moore**
Victor Lawrence	**Barry Morse**
Diane	**Jennie Linden**
Sanchez	**Martin Benson**
President Alvarez	**Peter Illing**
Hortel	**Gerard Heinz**
Delgado	**Michael Godfrey**
Vargas	**Peter Halliday**
Enrico	**John Garrie**
Pablo	**Louis Raynor**
Consuela	**Maria Roza**
Morales	**Norman Florence**
Sentry	**Clive Gazes**
Head Waiter	**Walter Randall**
Original Screenplay by	**John Stanton**
Directed by	**Leslie Norman**

THE SAINT arrives in San Pablo, a small South American Republic, and after a minor incident at the airport he is warned by the local police captain to stay out of trouble. Captain Sanchez goes to see President Alvarez and his right-hand man, Victor Lawrence, about the recent political troubles. Alvarez leaves Lawrence to sort it all out. That evening Simon is enjoying a drink outside the hotel when Diane, one of his flight companions, leaves the hotel furtively and he follows her to a local nightclub. Shortly afterwards Lawrence and Sanchez arrive; they are planning the downfall of the freedom fighter, Hortel. Sanchez is called away to the phone. Diane approaches Lawrence, pulls out a gun, and accuses him of causing her father's death. Simon intervenes before Diane can shoot him and he rushes her out of the club with the police in hot pursuit. They escape through the backstreets only to be stopped by the rebels. They are taken to see Hortel, the leader of the revolution party. Diane tells Simon that Lawrence is a powerful man, whose real name is James Foster, a business associate of her father's. He stole $200,000 from Diane's father's business resulting in her father going to prison, where he died. Simon returns to the hotel to pick up Diane's passport so that she can be smuggled out of the country. He manages to sneak in and collect the passport, but is caught by the police on his way out. He is taken to police headquarters, questioned and thrown into a cell. The police find the headquarters of the freedom fighters and attack, killing several of the men. They make several arrests but Diane and Hortel escape. They prepare a newssheet for the people telling them that Lawrence is a crook. Hortel leaves Diane in the hands of one of his men, Delgado. Lawrence returns to the prison to question Simon about Diane's whereabouts. Simon agrees to co-operate only as a ruse. He jumps Lawrence and makes his escape from the prison, in a police car. Vargas, who turns out to be a double agent, telephones President Alvarez telling him where he can find Hortel and Diane. Simon heads for Vargas's room unaware that he is a traitor. He arrives just after Captain Sanchez has taken Diane away. Simon teams up with Hortel and prepares to free Diane. Captain Sanchez questions Diane as to why she tried to kill Lawrence. Simon puts his escape plan into action, and changes places with one of the policeman. Sanchez questions Lawrence about Diane's accusations, while Simon goes to see President Alvarez and tells him about Lawrence's real identity. The President then calls Lawrence in, and both men talk unaware that Simon has a hidden recorder and that everything they say is being broadcast to the people. Hortel and the freedom fighters soon take charge with Simon dealing out justice to Lawrence.

THE HELPFUL PIRATE (1966)

Simon Templar	**Roger Moore**
Eva	**Erika Remberg**
Kolben	**Paul Maxwell**
Nikita Ruskin	**Vladek Sheybal**
Fran Roeding	**Anneka Wills**
Professor Roeding	**Redmond Phillips**
Uhrmeister	**George Pravda**
Major Carter	**Jack Gwillim**
Hotel Receptionist	**Michael Wolf**
Alexi	**Lawrence Herder**
Erich Braeur	**Ray Austin**
Pawnbroker	**Otto Diamond**
Screenplay by	**Roy Russell**
Directed by	**Roy Baker**

SIMON IS just about to leave London Airport, on a wet, cold morning, for a sunnier climate when he is stopped by two men. One has a gun. They take him by car to a small typewriter factory where he is reunited with Major Carter of British Intelligence. Carter introduces Simon to Fran Roeding, the daughter of Professor Roeding, a scientist working with laser technology. Fran has not heard from her father since he went to Hamburg 10 days ago on a shopping trip for antiques, apart from one call telling her he was on the trail of a fortune. Simon agrees to help Carter trace Roeding and leaves on the next flight to Hamburg. He checks into the same hotel that Roeding stayed at before he disappeared, and bribes the bellboy to give him the number of Roeding's room. Simon searches the room for clues and goes through the Professor's luggage. While he is doing this the room clerk enters and starts to collect Roeding's things. He is startled to see Simon and says that the Professor telephoned asking that his belongings be sent on to him. The room clerk is agitated and demands that Simon leave the room or he will call the police. Simon calls his bluff and the man backs down. Simon decides to stay in Roeding's room much to the clerk's annoyance. The clerk leaves and telephones a man called Kolben to warn him about Simon. Kolben then goes down to the cellar where he is holding Professor Roeding captive. Kolben leaves to meet up with Nikita Roskin, a Russian agent who is after Roeding. Roskin contacts his headquarters and warns them that Simon is after Roeding. Roskin arranges for one of his men to follow Simon. Later that day Simon goes out looking for antiques, the type that Roeding was searching for when he disappeared. Simon returns to the hotel unaware that he is being followed by Roskin's men. He stops off at the hotel bar for a drink where he is joined by Eva, an attractive young woman, who asks Simon to take her out on the town that evening. As he is returning to his room

Simon runs into Fran Roeding, who, tired of waiting for news of her father, decides to help Simon look for him. That evening, with Fran safely tucked away in his room, Simon takes Eva to several nightclubs, but on leaving the last one, Simon spots that he is being followed. Just at that moment Eva drags him to a nearby antique shop, where she spots a rare goblet, the type that Roeding was after. Eva tells Simon that the goblet will lead them to the fabulous treasure of a German pirate. Eva wakes up the store owner and buys the goblet. Simon breaks the goblet and finds a message inside in ancient German. Eva leaves with the note, and Simon starts to return to the hotel, giving the Russian following him the slip. The maid comes in to clean Simon's room and spots Fran. She calls the room clerk who goes to see Fran, and discovers who she really is. As Fran tries to leave, the room clerk knocks her out and then calls Kolben who comes over to collect Fran and take her to join her father. Simon returns to his room to find Fran gone. Eva calls on Kolben to tell him that she has another sucker ready for the phoney treasure game. Kolben tells her to wait until the deal with Roeding is complete. Eva mentions that the man is Simon and Kolben sends his man Erich to kill The Saint. Kolben calls on Roskin and makes a deal for Roeding and his daughter in return for £50,000. Eva returns home but is stopped by Simon on the way. She takes Simon to meet her father and they discuss the phoney goblet swindle. While they are talking, Kolben's man Erich, shoots at Simon but hits Eva's father instead. Eva then tells Simon where he can find Fran and her father. Simon goes to Kolben's house but finds it deserted except for Erich who attacks him. After a fight he tells Simon where Kolben is holding Professor Roeding and his daughter. Can Simon rescue the Professor and his daughter before the trade is made with the Russians?

Based on the 1962 short story.

THE CONVENIENT MONSTER (1966)

Simon Templar	Roger Moore
Anne Clanraith	Susan Farmer
Noel Bastion	Laurence Payne
Eleanor Bastion	Caroline Blakiston
Fergus Clanraith	Moultrie Kelsall
Willie	Fulton Mackay
Angus McGraw	William Holmes
Mrs Mongrieff	Anne Blake
Inspector Mackenzie	Ewan Roberts
Publican	Alistair Hunter
Pathologist	Brown Derby
First Reporter	Michael Graham
Second Reporter	Harry Littlewood
Screenplay by	Terrence Feely
Directed by	Leslie Norman

THE SAINT IS driving through Scotland. He stops off at Loch Ness, home of the legendary monster. Suddenly hearing a woman scream, he races to the water's edge where he comes across a young woman who points to the ground at a large foot-print, and then shows Simon a small dead dog. Simon walks the young lady, Anne Clanraith, back to his car; on the way they run into Willie, the local tramp, who says he has seen the monster. Simon drives Anne back to her house and on the way she tells him that she is secretary to an author, Noel Bastion. Simon drops Anne off at her house, where he meets her father who is not at all friendly. After Simon leaves, Anne's father accuses her of having an affair with Bastion. Simon stops off to see Bastion who introduces Simon to his wife, Eleanor, who strongly believes that the Loch Ness monster is real. She takes Simon into her trophy room where she shows him several of her hunting trophies. Their meeting is interrupted by a servant who tells them that Inspector Mackenzie is on the beach examining the prints left in the sand. Simon and Eleanor join him. The Inspector is not convinced that the killings are the work of the monster. Eleanor invites Simon to stay at the Bastion house, and he drives back to the inn to collect his things, giving the Inspector a lift on the way. Mackenzie asks indirectly for Simon's help. That evening as Simon prepares to leave the inn, he listens to the locals discussing the monster. Willie, the tramp, comes in and orders a whisky, and he pays with a £5 note. Simon questions Willie about the monster and Willie agrees to meet him later that evening in the castle ruins. Simon returns to the Bastion household where Eleanor runs some old film of the Loch Ness monster. She is still convinced that the monster exists. Bastion dictates several chapters of his book to Anne. She then tells him that she is planning to leave. Bastion tries to persuade her to stay and just at that moment Eleanor and Simon enter the room. Simon walks Anne back to her house across the foggy moor. They hear a sound behind them but cannot see anything, when suddenly they hear a man scream. Moving on through the mist Anne stumbles over Willie's lifeless body. They take the body to be examined by the local Doctor, who tells them that Willie was killed by an unknown beast. Eleanor tells the local press that Willie was killed by the Loch Ness monster. Mrs Bastion prepares to go on a big game hunt for the monster. Together with Simon she leaves for the Loch, and they set up camp near the water's edge. They are joined by Angus, a young farmhand, who wants to help out. Angus takes the first watch, while Simon goes to talk to Anne's father, Fergus. He was the last person to see Willie alive. Just as he is getting worked up over the accusations Simon is making, Anne arrives and Fergus storms off. Eleanor prepares for her shift on watch while Simon looks for clues at the castle ruins where Willie died. He finds a trap door which leads to an underground cellar where he finds some gas tanks and a large barbed club. As Simon is climbing out of the cellar a large rock is pushed down on him, which narrowly misses him. He returns to the house as Bastion is about to take his turn on watch, and the fog creeps in. Will the Loch Ness monster appear and claim another victim, or has someone just created a convenient monster?

Based on the 1962 short story.

Simon Templar and Eleanor Clanraith load up with heavy artillery, as they prepare to face the monster

THE ANGEL'S EYE (1966)

Simon Templar	Roger Moore
Mabel	Jane Merrow
Tom Upwater	Liam Redmond
Lord Cranmore	Anthony Nicholls
Jeremy	Donald Pickering
Malone	T.P. McKenna
Corbett	Frederick Abbott
Jonkheer	Cyril Shaps
Zullen	Terence Rigby
Van Effen	Martin Wyldeck
Police Sergeant	Arthur Gross
Receptionist	Katherine Schofield
Hotel Clerk	Steven Brook
Waiter	Jean Benedetti

Screenplay by	Harry W. Junkin
Directed by	Leslie Norman

SIMON CALLS at Cranmore House, a stately home. He has been invited by Lord Cranmore to stay for the weekend. He tells Simon that he is broke and that he must sell off some of the family jewels, in particular his most prized possession, a large diamond known as the 'Angel's Eye'. Cranmore asks Simon to accompany two of his staff to Amsterdam, to guard the stone until it has been cut and sold. Cranmore's nephew, Jeremy opposes the sale and plans to stop it. That evening two men break into the house to steal the diamond. Cranmore catches them in the act, and calls to Simon for help. After a brief struggle with Simon the men make their getaway. The next day, Simon along with two of Cranmore's staff, Mabel and Tom Upwater, take the plane to Amsterdam. They check into the hotel where Simon is approached by Jeremy who asks Simon to give him the diamond. Simon refuses and Jeremy leaves angrily. Simon drives Tom and Mabel to see Jonkheer, the diamond merchant. He notices that they are being followed and drops Tom off at Jonkheer's while he leads the other car away. Tom sees Jonkheer and leaves the diamond with him for cutting. Simon loses the other car and returns to pick up Tom. Meanwhile, Jonkheer calls his man Zullen, because he has a special job for him to do. The next morning Simon takes Mabel on a sight-seeing tour of Amsterdam, while Tom rests up at the hotel. They are followed by Zullen as they see the sights of the town. They return to the hotel to discover Tom very upset; he claims Jonkheer has stolen the diamond, but Jonkheer claims never to have seen Tom, or the 'Angel's Eye' before. Simon and Mabel go to see Jonkheer. Simon poses as Sebastian Toombs, a magazine writer, with Mabel as his photographer. He questions Jonkheer who denies having the diamond. He calls his man Zullen who recognises Simon, and they are forced to leave at gunpoint. Returning to the hotel they find that Tom has still not returned from the police station where he went to press charges against Jonkheer. Simon and Mabel go to the police, but they have no knowledge of Tom's visit. They return to the hotel where Mabel receives a message to phone a certain number. Mabel phones and is told by a man to come alone to a certain place. Simon follows at a discreet distance and sees Mabel being picked up by a man called Malone and taken to a remote windmill, where she is reunited with her father. Simon catches up with them and knocks out the two men holding Tom, and together they escape. Returning to the hotel Tom tells Simon that Jeremy is behind the plot to steal the diamond. Simon agrees to help Tom by stealing back the diamond from Jonkheer. Later that evening, after dinner with Mabel, Simon leaves to break into Jonkheer's office. He is nearly caught by Zullen, but suddenly Zullen is knocked out. Simon waits patiently for the next move. Can The Saint outwit the thieves? Several plot twists occur before The Saint can close the case of the 'Angel's Eye'.

Based on a 1954 short story.

Executive script editor for the series Harry W. Junkin prepares to read through the next script

THE MAN WHO GAMBLED WITH LIFE (1966)

Simon Templar	Roger Moore
Keith Longman	Clifford Evans
Stella Longman	Jayne Sofiano
Vanessa Longman	Veronica Carlson
Carl	Steven Berkoff
Ronald	Valentina Palmer
Chick	John D. Collins
Morris	Iain Blair
Tom	Barry Andrews
Ian	Hedger Wallace
Dr Morris	Geoffrey Lumsden
Pete	Barry Stanton

Original Screenplay by	Harry W. Junkin
Directed by	Freddie Francis

SIMON IS sent a message to meet a young lady in the park one morning. After a strange meeting with the girl, she presents him with a small white mouse, and he is told to observe it for 24 hours. Simon returns home to find a coffin in his flat, and inside the coffin a lifesize model of him. Suddenly a young girl appears armed with a gun; she fires at Simon but the gun only contains blanks. She tells Simon her name is Stella; she prepared the coffin and her sister Vanessa presented Simon with the mouse. Simon finds it all rather baffling. He sneaks out of the flat and follows Stella in her car, but loses her in the traffic. He catches up just in time to see the two sisters taking off in a helicopter. Simon questions the ground crew about the girls' flight plan. The girls return to their home base and to their father, Keith Longman, a wealthy businessman who is dying. Longman has strange plans for Simon's future, and he briefs his men and daughters. He will not tolerate interference from anyone, including his two daughters. Simon traces the helicopter to a small village in Cornwall, and he drives down taking along Mimi, the small white mouse. The trail has gone cold and he is about to give up when he spots the helicopter taking off from a nearby house. Simon waits until dark and then prepares to sneak into the house. Longman's daughter Stella decides to leave, but Longman insists that she stay and locks her in her room. Simon is caught by one of Longman's guards, but The Saint soon overpowers him. Longman assembles his men only to find one of the security guards missing, and so a search party is sent out. The Saint enters the house to find Longman preparing for a strange experiment. Unaware that he is to be a human guinea pig, Simon enters the laboratory and finds a huge gorilla in suspended animation. Meanwhile the guards have found Tom, the missing security man. Longman returns to the laboratory and catches Simon going through his things. He offers Simon a drink and starts to tell him that he is dying. Longman tells Simon that his time is running out due to poor health, and that he plans to freeze himself in suspended animation until a time when doctors have found a cure for him. Simon is gassed by security men, and upon awakening he finds that he is locked up with Stella. Longman tries to revive the gorilla from its frozen state but the gorilla is dead. Two guards are sent to

fetch Simon as the next guinea pig for Longman's experiment, but with the aid of Stella he escapes from the house only to run into Vanessa and the security men. Will Simon become Longman's next guinea pig, or is it the end of the road for the man who gambled with life?

Veronica Carlson and friends prepare to introduce Roger Moore as The Saint to *The Man Who Gambled With Life*

THE MAN WHO LIKED LIONS (1966)

Simon Templar	**Roger Moore**
Tiberio	**Peter Wyngarde**
Claudia Molinelli	**Suzanne Lloyd**
Franco De Cesarie	**Michael Wynne**
Inspector Galba	**Jeremy Young**
Vittoria Leale	**Michael Forrest**
Tony Allard	**Edward Bishop**
Beireeni	**Peter Elliott**
Serafino	**Nike Arrighi**
Guido	**Robert Russell**
Frascatto	**Steven Scott**
Princess Alexandra	**Phyllis Montefiore**

Screenplay by	**Harry W. Junkin**
Original Story by	**Douglas Enfar**
Directed by	**Jeremy Summers**

THE SAINT follows a party of tourists around the Colosseum in Rome. He is there at the request of Tony Allard, a reporter friend. Tony rushes up and tells Simon that he has just got a big scoop about 'the man who liked lions'. Suddenly Tony falls forward, killed by a knife in his back. The knife has the carved head of a lion on its handle. A policeman suddenly appears out of the crowd, questions Simon about the murder, and then warns him not to interfere in the murder investigations. Simon goes to Tony Allard's flat to search for clues, and while he is there he is attacked by two men. Simon gets the upper hand and the men run off. Simon finds a personal invitation to an art gallery exhibition, and he decides to go along as Allard. He is greeted by the gallery owner, Tiberio. Simon then introduces himself to Claudia Molinelli, the artist on display. Claudia was involved with Tony, and at the news of his death she rushes off. Simon returns to Tony's apartment, and there he finds Claudia with Tony's diary. She was instructed by Tony in the event of his death to hold onto the diary. Simon takes charge of it, but Claudia warns him that the little black book killed Tony and that it will kill Simon too. Claudia returns home and is surprised by Tiberio, who tells her off for leaving her guests at the gallery. He then questions her about going to Tony's flat. Simon goes through Tony's diary and sees that he has a number of appointments. Simon goes off to keep the first of them, with Signora Zambetti. He arrives to find the Signora dead of a heart attack. He then meets her niece, Serafino, and she tells him that her uncle also died recently. Serafino tells Simon that her uncle was found dead, supposedly a suicide, after 80 million lira was found missing from his business. Tony believed him to be innocent of the charge and was trying to help. Simon leaves the house and takes a taxi back to town, but he soon realises that he is being followed and orders the taxi to lose them. He proceeds to Tony's next appointment, with a man called Rudolpho Beireeni. Beireeni panics at the sight of Simon and leaps through his bedroom window, but Simon pursues him and traps him in an alleyway. Simon questions him about Serafino's uncle's death and the stolen money. Beireeni confesses that Serafino's uncle was innocent, and that it was the work of 'the organisation'. Simon asks him about the 'man who liked lions', but Beireeni claims never to have heard of him. Simon goes to the local zoo where he hopes to find a clue. There he runs into Tiberio, who confesses to being 'the man who liked lions'. Tiberio offers Simon $50,000 for Tony's diary, but Simon refuses. Simon returns to his hotel where he receives a visit from Inspector Galba, who returns Simon's passport and surprises Simon by offering him the freedom of the city. That evening Simon visits Claudia, and questions her about Serafino's uncle. She says that they were just friends. He also questions her about several dates in Tony's diary and gives her a chance to help find Tony's killer. Claudia invites Simon to a Roman period party at Tiberio's. He goes along and changes into the costume of a Roman guard. Tiberio offers Simon a drink, and arranges a display of wrestling for his guests. Simon questions Tiberio about the dates in Tony's diary, as several of the dates tie in with murders worldwide. Claudia tries to leave to call the police to help Simon but is caught by Tiberio's men. Simon tries to force Tiberio to leave at gunpoint but suddenly he collapses from a drugged wine, and Simon and Claudia are locked up in a room. Tiberio's man comes to collect them as Tiberio plans to put The Saint in a lion pit. Can The Saint triumph? Is it the end of the road for 'the man who liked lions'?

THE BETTER MOUSETRAP (1966)

Simon Templar	Roger Moore
Natalie Sheridan	Alexandra Stewart
Bertha Noversham	Madge Ryan
Alphonsa	Ronnie Barker
Colonel Latignant	Arnold Diamond
Milo Gambodi	Lisa Daniely
Bernie Kovar	Patrick Whyte
Tench	Eddie Byrne
Hugo	Michael Coles
Lady Haverstock	Aimee Delemain
Receptionist	Marika Rivera
Marie-Therese	Pauline Collins
Gendarme	Alan Downer
Fat Man	Robert Bridges
Banker	Tom Macauley
Mirelle	Vicky Hughes
Screenplay by	Leigh Vance
Directed by	Gordon Fleming

THE SAINT IS IN Cannes, gambling at one of the casinos. Meanwhile, a cat burglar is breaking into the room of the wealthy Lady Haverstock. A noise awakens her and she lets out a scream, just as the man is leaving. Simon, returning to his room, rushes to her aid. He telephones the police, and several other guests come to Lady Haverstock's room including Natalie Sheridan, who recognises The Saint. Colonel Latignant, of the Nice police arrives and takes charge. He questions Simon about the burglary, and is convinced that he is involved. Tench, the cat burglar returns to the hotel to meet his partner, Hugo. The next day Simon joins Lady Haverstock's companion Natalie, for cocktails, but they are interrupted by the very loud Bertha Noversham, and her friends. Simon makes a phoney excuse and leaves with Natalie. They are followed by Colonel Latignant's assistant, Alphonsa. Tench and Hugo prepare for the next robbery, but first they plan to plant some stolen jewellery in Simon's hotel room. Simon returns to his room while Tench is planting the diamonds. Tench tries to escape onto the next balcony, but Simon hears a noise and sees Tench hanging from the ledge. Simon goes to his aid but Tench slips and falls to his death. Colonel Latignant arrives and claims that Tench was Simon's partner in crime and that Simon killed him, but he has no proof. Latignant leaves to search Tench's hotel room and Natalie calls to see Simon in his room, where he is under house arrest. She covers for Simon while he slips out to investigate. While Latignant searches the room, Simon questions the hotel owner and discovers that Tench's partner was Hugo, who had left the hotel just before Simon arrived. Simon chases after Hugo but he escapes. Colonel Latignant receives a telephone call from a woman telling him he will find the jewellery in Simon's room. Simon manages to get back to the room just before Colonel Latignant arrives. Colonel Latignant arrests Simon and proceeds to take him to the station. Simon escapes, steals a police car and returns to the hotel to try and trace the leader of the gang. Hugo breaks into the apartment of actress Bernie Kovar to steal her jewellery. Simon telephones Colonel Latignant and tells him to come straight over to the hotel, and then stops Hugo leaving. They struggle and Hugo is knocked out. Colonel Latignant arrives at the hotel and together with Simon, they confront the leader of the gang.

Based on the 1963 short story.

LITTLE GIRL LOST (1966)

Simon Templar	Roger Moore
Mildred	June Ritchie
Brendan Cullin	Noel Purcell
Mullins	Shay Gorman
Brine	Maurice Good
Eugene Drew	Edward Burnham
Receptionist	Colette Dunn
Blaney	Leo Leyden
Mulloon	Gerry Duggan
Patrick	Peter Ellis
Tessa	Eve Belton
Sergeant Finnegan	Kevin Flood

Original Screenplay by	Leigh Vance
Directed by	Roy Baker

THE SAINT will always respond to a damsel in distress and so, while on holiday in Ireland, when Simon sees a pretty, young girl being chased by two burly and tough-looking men. He steps in to help her, and after a brief struggle, the two men, Brine and Mullins, end up in the river. Simon takes the girl, Mildred, to a nearby hotel in Dublin, where she tells him a fantastic story which Simon finds hard to believe. She tells The Saint that she is Hitler's daughter, and the two men are S.S. guards trying to resurrect the Nazi party. Simon persuades an old friend, Brendan Cullin, to hide Mildred in his remote cottage. Simon wants to know why Mildred is masquerading as Hitler's daughter. Later Brine and Mullins make a second attempt to kidnap Mildred. Simon later discovers that the two men are private detectives working for a wealthy property owner, Eugene Drew. They were hired by him to bring back his runaway daughter, Mildred. Mildred faces up to the fact that Simon doesn't believe her 'Nazi' story, and confesses that she is the missing daughter of Eugene Drew. The reason that she ran away was because she wants to marry a penniless young man, and her father wants to make her a ward of the court. Simon believes her story now, and is prepared to help her, so they start out on their journey to Brendon's cottage. The journey becomes a hazardous one when the two detectives make several more attempts to kidnap Mildred. They finally succeed, and a message is left behind at the cottage for Simon to meet them. Brine and Mullins have decided to go into business for themselves. They are holding Mildred for a large ransom. Simon must approach Drew to pay the ransom, he agrees, and Simon leaves with the money. Simon is not completely satisfied with the state of affairs, after all the tall stories Mildred told him, is she really, a little girl lost?

PAPER CHASE (1966)

Simon Templar	**Roger Moore**
Eric Redman	**Ronald Hines**
Hanya	**Penelope Horner**
Colonel Probst	**Niall McGinnis**
Rudolph Metz	**Gordon Gostlow**
Major Carter	**Jack Gwillim**
Kruger	**Carl Duering**
Dister	**Michael Beint**
Ernst Scherwin	**Steve Plytas**
Lieutenant	**Anthony Wager**
Receptionist	**Norma West**
Major	**John G. Heller**
Sergeant	**Hans De Vries**
London Policeman	**Paul Williamson**
Vopos	**Gordon Sterne**
Kraft	**Frank Maher**
Porter	**John Herrington**
Steward	**Carl Conway**

Original Screenplay by	**Harry W. Junkin**
Directed by	**Leslie Norman**

IT IS WESTMINSTER, London at 5 a.m. The Saint, returning home after a night on the town, stops off at Westminster Bridge, for an early morning stroll. He sees two men in conversation, one passes the other a piece of paper, the wind catches it and it blows towards Simon. One of the men rushes up towards him, very agitated and tries to snatch the paper back. At that moment a constable comes along and Simon returns the paper to the man. The next day Simon is at Wimbledon as the guest of Major Carter of the Foreign Office, who needs Simon's help. During the match he tells Simon that a man called Eric Redman has defected to Germany and taken top secret documents with him. Simon's involvement? The man Simon saw on the Embankment that day was Redman. Major Carter asks Simon to go to Germany to help his agents identify the defector. Simon reluctantly agrees and takes the next plane out. He goes to see Ernst Scherwin, an agent with the local branch of British Intelligence, who shows Simon several slides of men recently arrived in the country. Simon identifies Redman, and is then persuaded to bring him back. Simon takes the train to Leipzig, the last place Redman has been seen, his assignment to bring Redman back and destroy the papers. His travelling companion is Colonel Kurt Probst of the Secret Police who questions Simon, who is posing as a salesman. To escape Probst's questioning Simon goes to the restaurant car, but Probst follows. Returning to the compartment for his cigarettes, Simon finds a man going through his suitcase; he attacks The Saint and after a short struggle the man falls off the train. Redman's reason for defecting with the file was to use it in trade to secure his father's release

but he arrives to find his father already dead. He decides to return to England with the file, but before he can leave, Metz, of the Secret Police, arrives, demanding the file. Redman has passed it to Hanya, his father's assistant. Simon arrives at the flat and is questioned by Metz; then the police leave to question Hanya. Simon goes to Hanya's workplace and asks her for the file, but before he can get it Metz arrives. Simon causes a diversion by fighting with the police so the girl can get away. Uniformed police arrive and Simon is taken to the local station where he meets Colonel Probst again. Probst tells Simon that Metz is not with the police, but is a confidence man. Probst releases Simon, but retains his passport. Simon returns to Redman's flat to await Hanya's return. Colonel Probst picks up Metz and tortures him until he reveals that he planned to sell Redmans file – a list of agents – to the highest bidder. Metz followed Hanya to the railway station where she left a suitcase. Hanya returns to the flat but refuses to hand over the suitcase unless Simon takes her back to England. He agrees and they all head for the station. Colonel Probst has his guards all around the station, but Simon manages to sneak in and remove the file from the suitcase. He is caught by Probst but manages to escape in a police car. He picks up Redman and Hanya and they make a desperate bid to escape to the border, pursued by Colonel Probst and his men. They reach the border post, which is surrounded by guards. Can the trio escape across the border before the security guards catch them, or will someone else die before the paper chase is over?

FLIGHT PLAN (1967)

Simon Templar	**Roger Moore**
Mike	**William Gaunt**
Diane	**Fiona Lewis**
Nadya	**Imogen Hassell**
Landek	**Ferdy Mayne**
Flight Lieutenant Willis	**Jeremy Burnham**
Kovicek	**Tommy Duggan**
Colonel Zaglia	**Robert Crewdson**
Hassan	**Marne Maitland**
Ahmed	**Salmaan Peer**
Policeman	**Donald Oliver**
Corporal Buller	**Ray Lonnen**
Atar	**David Spencer**
Reeves	**Henry McGhee**
Dragisha	**John Casabon**

Original Screenplay by	**Alfred Shaughnessy and Anthony Squire**
Directed by	**Roy Baker**

SIMON ARRIVES back in London after a trip abroad. He is at the railway station and looking about he sees a young girl giving money to a nun collecting for charity. A nun with sandals! Suddenly the nun injects the girl with a hypodermic. As Simon rushes forward to aid the girl the nun disappears. A policeman is on the platform and takes the girl to a nearby hospital. The constable questions the girl. Diane Gregory, while Simon looks on. Afterwards Simon drives Diane to her brother's flat. but a man answers the door and claims that no-one called Gregory lives there. Back inside the flat the man, Ahmed, talks to Nadya, the girl who posed as a nun at the station. The two of them sneak out the back entrance of the flat. Diane shows Simon a photo of her brother taken outside the flat they have just visited. Simon goes round the back of the flat and enters. He lets Diane in and they find several letters addressed to Flight Lieutenant Mike Gregory. The phone rings, it's Mike. He tells Diane that he will be away on confidential business for a few days. Simon leaves her in the flat and drives down to Mike's post, Blakewell Airforce Base. where he talks to an old friend Flight Lieutenant Willis. Willis tells Simon that Gregory had been testing a new type of aircraft, the Osprey, but was court-martialled three months ago. Back at the flat. Diane

meets Nadya. who now claims to be Mike's girlfriend. While Diane is making tea. Nadya overcomes her with chloroform and two men arrive at the house to take Diane away. Simon tries to phone Diane at the flat and receiving no answer he goes round and is confronted by Ahmed waiting to kill him. Ahmed fires several shots at Simon. but The Saint disarms him and forces him to reveal where they are holding Diane. Simon forces Ahmed at gunpoint to take him to Diane. He releases her and locks up Ahmed and another man. While she was a prisoner Diane has overheard important information. She takes Simon to the Serpentine. the lake in Hyde Park, where they film four men in conversation. They take the film to an expert lip reader who makes out the word Osprey. Simon realises that they plan to steal the experimental plane from Blakewell, using Mike as the pilot. That evening Mike steals the plane. Simon and Diane arrive just after he has taken off, and they go to see Flight Lieutenant Willis, who alerts his men. Simon and Willis work out where Mike has to land the plane to refuel. Simon decides that he must go after Mike. His flight plan is to be flown to where the plane is, parachute into enemy territory, and bring back or destroy the plane.

ESCAPE ROUTE (1967)

Simon Templar	**Roger Moore**
Colonel Roberts	**John Gregson**
Penny	**Wanda Ventham**
Inspector Teal	**Ivor Dean**
John Wood	**Donald Sutherland**
Ann	**Jean Marsh**
Harry	**Jeremy Burnham**
Jim	**Terry Yorke**
Dave	**Romo Gorrara**
Maggie	**Vicki Woolf**
Snooper	**Tony Doohan**
Hal	**Eric Mason**
Wilson	**Edwin Brown**
The Judge	**Walter Horsbrugh**
Nicky	**George Zenios**

Original Screenplay by	**Michael Winder**
Directed by	**Roger Moore**

LONDON, LATE one evening. The Saint is seen breaking into a house by a policeman on patrol. He telephones Scotland Yard and Inspector Teal arrives and attempts to arrest Simon, who escapes and drives off in the police car. He goes to a nightclub, where he pays a couple of people to say that he was there all evening. Inspector Teal arrives and this time he arrests Simon without incident. Simon later appears in court and is sentenced by the judge to 10 years hard labour in Princetown Prison. Simon is placed in a cell with three other men, one of whom, John Wood, starts a fight which results in Simon being taken to solitary. Waiting for Simon in solitary is Inspector Teal – The Saint is working undercover for him. A dozen men have recently escaped from Princetown and Simon's job is to find out who is behind the escape plan. Simon is put on a work detail along with Wood and the others. Wood tells Simon that for a price, £50,000, he can get him out. A couple of days later while working in the rock quarry, a helicopter flies over and Wood tells Simon that this is it. The two men make a break for the helicopter, one of the guards tries to stop them, but is knocked to the ground. The two men are later transferred to a van which takes them to London to meet a man called Harry. He takes them to meet a woman called Ann. She asks them a few questions about which country they would like to live in, and then asks Simon where he has hidden the loot from his robbery. Simon takes Harry along with Dave, another gang member, to the nightclub where he left the diamonds. Penny, the club's singer appears, greets Simon and says that she has put the jewellery in a safe deposit box. Just before Simon and Dave leave, Simon slips a note into Penny's pocket. Penny calls Teal and arranges to meet him in Trafalgar Square. Unknown to her, she is followed by Harry. Harry returns to the flat and questions Simon about Penny's meeting with Teal, but Simon manages to bluff his way out of it. Simon and Wood are then transferred to the home of Colonel Roberts, the mastermind behind the escapes. Wood having paid his £50,000 fee is then prepared for his transfer to Europe. Simon questions Roberts about the escape route but the Colonel doesn't give much away. Harry returns to the nightclub to search Penny's things and finds evidence that Penny is the daughter of a former escapee. He telephones Roberts to warn him. Woods boards a boat expecting to be taken across the channel to France, but instead all he gets is a bullet. Penny collects the jewellery from Inspector Teal and awaits Simon's call with instructions for the meeting. Just as she leaves her flat she is intercepted by Ann and Harry. Ann assumes Penny's identity to lead the police on a false trail. Harry takes Penny to the hideout, where Colonel Roberts reveals that he knows who she is. Simon jumps Harry but gives in when Roberts threatens Penny with a crossbow. Simon is knocked out and when he awakens finds he is on board a boat. Will Simon take the one-way trip that Wood took, or will he get the upper hand in time to stop the men behind the escape route?

Roger Moore prepares to direct the next scene with co-star Wanda Venthem

THE PERSISTENT PATRIOTS (1967)

Simon Templar	Roger Moore
Jack Liskard	Edward Woodward
Mary Ford	Jan Waters
Anne Liskard	Judy Parfitt
Stewart	Richard Leech
Inspector Teal	Ivor Dean
Todd	Tenniel Evans
Jeff Peterson	Mike Pratt
Rogers	Patrick O'Connell
Benson	Nosher Powell
Lockhart	Michael Graham
Manservant	Hugh Morton
Dr Butcher	Eric Longworth
Original Screenplay by	Michael Pertwee
Directed by	Roy Baker

THE SAINT IS AT A foreign airport, awaiting a flight back to London. Among his travelling companions is Jack Liskard, the Prime Minister of a former British colony. Suddenly at the window a man appears with a gun, which he points at Liskard. Simon calls out a warning to Liskard to duck. Simon throws a bottle at the window, the man fires, misses and runs off, and outside he is shot by the airport police. A couple of days later at his Embassy, Liskard talks to his deputy while opening his mail. Suddenly, he rushes out of the house, and goes to see Simon. He shows him the letter he received: it's a blackmail note, about some letters Liskard wrote to a girl called Mary some time ago. Simon goes to see Mary. He arrives at her flat during a photographic session. The photographer, Jeff Peterson, leaves, and Simon questions Mary about the blackmail note. She offers to return Liskard's letters but then finds them missing. Simon reports back to Liskard about the missing letters and then returns home. He receives a mysterious phone call from a woman who says that if he wants the letters he must go that evening to an old church. Simon enters the church and is met by a man wanting £25,000 in return for the letters. Suddenly, Simon is attacked by a second man; he fights him off but the two men manage to subdue him, or so they think. Simon is taken in a car to see their chief. On the way there he jumps them and manages to find out that they work for Peterson, the photographer. Simon leaps out of the moving car and escapes. The Saint watches Mary's flat and sees her leave with the men who attacked him. He follows them to the river, and a boat moored on it. Suddenly, Peterson is behind him with a gun and he is taken to the boat and tied up. Peterson leaves to go back to town. Meanwhile Mrs Liskard receives a letter from the blackmailer, and she goes to discuss it with her husband. Simon manages to free himself from the ropes binding him and escapes via the river. Liskard tries to calm down his wife over the incident of the letters to Mary. Simon returns to the Liskard house, and on entering he hears a gunshot from Liskard's study. He enters the study and finds Liskard slumped on the desk with a gun in his hand, and on the table a suicide note. Was it suicide or murder? Inspector Teal is called in to solve the case, and with Simon's help, the case of the persistent patriot is closed.

THE FAST WOMEN (1967)

Simon Templar	Roger Moore
Cynthia Quillen	Jan Holden
Godfrey Quillen	John Carson
Enrico Montesino	Victor Maddern
Teresa Montesino	Kate O'Mara
Tordoff	John Hollis
Paddy	P.G. Stephens
Thelma	Valerie Bell
Inspector Daws	Donald Morley
Porter	Patrick Durkin
Barmaid	Vilma Ann Leslie
Night Watchman	Stan Jay
Stage Doorkeeper	Harry Brunning
Glenda	Mandy Mayer

Screenplay by	**Leigh Vance**
Directed by	**Leslie Norman**

THE SAINT IS IN England, at Brands Hatch, the home of motor racing. He watches a race between two women, deadly rivals in racing and also in love. After the race Cynthia Quillen takes Simon for a drink in the club bar, where she points out to Simon her husband, drinking with her rival Teresa Montesino. They go over and Cynthia introduces Simon to Teresa. That evening Simon takes Teresa dancing. After he escorts her home, she invites him in for a drink, and then asks him to help her kill Cynthia. The next day a man called Tordoff checks into a hotel near Brands Hatch – he has come there to kill Cynthia. That afternoon Simon watches her as she takes a test run around the circuit unaware that Tordoff is waiting with a high-powered rifle to kill Cynthia. Cynthia pulls into a pit stop out of sight of the killer. She is not feeling well and Simon offers to complete the test run for her. Tordoff, unaware of the switch, fires at the car as it rounds the corner, bursting the tyre. The car spins out of control, but Simon manages to stop just in time. Later when Simon examines the car he finds the bullet hole in the tyre and he manages to find the empty shell case in the woods. Simon returns to warn Cynthia that someone is out to kill her. Simon suspects Godfrey but Cynthia says no, it is Teresa. That evening Cynthia finds Teresa and Godfrey together again. She starts an argument and Teresa leaves. Simon goes to see Enrico, Teresa's father, to see if he has a motive for murder but Enrico says both he and his daughter would be happy to see Cynthia dead. That evening Tordoff has a drink in the hotel bar, and he is invited by one of the locals to a game of darts. Although Tordoff says he has never played darts before he manages to win six matches in a row. Simon hears about this and goes off to see him. Tordoff leaves his room just before Simon arrives. The Saint searches his room for clues. Tordoff tries to escape through the rear of the hotel but is stopped by Paddy, one of Simon's friends. Tordoff knocks him down and escapes in his car. Simon and Paddy chase after him in Simon's car, but they lose him at a railway crossing. Simon checks back at the hotel reception to see if Tordoff made any calls. They trace Tordoff to a theatre where he is billed as 'the World's Greatest Trick Shot'. Simon goes backstage to see Tordoff and questions him, but suddenly Tordoff attacks him and rushes off. Simon catches up with him and after a savage fight, during which Simon gets the upper hand, he convinces the man to talk, but just then Tordoff is shot in the back by a sniper. Paddy sees the killer drive off and he tells Simon it was Teresa's car. Simon is questioned by the local police and he tells them that the killer will make another attempt on Cynthia's life. He goes to see Teresa and questions her about Tordoff's murder, but she denies any knowledge of it. Paddy returns to work on Cynthia's car, and is later found by the night watchman knocked out. Later, Paddy telephones Simon, and tells him about the incident. He also tells him that Cynthia's car has been tampered with. Simon questions Enrico, but he denies tampering with the car. The next day the drivers prepare for the big race. Simon teams up with Inspector Daws to try and trap the killer. The race starts and after 40 odd laps Teresa is in the lead, followed by Cynthia, but suddenly the announcer says that Cynthia's car has crashed. Can Simon solve the case of the fast women before another person is killed?

Based on the 1963 short story.

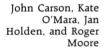

John Carson, Kate O'Mara, Jan Holden, and Roger Moore

THE DEATH GAME (1967)

Simon Templar	Roger Moore
Jenny Turner	Angela Douglas
Dr Manders	Alan MacNaughton
Vogler	George Murcell
Grey Wyler	John Steiner
Bill Bast	Bernard Horsfall
Inspector Teal	Ivor Dean
Gretl	Katherine Scholfield
Joe Halstron	Stuart Cooper
John Garton	Rick Jones
Duval	Michael Anthony
French Girl	Karen Ford

Screenplay by	Harry W. Junkin
Story by	John Kruse
Directed by	Leslie Norman

LONDON, late one foggy night: The Saint walks the streets. He hears a distant whirring noise and the sound of drums, and suddenly out of the mist come some marching toy soldiers. Simon bends down to touch them and suddenly they fire a gas pellet at him. Simon staggers back against a wall and an arrow narrowly misses him, followed by a bullet. He stumbles against a door, which opens: he enters the house which appears to be deserted, switches on the light and a sign saying 'Bomb' drops down. A voice then tells Simon that he has been gassed, shot at by an arrow and a bullet, and also electrocuted.

Roger Moore and Angela Douglas prepare to take part in *The Death Game*

Simon searches the house again but can find no trace of anyone, and then suddenly he is attacked by a young man. Simon knocks him down and suddenly a young girl arrives with tea. She tells Simon that their names are Grey and Jenny, and that they are students in a project called 'the death game'. They take Simon to meet their tutor, Professor Bill Bast. Jenny and Grey leave Simon with Bast, who tells Simon that he is worried about the death game, but he is interrupted by the arrival of Dr Manders before he can explain. Simon is persuaded to present the prizes to the death game winners. Dr Manders tells the winners, Grey, Jenny and Bast that they will be sent to Switzerland on an expenses-paid holiday as an additional prize. Bast appears upset and asks Simon to meet him back at the lab. Bast tells Simon that the death game started six months ago at colleges all around the world, and he is worried that there is something deeper behind it all. The phone rings and as Bast picks up the receiver the phone explodes, killing him. Simon takes Jenny with him to search Dr Manders' flat, where they find some college computer tapes which they take back to the laboratory. Before they have time to check the information, Dr Manders appears and attacks Simon with a sword stick. Simon receives a small cut and then fends off a further attack. Manders accidentally hits a power cable with the sword and is electrocuted. Simon decides to take Bast's place along with Grey and Jenny on the trip to Switzerland. They check in at the resort and are told that at midnight they are to play the death game. Simon goes to his cabin unaware that he is being watched on a video monitor. Gretl (one of the camp's organisers) calls on Simon to tell him he has been selected as a hunter for the evenings' death game. Simon wanders round the camp and finds the video monitoring room. He returns to his room now aware that he is being watched. Later that evening he warns Jenny about the video monitor, then goes off to 'kill' his victim in the death game. Simon 'kills' his victim, John Garton, and receives top marks in the game, followed by Wyler in second place and a man called Halstron in third. The three winners are invited to have dinner with Vogler, the man behind the death game. Vogler invites them to play the death game for real for a fee of $10,000. Gretl receives a message from London that Manders and Bast are dead, and she goes off to warn Vogler. Jenny overhears her and follows. Vogler decides to make Simon the first victim of Wyler and Halstron. He offers them the money to kill Simon, but just then two guards enter with Jenny. Simon and Jenny are given two minutes start before the others pursue them through the woods. Can they survive, or will the death game claim its first real victims?

THE ART COLLECTORS (1967)

Simon Templar	Roger Moore
Natasha	Ann Bell
Serge	Peter Bowles
Lucille	Nadja Regin
Marcel Legrand	Geoffrey Bayldon
Joseph	James Maxwell
Hans	Philo Hauser
Gunter	Richard Shaw
Mundt	Garfield Morgan
Bernard	Bryan Kendrick
Original Screenplay by	Michael Pertwee
Directed by	Roy Baker

THE SAINT IS IN Paris in winter and as he relaxes in a nightclub, he observes two attractive women talking near the exit. Outside two men attack the chauffeur of one of the women. The woman, Natasha, leaves the club, and is attacked by the men. Simon comes to her aid and chases them off. She asks Simon to drive her home, and when there she invites him to stay the night. She shows Simon the reason for the attack, several rare paintings, worth £1 million. The next day Natasha telephones Marcel Legrand, an art dealer, who wishes to buy the paintings. Marcel is visited by the police who warn him about a young girl trying to sell some phoney pictures. On his way to see Natasha, Marcel is stopped by two men and kidnapped. One of the men takes his place and continues to see Natasha. He examines the pictures and is convinced they are genuine, negotiates the price with her while Simon crates the pictures. The phoney Marcel drives away with the pictures, unaware that Simon is hiding in the back of the car. He drives to a remote area where his man is holding Marcel. While the two men are unpacking the pictures, Simon rescues Marcel and sends him off to fetch the police. The two men, Joseph and Mundt, unpack the case and find it empty, and then Simon appears and holds them at gunpoint. He locks them in the cellar, then Inspector Mathieu arrives with his Sergeant, and as Simon is taking them to the cellar the Inspector strikes him on the head knocking him out. Inspector Mathieu calls on Natasha to tell her that Legrand was found murdered, and his killer was Simon Templar. He then goes off to collect the paintings from where Simon left them, taking the paintings away as evidence. Natasha feels she needs a drink and while she is preparing it Simon appears. She screams and accuses him of murder, but he tells her that Legrand is alive and well, and then returns the paintings to her. The Inspector and his Sergeant are driving along, when the Inspector suddenly discovers that the picture frames are empty. They turn the car around to return to the house. The pictures change hands several times and before long its a case of picture, picture, who's got the picture, before Simon intervenes and the art collection is returned to its rightful owner.

Ann Bell and Roger Moore

TO KILL A SAINT (1967)

Simon Templar	**Roger Moore**
Paul Verrier	**Peter Dyneley**
Annette	**Annette Andre**
Andre	**Francis Matthews**
Sergeant Luduc	**Robert Cawdron**
Inspector Quercy	**John Serret**
Justine	**Pamela Ann Davy**
Bolande	**Michael Bilton**
Pierre	**Robert Gillespie**
Braddock	**Victor Winding**
Jacqueline	**Maggie Wright**
Theresa	**Valerie Leon**
Celeste	**Nita Lorraine**
Fellows	**Derek Bond**

Original Screenplay by	**Michael Winder**
Directed by	**Robert Asher**

THE SAINT IS IN Paris, browsing through the flea market. He is followed by Sergeant Luduc, waiting for Simon to break the law, but suddenly a car pulls up and a gunman fires several shots at The Saint. Simon and Luduc chase after him in Luduc's car, the car pulls into an underground car park, and there the gunman removes his hat, glasses and raincoat to reveal a beautiful young girl, who quickly switches to another car. Simon pulls into the car park and sees the girl. He questions her and she says that the car belongs to Paul Verrier. He examines the car and finds an earring; the girl drives off and Simon follows her. At the Verrier house Justine, Paul's wife, is just about to leave him. She says that he has no time for her. On her way out she passes Sergeant Luduc, who has come to question Verrier about the attempt on Simon's life. Verrier has several witnesses to say that he has not left the house. That evening at his club Verrier receives an offer from a man called Fellows for his club and his organisation, of seven million francs. Verrier refuses, and returns home with his assistant, André. While André is parking the car Verrier is greeted by his butler, who prepares him a drink which as he goes to open Verrier's cupboard explodes in his face, killing him. Among the debris is a drawing of the stick man. Verrier puts a price of 100,000 francs on Simon's head. The next day Inspector Quercy and Sergeant Luduc call on Simon in his hotel to arrest him, but they find him in bed attended by two ladies from the Paris Symphony Orchestra. Quercy accuses Simon of the attempt on Verrier's life, but the ladies are Simon's alibi that he has not left the hotel. Quercy leaves the hotel frustrated, with Sergeant Luduc staying behind to watch Simon. Verrier hires a professional killer called Bolande to kill Simon. Later that day Simon goes out followed by his faithful watchdog Sergeant Luduc. As they leave the hotel Simon spots Annette, the girl from the car park, entering the hotel. He makes an excuse to Luduc and follows her back into the hotel. Simon follows Annette to his room. She proceeds to wreck the room, and Simon questions her as to why she shot at him with blanks. She tells Simon that her father was killed by Verrier during a bank raid. Meanwhile, Bolande prepares to kill Simon. Bolande approaches Simon's room via the balcony; he fires at Simon and misses. He tries to escape but runs into Inspector Quercy and Sergeant Luduc. He fires at them and they shoot back, killing him. Back at Verrier's club, he speaks to Fellows who sympathises about the bombing. He also increases his offer on the club to nine million francs. Verrier telephones London and sends for Braddock, another professional killer. Fellows goes to see Justine, whom he accuses of hiring The Saint to kill Verrier. Simon decides to go and see Verrier, so he goes along to his club. Verrier's men try to stop him, but he overpowers them just as Verrier appears. Verrier mistakes Simon for the killer, Braddock. He then hires Simon to kill himself for the sum of $200,000. How will Simon earn his money? Will the real Braddock appear and try to kill a Saint?

THE COUNTERFEIT COUNTESS
(1967)

Simon Templar	Roger Moore
Nadine/Yvette	Kate O'Mara
Mireille	Alexandra Bastedo
Alzon	Philip Madoc
Carl	Derek Newark
Inspector Teal	Ivor Dean
Warburg	Henry Soskin
Riles	David Kelsey
Larry	Ray Brown
Barman	Gertan Klauber
Maurice	Cliff Dickins
Gendarme	Terry Mountain

Original Screenplay by	Philip Broadley
Directed by	Leslie Norman

ONE MORNING AS The Saint drives along a country lane through the English countryside, he hears a small plane fly overhead. The engine splutters and then fails, and the plane crashes in a field nearby. Simon rushes to the pilot's aid and the man shoots at him. And so begins the case of the counterfeit Countess. The pilot runs off, but he is picked up by two men in a car nearby. Simon examines the plane wreckage and finds a bundle of £5

Simon and Mireille plan to recover the counterfeit plates from the Countess

notes parcelled up, so he takes down the plane's number and leaves. The driver of the car which picked up the pilot makes an urgent call to Paris to a man called Alzon and he informs him of The Saint's involvement. Alzon then calls

Switzerland and speaks to the Countess. Simon examines the money and after several tests he discovers that it is forged. He checks with Inspector Teal who traces the pilot's address from the plane's call sign. Simon goes to the address in Chelsea where the pilot lives. He finds the pilot dead, telephones Scotland Yard, and while he is searching the flat, two men break in and tackle him, but he soon gets the upper hand and subdues them just as the police arrive. The next day he flies to Paris, to follow up an address he found in the flat. This leads him to the pilot's girlfriend. He calls at the flat and finds the girl, Mireille out. Her flatmate, Yvette, says that she can be found at the Black Cat nightclub. After Simon leaves, Yvette telephones Alzon and warns him that Simon is on his way over. Alzon then telephones the Countess again, and she tells her man Carl to make a delivery to Alzon, and then to kill Simon Templar. That evening at the club Simon questions Mireille about the pilot, Miles Chapman. He pretends to be a friend of Chapman. Alzon calls Mireille into the office and tells her to keep Simon occupied until Carl arrives. Yvette arrives with Carl and they join Simon for a drink. After several drinks Yvette invites them back to her flat for breakfast. While Simon is dancing with Yvette Carl slips something into his drink. Simon switches drinks with Yvette and then appears to be drugged. He questions Carl about the forged notes and Carl mentions an address in Switzerland. Simon then pretends to collapse. Carl drags him outside where he plans to kill him, but suddenly Simon jumps him and is about to take him in when Alzon appears with a gun. He plans to kill Simon, but Mireille suddenly appears with the police and the two men run off. That evening Simon goes to the Countess's villa; he breaks in and finds the printing press and plates. Carl appears and Simon is knocked out. He wakes up in the Countess's bedroom. She has gone to fetch Carl and Alzon. Simon escapes through the window and drives off in an old car unaware that the brakes have been tampered with by Carl. As he drives down the winding mountain road, the brakes go and suddenly the car is racing out of control, heading towards the cliff edge. Is this the end of the road for The Saint?

INTERLUDE IN VENICE (1967)

Simon Templar	Roger Moore
Helen	Lois Maxwell
Foots Fortunati	William Sylvester
Cathy	Quinn O'Hara
Prince Ubaldo	Paul Stassino
Goldilocks	Joyce Blair
Don Battista	Richard Warner
John Allardyce	Robert Ayres
Inspector Gambetti	Patrick Troughton
O'Mallamo	Derek Sydney
Carlo	Earl Green
Toni	Hal Galili
The Nun	Tita Dano
Original Screenplay by	Paddy Manning O'Brine
Directed by	Leslie Norman

THE SAINT IS IN Venice and, late one night, as he walks down the alleyways and side streets, he sees a young girl struggling with a man. Simon intervenes and the man pulls out a knife. He lunges at The Saint but Simon disarms him and he runs off. The young girl introduces herself as Cathy Allardyce. Simon takes Cathy home and leaves her with her father and stepmother. Cathy, and Helen, her stepmother, argue about Cathy's recent behaviour. Meanwhile, the thug, Carlo, reports to his boss 'Foots' Fortunati about the failure of his mission and Simon's interference. The next day Simon takes Cathy and Helen on a sightseeing trip around Venice while John Allardyce is away on a business trip. Helen questions Simon about his intentions and Simon says he is just a friend. 'Foots' goes to see Prince Ubaldo. He uses the Prince's name to attract customers to his nightclub. He tells the Prince that he must seduce Cathy, and that evening the Prince engages Cathy in conversation. He invites her and Helen to be his guests that evening at the club. Simon takes the two ladies along to the Casino, where the Prince takes the ladies off for a drink. Simon tries his luck at the gambling tables and he is approached by Goldilocks, the Prince's ex-girlfriend. The Prince persuades Cathy to leave with him and he takes her to his villa. Simon leaves the table a winner. Meanwhile Cathy is being wooed by the Prince. Goldilocks tells Simon where the Prince and Cathy have gone. Simon leaves with Helen to find Cathy, but just as they arrive at the Villa they hear two shots. They enter and find Cathy dazed, standing over the Prince's body with a gun in her hand. Simon questions Cathy about where she got the gun, but she cannot remember. Simon sends the ladies to stay with a friend, Don Battista. While he removes all traces of Cathy having been at the Villa. Simon hides when the police arrive and then escapes in their motorboat. He believes that Cathy was to be the innocent victim of a blackmail plot. Simon returns to the girl's apartment to collect some of her things. While he is packing Goldilocks arrives, and Simon quizzes her about the blackmail plot; Goldilocks accidentally lets slip the name, Carlo. He was the man Simon had the fight with in the alley the previous night. Simon gets Carlo's address from Goldilocks and goes to see him. Simon questions Carlo and discovers that blackmail photos were to be used on Cathy. Simon destroys the photos and then while struggling with Carlo one of 'Foots' men appears and throws a knife, which hits Carlo in the back. The next day Simon discovers that 'Foots' was previously involved in a murder case, but let off on insufficient evidence. Don Battista takes the ladies away the next day to a small village, where they are met by phoney police officers who attack Don Battista, and take away Cathy and Helen. Simon visits Don Battista in the local hospital, and then speaks to the local police chief, Inspector Gambetti. He warns Simon not to take the law into his own hands, and he also tells him that he is keeping a close watch on Fortunati waiting for a chance to catch him. Helen and Cathy are held prisoner in the basement of 'Foots' casino. Cathy tries to escape but is recaptured by 'Foots'. Allardyce returns from his business trip. Simon questions him and discovers that he was responsible for the accidental death of 'Foots' brother. Now 'Foots' is out for revenge. Simon sneaks into the casino to find the girls. He is led to Cathy by one of Fortunati's men. He knocks the man out, but is then caught by another of the gang and taken at gun point to see 'Foots'. Two people die before Simon's interlude in Venice is over.

SIMON AND DELILAH (1967)

Simon Templar	Roger Moore
Roberto Vittorini	Ronald Radd
Beth	Lois Maxwell
Serena Harris (Delilah)	Suzanne Lloyd
David Bradley	Guy Rolfe
Tig Jordan	Leon Greene
Hal Ward	David Healy
Herbert Wheeler	Patrick Holt
Serio	John Collin
Renzo	Ray Chiarella
Toni Amato	Peter Birrel
Inspector Crepi	David Nettheim
Electrician	Gino Meldazzi
Maria	Vicky Hughes
Original Screenplay by	C. Scott Forbes
Directed by	Roy Baker

THE SAINT IS IN Rome visiting the film set of the latest biblical epic. Delilah. Simon sees a display of bad temper by the leading actress Serena Harris as she storms off the set. He is introduced by the film's publicist. Beth to the harrassed producer of the movie. Roberto Vittorini. Moments later two men sneak into the studio and knock out one of the technicians. They then kidnap Serena at gunpoint, also taking along her leading man Tig Jordan. Simon intervenes but the men get away. Shortly afterwards. Vittorini receives a ransom note with instructions not to call the police. Simon goes to see Toni Amato, one of the studio technicians, but his flat is empty. While searching the flat Maria, Amato's girlfriend, comes in and Simon questions her. but she does not know where Tony is. Tony has run off to join the rest of the gang. Meanwhile Simon is convinced that the kidnapping is an inside job, and that someone besides Amato is involved. Vittorino asks Simon to negotiate with the kidnappers on his behalf. Simon is approached by Sergio, one of the gang. but Simon refuses to pay the ransom until he is sure that Serena is unharmed. Sergio agrees to take him to see her. unaware that Simon has a hidden tape recorder on him which is recording all of the street sounds. He sees that Serena is well and returns to the studio. Beth, working on Simon's instructions, proceeds to question the other members of the crew including Serena's fifth husband. Herbert Wheeler. She discovers that almost everyone on the production disliked her. Simon and Beth drive off trying to retrace the journey that the kidnappers took using the various sounds picked up by the tape recorder. The trail leads them to an old warehouse, where Simon finds clues that Serena was there, but the warehouse is empty. Simon returns to the studio to await further developments. The gang make contact again, and this time Serena's husband, Herbert, will make the delivery. He leaves with the money and with Simon and Beth following close behind. Wheeler drops off the money, which is picked up by one of the men and taken to the gang's headquarters, where they start to divide it up. Simon sneaks in and tackles the men and with Delilah's help. overpowers the gang. Simon returns Serena and the money to the studio where he has a final confrontation with the person behind the kidnapping plot.

ISLAND OF CHANCE (1967)

Simon Templar	Roger Moore
Marla Clayton	Sue Lloyd
Dr Charles Crayford	David Bauer
Arlene Bland	Patricia Donahue
Jan Vanderfelt	Alex Scott
Vargas	Milton Johns
Grant	Thomas Baptiste
Inspector	Christopher Carlos
Pete	Norman Jones
Cody	Richard Owens
Rig	Kenneth Gardiner
Barman	Danny Daniels
Calypso Singer	Tommy Eytle
Maître d'Hôtel	Charles Hyatt

Original Screenplay by	Leigh Vance
Directed by	Leslie Norman

THE SAINT is in the Caribbean. He has come at the request of a friend, Frank Cody. Simon waits for him in one of the local bars, but as Cody enters he is shot at by a man with a blowpipe. Before he can tell Simon why he sent for him, he collapses and dies. The local police Inspector questions Simon about Cody's background. Simon tells him he received a cable ten days ago asking him to come over on a big money deal. Cody worked for Dr Charles Krayford, a scientist working on a new serum against disease. Simon goes to a local bar for a drink, but unknown to him he is followed by the two men who killed Cody. One of the men deliberately bumps into Simon and pulls a gun on him. They start to leave, but Simon jumps the man and after a short struggle the man escapes dropping the blowpipe. Simon goes to the local police and leaves the weapon with them. The following day he goes to see Krayford. He has a companion on the trip, Marla Clayton, a photojournalist who was at the nightclub when Cody died. At the Krayford house Arlene Bland, the housekeeper, prepares for the arrival of Simon. After a brief meeting with Krayford Simon is given Cody's room. He examines it for clues. He finds some photos, one of which is a photo of Cody's killer on board a boat. Simon and Marla go to the harbour to look for the boat. They trace the boat, and then the home of the man, Pete. Simon searches through his belongings but does not find anything of use. He is unaware that he is being followed by Jan Vanderfelt, one of Krayford's men. Meanwhile,

Pete is collecting snakes. That evening after dinner Simon questions Krayford about his staff, and asks him for a list of his benefactors. Vanderfelt angrily tells Krayford to get rid of Simon and the girl. That evening Simon sleeps peacefully unaware that a deadly snake is crawling up his bed, but he awakens just in time and shoots it. Simon questions Krayford about the incident, but he denies any knowledge of it. He also claims not to know about Cody's death. Krayford questions Vanderfelt about Cody's murder. Arlene overhears the conversation and is warned by Vanderfelt to keep quiet, but she refuses and Vanderfelt knocks her out. The next day Simon and Marla puzzle over the mystery of Cody's murder. They drive to the Martelu Tower, a local landmark that was in Cody's photographs. They hope to find a clue somewhere in the ruins. Simon finds a trap door in the ruins which leads to an underground cellar. There he finds several boxes filled with gold bullion. He then finds the dead body of Arlene. Suddenly, he is attacked by Vargas, one of Vanderfelt's men. Simon knocks him out and is then attacked by a second man. Simon subdues both men and questions them about the gold bullion. He discovers that the gold came from a plane crash several years earlier, and that Krayford with the help of Vanderfelt has been using the gold to fund his experiments. Simon returns to the house for a showdown with Krayford and Vanderfelt. His friend, Frank Cody must be avenged.

THE GADGET LOVERS (1967)

Simon Templar	Roger Moore
Smolenko	Mary Peach
Fenton	Campbell Singer
Igor	Glynn Edwards
Ivan	Nicholas Donnelly
Muller	John Bennett
Colonel Wing	Burt Kwouk
Vogel	Vernon Dobtcheff
Anton	Wolf Frees
Blagot	Maurice Browning
Klaus	Stephen Hubay
Mollière	Peter Burton
Gretchen	Trudi Neilson

Original Screenplay by	John Kruse
Directed by	Jim O'Connelly

IN A trendy Berlin nightclub, Simon is having a quiet drink when he spots William Fenton, of British Intelligence, letting his hair down. Suddenly, a man points a gun at Fenton through the curtains, but before he can fire, Simon spots him and throws a knife at him. Fenton calls the police and then starts to question the man to find out who paid him. Fenton tells Simon that 13 Russian agents have been killed in the past four months. Fenton tells the assassin to contact his control via the small transmitter he has with him and say that Fenton is dead. As he transmits the message the gadget explodes killing the man. Simon suspects that someone close by set off the explosion and goes to check up on the barman, but he has disappeared. Fenton takes Simon to security headquarters, where agent Muller demonstrates the latest technology in gadgets. Fenton tells Simon that someone is killing off Russian agents and making it look like the work of the British. Fenton receives a message that a top agent called Colonel Smolenko, is leaving Berlin for Paris on the midnight train, and that the barman has been traced to the railway station. Simon has ten minutes to catch the train and he makes it with seconds to spare. Simon's job is to find the Colonel and then protect him from the assassin. He traces the Colonel's carriage and is then surprised when he discovers that the Colonel is a woman. Simon talks the Colonel into letting him stay. He sends for some tea. The steward arrives with a tray, and suddenly Simon attacks the man. He's recognised him as the barman from the nightclub. Simon grabs the tea set and hurls it out of the window, seconds before it explodes. The barman escapes from the carriage and is shot down by the Colonel's security guards. The Colonel decides that Simon has his uses, and when the train pulls into Paris, Simon is dressed as the Colonel and she is posing as his assistant. They check into a hotel and then one of the local Russian agents arrives, Comrade Blagot. He is in charge of the local factory making gadget bombs. He takes Simon and the Colonel to his record shop, the cover for his factory, and he shows Simon the latest in miniature cameras. While Simon is taking pictures around the record shop, Blagot rushes off. Simon throws the camera out of the window, and it explodes. They return to the hotel and that evening Simon takes the Colonel dancing in a nightclub. On returning to the hotel he orders room service, while the Colonel opens her mail. Suddenly one of the letters starts to turn brown and ignites. Simon snatches it and throws it out of the window — it explodes. It was made of plastic explosive, another deadly weapon from the unknown enemy. The letter was postmarked Switzerland, so the next day Simon and the Colonel fly there to try and uncover the factory and the mastermind, who is obviously a gadget lover.

A DOUBLE IN DIAMONDS (1967)

Simon Templar	Roger Moore
Lord Gillingham	Cecil Parker
Charlie Hallowes	Jack Woolgar
Kate Summers	Yolande Turner
Veronica	Cathy Graham
Pierre	Anton Rogers
Mary	Ilona Rogers
Valerie	Vicky Graham
Nicholas	Ferdy Mayne
Mercier	Howard Gournay
Garton	John Clive
Michelle	Yvette Herries
Sergeant Knox	Alan Haywood
The Steward	Tim Barrett
Pilot	Brian Harrison
Chief Inspector Teal	Ivor Dean

Screenplay by	Harry W. Junkin
Story by	Donald and Derek Ford
Directed by	John Gilling

THE SCENE IS Hatton Gardens, London, the heart of the jewellery centre of England. Simon calls on Charlie Hallowes to collect a pair of personalised cuff links. While he is there Charlie shows him a copy of a necklace he is making for Lord Gillingham, the original of which is worth £200,000. Simon leaves and drives off, but he then discovers that he has left something behind and starts to drive back. Meanwhile Lord Gillingham's assistant Kate calls to pick up the copy, she acts strangely and Charlie becomes suspicious. He tries to telephone Lord Gillingham, but Kate strikes him on the head with a silver goblet, killing him. Kate leaves and is picked up by another member of the gang, Garton. Simon returns and finds Charlie dead; he calls in the Yard, and Chief Inspector Teal takes charge of the case. Simon and Teal call on Lord Gillingham just as he is about to start a fashion show. One of the models, Valerie, is wearing the necklace. After the show Simon examines the necklace and discovers that it has been switched. Simon leaves Teal baffled over the switch while he follows Valerie to her flat. Simon discovers that Valerie is actually Veronica — the girls are twins — and they tell Simon that they were paid £1000 by Pierre, the show designer, to switch the necklaces. They tell him that Pierre has left for Paris. Pierre goes to see a man called Nicholas, a wealthy dealer who plans to buy the necklace. The only problem is that someone has pulled a double switch on Pierre. Simon goes to see Lord Gillingham, who tells Simon that he has just received a phone call telling him he can have the diamonds back for £10,000. The diamonds change hands several times before The Saint's intervention, and Charlie's killer is brought to justice.

Cecil Parker and Yolanda E. Turner try to pull a switch on The Saint

THE POWER ARTIST (1967)

Simon Templar	**Roger Moore**
Cassie	**Pauline Munroe**
Vogler	**George Murcell**
Chief Inspector Teal	**Ivor Dean**
Finlay-Thorpe Jones	**Tristram Jellinek**
Perry Loudon	**Peter Bourne**
Shard	**John Bown**
Clay	**John J. Cairney**
Carter	**George Roubicek**
Sergeant Knox	**Alan Hayward**
Clerk	**Anthony Dawes**
Jack	**Charles Rea**
Taxi Driver	**Tommy Godfrey**
Policeman	**Michael Pemberton**
Dolly Girls	**Caron Gardner**
	Charlotte Selwyn

Original Screenplay by	**John Kruse**
Directed by	**Leslie Norman**

THE SAINT is on his way home by taxi. Suddenly, the driver diverts the cab to a house in Chelsea. The cabby tells Simon that if he likes adventure he is to go to the top floor flat and ask for Perry Loudon. Simon climbs to the top flat and on entering he finds a young man working on a metal sculpture. The man, Loudon starts shouting at Simon saying that he took Loudon's girl away from him but Simon has never seen the boy before. Simon goes close up to the boy and Loudon realises that this is not the Simon Templar that he knows. Before he can say anything else he is killed by a knife in the back. Two men enter the room and fire a pellet gun at Simon, he falls down and the men proceed to wreck the flat, and put Simon's fingerprints on the murder weapon. Simon, awakens just in time to hear a police car pull up outside, but he manages to hide the body just in time. Chief Inspector Teal arrives and questions Simon about Loudon's whereabouts. He tells Simon that he received a call telling him that Loudon and Simon were fighting in the flat. Teal searches the flat looking for Loudon. He goes into the bedroom where he sees a body in the bed. He pulls back the cover to reveal a young girl, and both he and Simon are surprised. Teal leaves embarrassed, and Simon follows, only to return when Teal has left. Simon returns to where he left Loudon's body. The young girl, Cassie, sees the blood and faints. When she recovers, Simon asks her to help. He calls up a friend and arranges for him to collect one of Loudon's sculptures. The men call to collect it, and are followed by the killers. Simon works out that someone set up an elaborate plan to kill Loudon and frame him. On the wall by Loudon's telephone is the name Simon Templar and a number. Simon rings the number and a man claiming to be The Saint answers the telephone. Simon traces the man and goes round to see him but 'Simon Templar' is dead, he leaped out of the window, a suicide, the local constable says. Simon and Cassie return to Loudon's flat to find Inspector Teal waiting for them. Teal questions Simon once again about Loudon, and as they leave the flat they run into a group of Loudon's beatnik friends who take over the flat for a party. In the flat Simon finds two cheques, one for £700 from a man called Findlay-Thorpe Jones. Simon goes to his house to see him while Cassie waits outside in the car. He questions Jones about Loudon's murder, but all that Jones will say is that now his sculpture will increase in value. Waiting outside the house Cassie hears voices coming from the basement of the next house. She waits until Simon returns and then shows him two men who are in the flat with video equipment recording what goes on in Findlay-Thorpe Jones' apartment. Simon realises that they have a video camera inside Loudon's sculpture. One of the men leaves with a video tape and Simon and Cassie follow. He leads them to an exclusive hotel where the man drops off the tape. Simon tries to bluff his way into the hotel while waiting for someone to collect the tape. The lift comes down from the penthouse and a man picks up the tape. Simon makes a dash for the lift and heads for the penthouse. Simon leaves the lift and is surrounded by four men, who grab him and take him to see Adolph Vogler, an old enemy. Vogler confesses that he is behind the plot to frame The Saint. Vogler tells Simon he 'bugged' Findlay-Thorpe's statue to get information on him. He also tells him that he will not kill him but he will hand him over to the police. His men try to sedate Simon but The Saint fights them off and escapes into the lift. Vogler calls Scotland Yard and Inspector Teal is waiting for Simon when they return to Loudon's flat. He takes Simon and Cassie to where the sculpture has been stored. Teal eagerly opens the box to find the case empty. Simon and Cassie return to Loudon's flat where they find the party in full swing. One of the party revellers knocks over a statue and breaks the plaster to reveal a human hand. Simon asks them to help him. He returns to Vogler's hotel taking along all the party people, and while they take over the hotel reception, Simon makes his way to Vogler's penthouse. Simon breaks in from the balcony, and comes across one of Vogler's men asleep. Simon puts him right out. The hotel clerk calls Scotland Yard. Simon discovers where Vogler has hidden the video tapes which were to be used for blackmail, and he destroys them. Cassie brings the revellers up to the penthouse just as Vogler appears. The revellers take over the penthouse, and shortly afterwards Inspector Teal appears. Simon warns Teal who Vogler is and then reveals Loudon's body in a cupboard, where he had placed it only moments before. Simon leaves Teal to wrap up the case. For The Saint this case is over, and the power artist is through.

This episode is a sequel to *The Death Game*.

WHEN SPRING IS SPRUNG (1967)

Simon Templar	Roger Moore
Joanne Dell	Toby Robbins
Marie Spring	Ann Lynn
Colonel Hannerly	Allan Cuthbertson
Chief Inspector Teal	Ivor Dean
Vulanin	George Pastell
John Spring	Gary Watson
Peter Quentin	Harvey Ashby
Watters	Douglas Livingstone
First Sleuth	Brian Mosley
Prosecuting Council	Eric Dodson
The Judge	Kenneth Edwards
Doctor	John Frawley
Russian Guards	Les Crawford
	Peter Brace

Original Screenplay by	Michael Pertwee
Directed by	Jim O'Connolly

SIMON IS ON the French Riviera, saying goodbye to a past love. As he leaves the airport he rescues a young girl from a drunken suitor. Simon offers her a lift, and while driving along she informs Simon he has just walked into a trap. The girl, Joanne, takes him to a country house where he is introduced to Colonel Hannerly of British Intelligence. The Colonel tells Simon that he believes the Russians will approach him to help free their man John Spring, a Russian agent. Hannerly asks Simon to work for the Russians and help Spring escape. As he is now a double agent working for the British, Simon agrees, and later that day he returns to London with Joanne. The next day Simon is approached by Marie, the wife of John Spring, who asks Simon to help her husband escape. The Saint agrees for the sum of £10,000. Simon calls in on Inspector Teal, and informs him that he was approached by Mrs Spring. Teal warns Simon to stay away and not interfere. On leaving the Yard Simon is stopped by a man wanting a light. He lights the man's cigarette and as the man blows the smoke at him, Simon collapses. Simon is taken to see Vulanin, a Russian agent. He questions Simon about his trip to Scotland Yard. Simon tells the truth and is then asked by Vulanin to help Spring escape. Simon ups the price to £15,000. Simon returns to the Yard to speak to Teal, pretending that he does not know that he has been followed by Teal's man. Leaving the Yard Simon goes on a shopping trip and buys several items. Marie visits her husband in gaol and warns him about the impending escape plan Simon has arranged for 4 o'clock the next day. Simon visits the court that Spring will be taken to the next day, and posing as a tourist he manages to slip a pill under Spring's chair in the dock. Inspector Teal's man reports back convinced that Simon is about to help Spring escape. Later that day Simon leaves the flat in disguise, with Joanne. During the trial Spring slips the pill into his mouth and shortly after collapses. An ambulance arrives to collect Spring and take him to the nearest hospital. The ambulance driver and nurse are Simon and Joanne. A police car follows the ambulance, but Simon manages to lose them. Simon returns to his flat with Joanne and Spring. Chief Inspector Teal is confused, he is convinced that Simon is involved, but has no proof. Simon receives instructions from Vulanin for Spring and Joanne to go to a house in Streatham. Simon waits a couple of minutes and then follows them. Several plot twists occur before the case is closed.

THE GADIC COLLECTION (1967)

Simon Templar	**Roger Moore**
Turin	**Peter Wingarde**
Diya	**Georgia Brown**
Sukan	**Michael Ripper**
Inspector Yolu	**Martin Benson**
Ahmed Bayer	**Andre van Gysegham**
Ayesha	**Nicole Shelby**
Geoffrey Bane	**Hedger Wallace**
Kemal	**Henry Sodkin**
Omar	**Paul Darrow**
Zoltan	**Geoff Cheshire**
Old Man	**Andreas Malandrinos**
Directed by	**Freddie Francis**

SIMON IS IN Turkey visiting a friend Geoffrey Bane. He is looking around at the exhibits at the Silbakin Museum when a young girl enters and goes over to look at a piece known as the Gadic Collection. A man enters the room and the girl hides. She then tries to run off. The man tries to follow her. Simon trips him and stops him, and the girl gets away. The Saint finds some photos that the girl dropped – they are of the Gadic collection. Bane takes Simon to see the general manager of the museum and they discover from Omar, a clerk, that the collection was recently cleaned by a man called Kemal. That's when the photos were taken so that a copy could be made of the collection. Simon and Bane go to see Kemal in his shop. He is not there so they start to search the place. When the girl from the museum, Ayesha comes in, she also starts to look for something. The man from the museum has followed her there and again he tries to attack her. Simon chases him off and then questions the girl about her uncle, Kemal. They escort her home to her uncle, via the local ferry. Simon shows Kemal the photos and they accuse him of making copies of the collection. They warn him not to do it again, and leave. After they have left Ayesha tells her uncle about the attack. Bane returns to the museum to work and he takes out the Gadic collection to examine. He telephones Simon and asks him to come right over as he has made an important discovery. Simon arrives to find Bane dead. Shortly afterwards the police arrive, and Simon is put under arrest. Simon is taken back to the station and questioned by Inspector Yolu. The general manager of the museum is sent for and he vouches for Simon and so he is released. Simon plans to take the ferry back to see Kemal, to question him further. On board the ferry he is questioned by Sukan, a man looking for the collection. Simon returns to his hotel where he finds a young woman waiting for him in his room, who also questions him about the collection. Sukan goes to see Turin, a wealthy man who wants the collection at any price. Later Simon runs into Sukan who takes him to see his employer. Turin is convinced that Simon has the collection and he has his men take Simon down to the basement into a special cell with sharp spikes on the walls. Suddenly the walls of the cell start to close in on Simon. Is this to be the end of The Saint?

LEGACY FOR THE SAINT (1967)

Simon Templar	Roger Moore
Chief Inspector Teal	Ivor Dean
Charlie Lewis	Alan MacNaughton
Tony	T.P. McKenna
Ed Brown	Reginald Marsh
Penny	Stephanie Beacham
Ashford	Kenneth Farrington
Pietro	Edward Brayshaw
Mark	Bruce Boa
Dickie	Brian Coburn
Original Screenplay by	Michael Winder
Directed by	Roy Ward Baker

ED BROWN is a retired big-time gangster, who enjoys life until he is blown up inside his Rolls Royce. Simon Templar finds the wrecked car, and is later asked to fly to Switzerland to break the news to Ed's daughter, Penny. Ed's will is an unusual one – it has been recorded on a home movie. It is shown to Simon, Penny, and to his friend Charlie, a crooked lawyer. Also at the screening are four of Ed's gangster rivals, Tony, Pietro, Dickie and Mark. In Ed's will he tells his rivals that he has deposited £1,000,000 in a bank in Switzerland, and whichever one of them can match it can claim it. Simon realises that the various gangs will be after the money. Simon discovers that £1,000,000 worth of gold is being transported from Southampton to London in a week's time, and it looked as though Ed was planning to steal it. Penny is horrified to learn the truth about her father. The various gangs

decide to go ahead with the robbery, but they decide to hold Penny hostage in case Simon decides to interfere. Simon decides it's best to be involved in the robbery from the inside and, for Penny's sake, he offers to help the gangs with the robbery. They accept the offer, but warn him if he tries any tricks they will harm Penny. It is not long before the different gangs start to squabble with one another, and Mark is the first to get bumped off. The plan to hi-jack the bullion goes ahead, with Simon in the role of a policeman. The gold bullion robbery is a complete success. But which of Ed Brown's rivals will walk away with the loot? Did Ed trick Simon when he left a legacy for The Saint?

Simon Templar and Penny outline the plan for the bullion robbery

THE DESPERATE DIPLOMAT (1968)

Simon Templar	Roger Moore
Chief Inspector Teal	Ivor Dean
Walter Faber	Robert Hardy
Sara Douglas	Susan Farmer
Jason Douglas	John Robinson
Eddie Margoles	David Cargill
John Chatto	Kenneth Gardiner
Carla Lawrence	Lorna Wilde
Dunn	Leslie Crawford
Healey	Terry Plummer
Julie	Maggie London
Telephone Operator	Yutte Stensgaard

Original Screenplay by	Terry Nation
Directed by	Ray Austin

LATE ONE EVENING Simon is driven by the police to see Chief Inspector Teal at a derelict house in London, a house where a murder has been committed. Teal asks Simon if he knows the dead man. Simon recognises the man but tells Teal he does not. The man was an aide to Jason Douglas, a diplomat who has disappeared with three quarters of a million dollars. Teal hands Simon an envelope addressed to him but the only thing inside is a foreign coin. Teal tells Simon that the man was tortured before he was killed. Simon leaves; outside the house he examines the coin, and then he takes an identical coin out of his pocket. Simon is unaware that he is being watched by two men. The next day Simon goes to a trendy boutique to see the owner, Sara, Douglas's daughter. He tells Sara that her father's man was murdered and that the coin was a call for help from Douglas. Simon leaves and shortly afterwards one of the two men following Simon enters the shop. The man, Eddie, questions Sara about her father. Sara runs out of the shop straight in to the arms of the other man Walter Faber. Later that evening Simon receives a call from Sara, who tells him that she is being held by Faber. Faber gives Simon instructions to drive to a remote part of the country where they will exchange Sara for information of Douglas's whereabouts. Simon drives to a small lake and there on the other side is Faber and Sara. Faber's man, Eddie, sneaks up behind Simon ready to kill him as soon as he reveals the hiding place of Douglas. Simon hears Eddie behind him and turns round to tackle him. Faber fires but shoots Eddie by mistake. During the distraction Sara makes a break in Faber's car. He chases after her but she gets away. The next day Simon and Sara fly to Geneva, Switzerland, as this was the last place that Douglas was seen. They check into a hotel and

wait, and later that day Simon receives a call from John Chatto, Douglas's aide. He gives Simon instructions to drive to the place where Douglas is. Simon is unaware that Faber has been listening in on the extension, and they arrive at the house where Douglas is only to find that Faber has got there first. Faber holds Simon at gunpoint while his man goes to look for Sara. She sees the man coming out of the house and hides in the woods. Simon tells Faber that she is waiting back at the hotel for him. Simon pretends to co-operate with Faber, but when he has the chance he jumps Faber and his men. He almost gets the upper hand, when suddenly Faber holds a gun to Chatto's head. Simon gives in and is taken to the cellar. Sara sneaks into the house to look for Simon and her father. Simon manages to free himself and Chatto and then he questions Douglas about the stolen money. Douglas says the money was to have been used to help the poor people of an African country. Faber captures Sara, and then two of his men come down to the cellar. They take Chatto and Douglas upstairs to see his daughter. Faber sends Chatto to fetch some medicine to take care of Douglas's wounds, and meanwhile Simon prepares a trap in the cellar for Faber's man. Faber tells Sara that she and her father will be released if he tells him where the money is hidden, but that Simon must be killed. Douglas reveals the hiding place is in the house, and Faber's man takes Sara back to the cellar. The man prepares to shoot Simon, but Simon has rigged the staircase and he falls down. Simon picks up the man's gun and goes after Faber. Faber's man shoots it out with Simon while Faber escapes in his car. Simon pursues him, but more people will die before the case is closed.

THE ORGANISATION MAN (1968)

Simon Templar	Roger Moore
Jonathan Roper	Tony Britton
Kate Barnaby	Caroline Mortimer
Leander	Glynn Edwards
Mr Spode	Norman Bird
Cable	John Collin
Craddock	Simon Lack
Major Carter	Mark Dignam
Captain Yates	Terence Edmond
Mason	Tony Caunter
Original Screenplay by	Donald James
Directed by	Leslie Norman

THE SAINT is walking through a London park early one morning when he spots his quarry walking towards him. Simon draws out a gun and shoots the man six times at point blank range, and then walks away. A few days later Jonathan Roper runs a home movie of Simon shooting the man called Spode. Roper invites Simon to visit him at his home in the country. He asks Simon if Spode was the first man that he had killed, and Simon replies that there were others. Roper shows Simon round his house. He has a small international Army, combat ready and trained to kill. He asks Simon if he would like to join his organisation. Simon agrees. The next day, Simon is put through his paces by Leander, one of Roper's Lieutenants. The training goes on for a week and one morning while out for a run Simon manages to lose the rest of the team. He slips into the local pub, where he is greeted by his undercover contact, Kate. Simon rejoins the team training in combat and later is invited by Roper to join him for a drink. Roper tells Simon that he will keep a close watch on him as he wants him to succeed. That evening Simon sneaks out of the camp and is picked up by Kate, who takes him to see Major Carter of Military Intelligence. Simon's assignment is to find out why Roper is building up a private army. During the meeting the 'dead' man, Spode, appears – he is one of the Colonel's men. While Simon is out of the camp Leander and another man, Cable, discover that someone has left the camp. Kate returns Simon to the camp to complete his assignment, but waiting in the bushes are Leander and Cable. Simon manages to sneak past them without being noticed. The next day at a government building Spode receives a man called Craddock, who is a defector. Spode must obtain from him a list of his contacts. The next day at combat training Leander picks on Simon to tackle him with a knife. Simon defeats him under the watchful eye of Roper. Simon is informed by Roper that he will lead a mission that evening. Simon and his men are assigned to hi-jack a military vehicle and the plan goes without any problems. Roper appears and examines the contents of the vehicle – inside are a number of Army kilts. On his way back to the camp Simon diverts to the pub to see Spode, unaware that he is being followed by Cable. Simon talks to Spode about the uniforms but they are uncertain what they will be used for. Simon starts to leave but runs into Cable holding Kate at gunpoint. He disarms him, and as Cable comes at him with a bottle, Spode shoots him. The next day, Simon puts his men through their paces, dressed in their highland regiment uniform. Roper's plan is that his men will replace the guards that are watching over Craddock. Roper's men divert the genuine guards, and then Simon's men replace them. Just after the switch Kate is captured by Leander. Will Roper's men succeed in releasing Craddock. Will Kate reveal Simon's involvement with the Army? Can The Saint stop Roper before the organisation man gets away with his plan?

THE DOUBLE TAKE (1968)

Simon Templar	Roger Moore
Eugene Patroclos	Gregoire Aslan
Annabel	Kate O'Mara
Annabel	Denise Buckley
Bainter	Blake Butler
Pat Hurst	Michael Robbins
Girl at Airport	June Abbott
Hotel Clerk	Michael Mellinger
Chuck Spendelton	Iain Blair
Party Guests	Martin Wyldick
	Geoffrey Morris
	Rose Alba

Original Screenplay by	John Kruse
Directed by	Leslie Norman

THE SAINT flies into Greece on his way to Beirut. On his way to change planes he is told that he is the ten millionth passenger and that there is a small presentation to be made to him. At the side entrance to the airport he is met by a man with a gun. The chauffeur and the phoney hostess, Annabel, take him to see Eugene Patroclos, a wealthy businessman. He tells Simon that he is being impersonated by an exact double, who is changing several of his business deals. Patroclos offers Simon $100,000 to find the impostor. Simon declines the offer but decides to stay overnight. Checking into a hotel, he receives a note to leave town, followed up by threats from two men with guns. Simon disarms them, and returns to Patroclos to accept his offer. Patroclos sends Simon to London, the last place where the imposter had been seen. As Simon drives to his flat he sees the impostor with his secretary arriving at a large house. Simon telephones Patroclos in Greece who tells him to watch the impostor closely. That evening Simon gate-crashes a party given by Patroclos. He is approached by the impostor with a deal. He wants Simon to trace the man who has been impersonating him! Patroclos requests Simon to stay at his house and not leave. Later that evening Simon sneaks in to Patroclos's bedroom and steals an important notebook from his safe. He switches off the alarm system and slips out of the house. Simon drives to the airport and hands over the notebook to be put on the next flight to Greece. After he leaves, Patroclos appears and retrieves the notebook, but unknown to him, Simon was watching. The next day Simon receives a cable from Patroclos saying, 'notebook received, arriving soon'. Patroclos questions Simon about his missing notebook. Simon, Patroclos and his secretary, Annabel, fly to Greece to have a showdown with Patroclos! They arrive at his office just after he has left for the airport. They race after him only to arrive just as his plane takes off. Simon questions the two Annabels but is no wiser to what is going on. Simon leaves confused.

Shortly afterwards he receives a cable saying that Patroclos's plane has crashed. Can Simon solve the riddle of the two Patrocloses and what of the two Annabels. Simon needs all of his skill to unravel the mystery of the double take.

Simon Templar tries to solve the mystery of the two Eugene Patrocloses

THE FICTION MAKERS (1968)

Simon Templar	Roger Moore
Amos Klein	Sylvia Syms
Galaxy Rose	Justine Lord
Warlock	Kenneth J. Warren
Frug	Philip Locke
Monk	Tom Clegg
Bishop	Nicholas Smith
Nero Jones	Roy Hanlon
Finlay Hugoson	Peter Ashmore
Carol Henley	Caron Gardner
Rip Savage	Frank Maher
Carson	Graham Armitage
Ma	Lila Kaye
Pa	Joe Gibbons
Screenplay by	John Kruse and Harry W. Junkin
Directed by	Roy Baker

SIMON IS AT the film première of a new action series based on the best selling novels by Amos Klein. He is the escort of starlet, Carol Henley. Simon talks to Finlay Hugoson, the publisher of Klein's novels. He wants to speak to Simon privately so they return to his office. As they are about to enter Simon sees the light go out. He rushes in and is confronted by two men. He tackles them, but they get away. Hugoson discovers that all that was taken was Klein's home address. Hugoson wishes Klein's identity to be kept a secret and asks Simon to drive down and keep an eye on Klein. On arriving at the house Simon discovers that Amos Klein is a woman. 'Amos' shows Simon a letter that she received asking for assistance, with a cheque enclosed for £50,000. The police call at the house to question Amos Klein. Simon becomes suspicious, and makes a break for it with 'Amos'. The policeman fires a dart gun at him and Simon collapses. When Simon awakens the next day, he finds himself in a large country house, where he is attended to by Galaxy Rose, a young woman who is there to see to his every need. She then takes him to see Warlock. Warlock, and Galaxy Rose are both names out of Amos Klein novels. Warlock mistakes Simon for Klein, and 'Amos Klein' is mistaken for Simon's secretary. Warlock wants Simon to devise a plan to break into Hermetico, a colliery in North Wales that has been turned into a Fort-Knox style security vault for gold, jewels and cash. Simon returns to his room to start thinking about a plan for Hermetico, and also a plan to escape with 'Amos' from Warlock. That afternoon he goes on a tour of the grounds with Galaxy, and he makes a point of noting the security system. That evening he breaches the security system, and with 'Amos' he makes his escape in a car, crashing through an electrified fence. They travel for a couple of miles before the car breaks down, unaware that Warlock is close behind them controlling the car. They escape from the car just before Warlock arrives. Simon and 'Amos' are chased through the woods by Warlock's men with dogs. They reach a small cottage and as they are about to borrow a car, Warlock and his men arrive. The next day Simon and 'Amos' are taken by Warlock to his cellar, where they are threatened with death unless Amos Klein comes up with a plan to rob Hermetico. Simon and Warlock pay a visit to Hermetico posing as prospective clients and they are given a tour of the underground base. Back at Warlock's base Simon and 'Amos' come up with a plan to breach the security. The next couple of days Simon puts Warlock's men through an elaborate plan to break into Hermetico. After intense training Warlock and his men are ready. Warlock's man, Frug, discovers who Simon really is just as they are about to leave. Warlock leaves 'Amos' tied up with a lazer gun pointing at her. If Simon's plan does not work she will be killed. Will Simon's and 'Amos's' plan to break into Hermetico work or will the fiction makers' plot end in disaster for its authors?

THE TIME TO DIE (1968)

Simon Templar	Roger Moore
Mary Ellen Brent	Suzanne Lloyd
Steven Lyall	Maurice Good
Dinny Haigh	John Barcroft
Charlie Mason	Terence Rigby
Martin Graves	Freddie Jones
Donna Sumrie	Monica Gray
Laura Carlton	Linda Marlowe

Original Screenplay by	Terry Nation
Directed by	Roy Ward Baker

SIMON IS driving along with journalist Mary Ellen Brent. She is going to write an article for her paper on The Saint. She finds a gift-wrapped box in the car and inside the box is a snake. The snake is harmless, but inside is a note saying that this is just the beginning. Back at his flat Simon goes through a list of possible suspects with Mary Ellen. He then receives a phone call from the mystery man planning to kill him. Simon takes Mary Ellen home, unaware that his flat is being watched. The man waits till Simon has driven off, then he sneaks into the flat and prepares a booby trap for Simon. Mary Ellen discovers that she has left her notebook in the flat and they return to collect it. Simon sees a flashlight through the window and sneaks round the back. He catches Charlie Mason, a small-time crook, preparing a surprise for him. Simon questions Charlie about his employer and Charlie says that he just received a note telling him what to do, with the payment enclosed. That night Simon goes to see Martin Sumrie, an ex-con who has reason to want The Saint dead. Simon breaks in to Sumrie's shop, and is suddenly confronted by Mrs Sumrie holding a gun on him. He questions her about her husband and then starts to look for him. He finds him behind a curtain, laid out in a coffin. The next morning, Simon opens his door to find a wreath pinned to it with the message Simon Templar R.I.P., died Thursday – that's two days away. Simon then receives a call from Charlie Mason, who says that he's received another note, and he tells Simon the address that the note says to go to. Simon will go in Charlie's place, but unknown to Simon, Charlie is about to pull a double cross. Simon goes to the address, a derelict country house. The house appears to be empty, but suddenly Simon hears a noise upstairs. At the top of the landing is Charlie, he sways, and then falls down the stairs, dead. The telephone rings, but there is no one there, just a distant sound of a music box. Behind Simon a door slams and a man runs off. Simon chases him only to discover it's Mary Ellen, still after a story. Dinny Haigh of the Yard visits Simon just as Mary Ellen is leaving the flat, and as she stands in front of the door several shots are fired at her. Simon drives her home and then goes to see Laura Carlton. Laura is Charlie's girlfriend, and she arranges to meet Simon in an underground car park. She tells him that Charlie told her that the mystery man parks his car there. They wait in silence, and suddenly the man drives in. As he walks past them, Laura accidentally makes a noise and the man sees them, and fires at Simon. A stray bullet accidentally hits and kills Laura. Simon goes to see Dinny, and while he is there he receives a phone message from Mary Ellen saying she is waiting at the flat. He returns home to find the flat wrecked, and Mary Ellen gone, with a message scrawled on the wall, giving the time to die. Can Simon save Mary Ellen from the mysterious killer, and what of the hearse that waits outside Simon's door? Is it really the time to die for The Saint?

THE MASTER PLAN (1969)

Simon Templar	Roger Moore
Cord Thrandel	John Turner
Jean Lane	Lyn Ashley
Mr Ching	Bert Kwouk
Fish	Christopher Benjamin
Max	Robert Morris
Tony Lane	Paul Greenhalgh
Dr King	James Locker
Nurse	Brenda Kempner
Porter	Leslie Anderson
Van Driver	Edwin Brown
Original Screenplay by	Harry W. Junkin
Directed by	Leslie Norman

SIMON OFFERS to help a young girl, Jean Lane, find her brother, Tony. The search takes them to a nightclub in Soho, where Simon comes up against Cord Thrandel, a vicious criminal. A handshake from Thrandel lays Simon out. Thrandel's ring contains a tiny hypodermic needle with a drug solution in it. Simon is taken to a cell and locked up with Jean. Cord leaves and goes looking for Tony. He visits a man called Fish in his antique shop. Simon recovers to find he is locked up in a padded cell. Cord traces Tony to his flat and savagely beats him up. Back at the club Simon devises a way out of the cell. One of Cord's men tries to stop them, but Simon disarms him and finds out where Tony lives. He goes off to see him with Jean. They arrive at Tony's flat to find him knocked out on the floor next to the gas fire, with the gas on full. Simon calls an ambulance and Tony is taken off to hospital. Jean thinks it's attempted suicide, but Simon says it is attempted murder. Simon calls on Fish, the antique dealer. As he leaves, Cord arrives. Simon sneaks round the back of the shop, and listens in to the conversation between Fish and Thrandel. He overhears something about a shipment to be collected from a warehouse. Cord returns to the club, to discover that Tony is alive and in hospital. He takes his man, Max, with him and drives round to the hospital, and posing as a doctor he sneaks into Tony's room preparing to finish him off. Jean arrives and interrupts him. He knocks her out and leaves just before Simon arrives. Simon drives Jean home, and then heads for the warehouse. He opens a crate containing plaster statues and he breaks one open to find heroin. He switches labels on the crates and leaves just before Thrandel and his men arrive. Thrandel opens the crate to find his statues missing. Simon goes to see Tony and discovers that Thrandel has blackmailed him into working

for him. As Simon leaves the hospital Thrandel appears and takes him away at gunpoint. Thrandel wants to know where his drugs are. He gives Simon the chance to reveal where they are hidden, or Jean, who is held prisoner, will be killed. Does Simon have a master plan that will save the day?

Lyn Ashley, Roger Moore and Burt Kwouk are all involved in *The Master Plan*

THE PEOPLE IMPORTERS (1969)

Simon Templar	Roger Moore
Bonner	Neil Hallett
Laura	Susan Travers
Slater	Gary Miller
Jackson	Ray Lonnen
Suresh	Salmaan Peer
Malia	Imogen Hassell
Chaudri	Nik Hassall
Kumar	Shivendra Sinha
Hima Dri	Kevork Malikyan
Mrs Reynold	Joan Newall
Harry	Michael Robbins
Sam	Ron Pember
Mr Sen	Julian Sherrier
Photographer	Christopher Sandford
Roberts	John Downing
Doctor	Michael Da Costa
Ministry Man	John Garvin

Original Screenplay by	Donald James
Directed by	Ray Austin

THE SAINT IS out fishing when an unexpected catch leads him into a vicious racket of smuggling illegal aliens into Britain. Simon is out on a charter boat after a successful day's fishing; returning home, the fog sets in. In the fog another boat nearly collides with his and he hears a shot and the sound of something being thrown overboard. He searches the water and drags out the body of a dead man. The next day Simon visits the local Yacht Club, where he starts up a conversation with an attractive girl, Laura, who is waiting for a man called Bonner. He is the man behind the illegal immigrant racket. Bonner arrives and makes his apology to Laura for he must leave on urgent business. Simon offers to give Laura a lift back to town, which she accepts. Bonner's urgent business is to take the latest cargo of immigrants to London, as his partner, Slater, is having trouble with the police, and has also lost a couple of immigrants. On the drive to town Simon questions Laura about Bonner, and he learns that he is a boat-broker who hasn't sold a boat in months, but still seems to be making lots of money. Unknown to Simon, all is not well with Bonner as he is being blackmailed by his partner, Slater. Simon is convinced that Bonner is behind the shooting of the Asian man, and the trail leads him to a clearing-house used by Bonner. He finds a very ill Asian named, Chaudri, who rejects his offer of a doctor. Before Simon can do anything to help the man, Chaudri is shot by a gunman. Simon escapes, and, when he returns with a doctor, he discovers that the dead man had smallpox. Simon must now trace the other Asians who were staying at the house before they infect others. Bonner is also out hunting – he is after Malia Gupta, a lovely Asian girl. He wants her to lead him to her

brother, Suresh, who plans to go to the authorities about Bonner and Slater. Simon manages to track down Suresh at the same time that Bonner finds him. The case of the people importers is about to come to a climax.

THE SCALES OF JUSTICE (1969)

Simon Templar	Roger Moore
Gilbert Kirby	Andrew Keir
Anna Kirby	Jean Marsh
Elliott Stratton	Mark Burns
Mrs Stratton	Gillian Lind
Neal Lammerton	John Barron
Carl Howard	Geoffrey Chater
John Ramsey	Ronald Leigh-Hunt
Jim Cowdry	Victor Maddern
Mac	Leon Cortez
Sir John Mulliner	John Boxer

Original Screenplay by	Robert Holmes
Directed by	Robert Asher

THE SAINT IS driving through London in a Rolls Royce belonging to Sir John Mulliner. He is in London at Sir John's request. The car stops to pick up Sir John and as he leaves his office he brushes past a blind man. Inside the car he shows Simon a postcard he has just received – on the one side, the scales of justice, and on the other the word 'you'. Sir John starts to tell Simon why he has asked for his help, but suddenly he collapses. Meanwhile, an influential group of businessmen await Sir John and Simon. They are there at Mulliner's request. Simon arrives at the meeting and informs the group that Sir John is dead. Gilbert Kirby tells Simon that recently 5 directors of the company have died. Young Elliott Stratton tells Simon that his father was the first to die. Simon informs the group that he will investigate the case. Simon goes to see the coroner but the Doctor can find no trace of foul play. He then goes to talk to Sir John's chauffeur, Jim, but he still has nothing concrete to go on. Simon is convinced that five dead men in five months is no accident, and he decides to investigate each death. He goes to see Mrs Stratton and Elliott, and takes along Kirby's daughter, Anna. Elliott finds a postcard similar to the one Sir John received in his father's room. Simon goes with Anna to see a nightwatchman who was hurt in an accident recently in one of Sir John's warehouses. He finds the man unconscious, and suddenly a shot is fired at Simon. He chases after the gunman, and the man fires at him again, then disappears. Simon hears Anna scream; he goes to her aid, and she says the killer brushed past her on his way out of the factory. The next day Neal Lammerton visits Kirby and tells him not to let Simon interfere in Combined Holdings business. He leaves and as Kirby goes through his morning mail he finds he has been sent one of the 'scales of justice' postcards. Simon and Anne go to see Lammerton at a charity function for the poor. A blind beggar enters the room who was also around when Sir John died. He points a stick at Lammerton and fires a silent weapon. Lammerton rises from his chair, and then collapses – he is dead. Simon finds a tiny dart in Lammerton's chair, which he takes along to the coroner who then confirms that a similar dart killed Sir John. Simon speaks to the Combined Holdings board and warns them that they are in danger and should stay at home. Kirby cannot do that as he is to be made Lord Mayor of London the next day. Simon keeps a close watch on Kirby during the ceremony, but he later discovers that an unsuccessful attempt was made on Kirby's life with a poisoned dart. He examines photos of the ceremony and discovers a man with a weapon on the Combined Holdings float. The killer is someone in the company. Can Simon find the killer before another member of the board is killed by the 'scales of justice'?

WHERE THE MONEY IS (1969)

Simon Templar	Roger Moore
Ben Kersh	Kenneth J. Warren
Jenny Kersh	Judee Morton
Jean Latour	Sandor Elés
German	Derek Newark
Arnie Garnett	Warren Stanhope
Frank Lomax	John Savident
Largo	Tony Wright
Lila Prentice	Jane Bates

Original Screenplay by	Terry Nation
Directed by	Roger Moore

BEN KERSH IS a much-married American movie producer. He is the father of an attractive, if somewhat wayward young girl, Jenny. Ben appeals to Simon for help when Jenny is kidnapped. He is worried for her safety, but realises that paying the ransom may not necessarily mean her safe return. The ransom demand arrives – it's a short film showing Jenny held prisoner. She pleads with her father to pay the ransom. The film was delivered along with the day's rushes of a film that was shot on location in Nice the day before. Simon feels that someone in the studio is involved in the kidnapping. The instructions from the kidnappers are followed, and Simon acts as a go-between for the two parties. He goes to Nice and checks into a hotel with the ransom money, to await further instructions. Simon receives a call from the kidnappers to go to a remote, deserted airfield. He has taken along his own precautions – he has on him a specially designed wristwatch, provided by the studio's special-effects man, Lomax. The watch is actually a miniature camera. On the way to the airport there is an attempt to hi-jack the money, but Simon escapes. He arrives at the airport and is confronted by two men, a young man called Latour, and the other a tough looking German. Simon refuses to hand over the money until he is sure that Jenny is safe. He insists on seeing her, and the two men reluctantly agree. They blindfold him and he is taken to a remote farmhouse, where he sees Jenny. She is being guarded by a tough-looking man called Largo. Simon is returned to the airport, but unknown to the gang he has been taking photos all the time with his trick watch – photos that will enable him to trace the whereabouts of the farmhouse. Simon sets out on his journey to find the farmhouse to rescue Jenny. Does she really want to be rescued, or would she rather be where the money is?

Roger Moore prepares to direct another Saint episode

THE EX-KING OF DIAMONDS (1969)

Simon Templar	**Roger Moore**
Rod Huston	**Stuart Damon**
Henri Flambeau	**Ronald Radd**
Janine Flambeau	**Isla Blair**
King Boris	**Willoughby Goddard**
Colonel Rakos	**Paul Stassino**
Gregorio	**Jeremy Young**
Franco	**Anthony Stamboulieh**
Lafitro	**Alan Rowe**
Ben	**Ray Chiarelle**
Alba	**Karen Young**
Henriette	**Jacky Allouis**
Josette	**Carol Friday**
Young Man	**Derek Smee**
American Lady	**Araby Lockhart**

Original Screenplay by	**John Kruse**
Directed by	**Alvin Rakoff**

SIMON FLIES to the Côte D'Azur at the invitation of King Boris, the ex-King of Slavonia. He has invited the wealthy and famous to join him at baccarat in his casino. Driving along the road in a vintage car, Simon is challenged to a race by Rod Huston, a wealthy Texas millionaire. Simon wins the race and finds he has made a new friend. Colonel Rakos, the King's aide, is up to something. He negotiates a deal for the King, but the price is $1 million. That evening at the casino Simon runs into Rod once more. Simon tries his luck at cards and wins again. He then meets Janine Flambeau and her father, Henri, the famous mathematician. Their meeting is interrupted by the grand entrance of King Boris. Simon invites them to watch while he plays baccarat with the King. After several hands, with the King winning constantly, a break is called and Simon talks to Henri. Both men are convinced that the King is cheating. When the game resumes Henri sits in on a couple of hands. After a short while he leaves the casino with Janine and they go to the factory where the cards are printed. Henri is determined to find the truth. Janine goes into the factory to look around and is knocked out. Outside Henri is attacked by Colonel Rakos and his men who plan to kill him. Simon and Rod arrive just in time to save him, but after a brief struggle the Colonel and his men escape.

Simon and Rod check out the factory, but there is no sign of Janine. They examine the playing cards and find that they have been marked. They also find an underground cellar which leads out to the sea, and in front of them is moored the king's yacht. Suddenly, a frogman appears and attacks Simon, but The Saint soon has him subdued. The man reveals that Janine is held prisoner on the yacht. Simon plans to disrupt the King's plan to win at gambling, and the next evening, at a costume party at the casino, Henri sits down to play. Simon has fixed it so that the King will be unable to tell in advance what the cards are, and the game will be played on skill alone. Simon and Rod prepare to rescue Janine, posing as two of the Colonel's men. They make their way to the yacht, and on board they discover that ex-King Boris is preparing a revolution so that he can return to his country. Simon and Rod rescue Janine, but are attacked by the crew on the way out. They overpower the crew and leave the ship. Meanwhile Henri uses his skill as a mathematician to defeat the King at cards. With the ex-King broke, he has little chance of overthrowing the government.

Although this episode is reminiscent of an earlier Roger Moore series, *Maverick*, it is much more likely that it was the pilot for Moore's next series, *The Persuaders*.

VENDETTA FOR THE SAINT (1969)

Simon Templar	Roger Moore
Allessandro Destamio	Ian Hendry
Gina Destamio	Rosemary Dexter
Lilly	Aimi Macdonald
Marco Ponti	George Pastell
Dona Maria	Maria Burke
Don Pasquali	Finlay Currie
James Euston	Fulton Mackay
Major	Alex Scott
Lo Zio	Peter Madden
Doctor	Anthony Newlands
Marescello	Guy Deghy
Bank Manager	Edward Evans
Cirano	Steve Plytos

Screenplay by	Harry W. Junkin and John Kruse
Directed by	Jim O'Connolly

THE SAINT is in Naples. The saying goes 'see Naples and die'. and for The Saint it almost comes true. One evening while he is having a drink in a nightclub he stops a fight when three men attack another over a supposed mistaken identity. The man, James Euston, leaves the club and as he walks down a side street he is attacked and killed by the chauffeur of Allessandro Destamio. Euston recognised Destamio to be a man called Dino Cartelli, supposedly killed in a bank robbery several years earlier. The next day Simon sees Euston's photo in the papers and decides to investigate the case. He returns to the nightclub to question the barman about the incident. but the man is too afraid to speak. Simon returns to his hotel to find his room ransacked, then there is a knock on the door. It is Destamio's chauffeur, who requests that Simon go with him to see Destamio. Simon agrees and is taken to the airport where. after a short flight. he is met by a friend of Destamio's. Lilly. Simon questions Destamio about his past. and about Euston calling him Cartelli. Angrily, Destamio denies ever having heard the name. Lilly drives Simon back to the airport and on the way she tells him that she is afraid of Destamio. but does not have the money to leave him. Simon gives her $500. Simon returns to Palermo. and goes to see the manager at the bank where Euston and Cartelli worked. The manager tells Simon that Cartelli was killed by a shotgun blast in the face. Simon leaves the bank and is attacked by two of Destamio's men. Simon overpowers them. but when the police arrive. he is arrested and the men let go. He is questioned privately by Marco Ponti. an official of the police force. who tells him that Destamio is a high ranking member of the Mafia. Marco asks Simon for his help later that day over a meal. He points out a young girl. Gina, and tells Simon that she is the niece of Destamio. Later that day Simon pays a call on Gina and her aunt pretending that he has been sent by Destamio. Dona Maria invites Simon to stay for dinner. and later while Simon is persuading Gina to take him sightseeing. Dona Maria telephones Destamio and discovers that Simon is a fake. Two of Destamio's men are sent to deal with him. After the meal Simon leaves. and aware that Dona Maria is acting strangely. he drives off. A tell tale clue warns Simon just in time that there is a bomb ticking away under the hood of his car. He leaps out of the car just before it explodes. The next day Simon calls on Maria to go sightseeing. much to the surprise of Dona Maria. Destamio arrives with Lilly. but sends her off to the hotel while he and the rest of the Mafia members go to see Don Pasquali. the dying head of the Mafia. He must chose someone to replace him. and Destamio is the favourite choice. Simon tells Gina the truth about her uncle. At first she refuses to believe him. but later she agrees to help. Simon returns to his hotel and is warned by Lilly that Destamio is out to kill him. Simon is suspicious about Destamio. and goes to the family vault to check on him. and on entering the vault he is attacked by Destamio's men. When he wakes up he is questioned by Destamio. and then taken to see Don Pasquali. Simon realises that he may never leave the house alive. Will the Mafia's vendetta against The Saint end in bloodshed?

Based on the 1964 novel

THE PORTRAIT OF BRENDA (1969)

Simon Templar	**Roger Moore**
Diane Huntley	**Anna Carteret**
Chief Inspector Teal	**Ivor Dean**
Josephine	**Anne De Vigier**
Johnny Fox	**Trevor Bannister**
Mrs White	**Petra Davies**
The Guru	**Marne Maitland**
Mrs Blondel	**Hazel Coppen**
Opera Singer	**Tina Ruta**
Ashok	**Larry Taylor**
Tony	**Dave Prowse**
Postman	**Harry Littlewood**

Original Screenplay by	**Harry W. Junkin**
Directed by	**John Gilling**

SIMON RECEIVES a call from Alan Williams, an artist, who asks Simon to come over. He needs his help, so Simon arranges to visit him. When he arrives he finds Williams dead, with a knife sticking out of his back. Simon searches the place looking for a clue to the murder, but his search is interrupted by the arrival of Josephine, a model. Together they search the place, and they find the start of a message scrawled on the floor by Williams. 'Brenda's p' is all that Williams had time to write. Josephine identifies this as a reference to the painting of a beautiful girl called Brenda. The telephone rings and a recorded message asks Williams to go over to the recording studio. The message is from pop singer, Diane Huntley. Simon leaves Josephine to call the Yard and ask for Chief Inspector Teal, while he goes over to meet Diane Huntley. Diane is unaware that Williams is dead, and she assumes that he had told Simon about the meeting. She takes him to a meditation session held by a Guru. Simon is convinced that the Guru is somehow connected with the racket onto which Williams had stumbled. Simon is amazed at the large sums of money the Guru's disciples donate. The money is collected by the Guru's personal assistant, Mrs White. Simon breaks the news of Williams' death to Diane, and he then takes her to Williams' studio. Diane is able to give Simon more information about Brenda: she was Williams' younger sister, a singer, who committed suicide. Diane also tells him that she and Brenda had the same agent, Johnny Fox. Simon returns to the recording studio, where he is attacked by a man called Tony. While he is struggling with him another man sneaks up and knocks Simon out. Josephine arrives and helps revive Simon. They return to the studio and examine the portrait, and behind it they find a letter containing information about the Guru, Brenda's bank account, and a cottage in the country. It was for this letter that Williams was killed. The Saint has a mystery to solve, and in the process, another attempt is made on his life. Slowly, the pieces of the puzzle fit together, and finally it is a record which puts an end to the case that started with the portrait of Brenda.

THE WORLD BEATER (1969)

Simon Templar	**Roger Moore**
Kay Collingwood	**Patricia Haynes**
Justin Pritchard	**John Ronane**
George Hapgood	**James Kerry**
Harold Laker	**George A. Cooper**
Mr Hapgood (Snr)	**Eddie Byrne**
Tom Stevens	**William Wilde**
Dilys	**Rosemary Donnelly**
Rally Officials	**Anthony Sheppard**
	Clifford Earl
Original Screenplay by	**Donald James**
Directed by	**Leslie Norman**

SIMON IS INVITED by George Hapgood to test drive his new sports car and put it through its paces. He agrees, and the trial is watched over by Harold Laker, a man who is prepared to invest a lot of money in the car if it passes its test. Simon takes the car out and at first it performs well under his expert hands, then suddenly the steering goes and Simon loses control and crashes into a tree. Later when the car is examined by Simon and Hapgood back in the garage, they discover that it was sabotaged. Just then George's cousin, Justin Pritchard, arrives. He too has a new sports car that he wants Laker to invest in. Hapgood tells Justin that he is quitting the racing game. Justin wants Simon to race for him, but before he can ask him, Simon drives off. He goes to the offices of Kay Collingwood, a lady whose various schemes have involved Simon before.

Simon saw Kay drop Justin off at the Hapgood place earlier that day. Kay tells Simon that she is just a business associate of Justin's. Simon accepts Pritchard's offer to drive in Laker's rally, but first he wants to take the car out for a test run. Simon puts the car through her paces, then suddenly a van pulls out in front of him, and tries to force him off the road. Simon returns the car to Pritchard and then goes off to see Hapgood. He asks him why someone would want to sabotage both cars, but George does not know. Later that evening a man sneaks into Pritchard's garage, and tampers with the car that Simon will drive in the rally the next day. Can Simon uncover the real reason behind the sabotage, before the race, and before there is another accident. Will he discover which of the cars is the real world beater?

John Ronane and Roger Moore prepare to test the world beater on the track

INVITATION TO DANGER (1969)

Simon Templar	**Roger Moore**
Reb Denning	**Shirley Eaton**
Brett Sunley	**Robert Hutton**
Ramon Falconi	**Julian Glover**
Moreno	**Bryan Marshall**
Al Vitale	**Charles Houston**
Marty Bressett	**Warren Stanhope**
Peter Rendo	**Les Crawford**
Inez	**Ros Drinkwater**
Carson	**Dennis Chinnery**
Original Screenplay by	**Terry Nation**
Directed by	**Roger Moore**

SIMON IS in London at an exclusive gambling casino. As he plays he surveys the high security used in the casino. His friend Marty Bressett points out an attractive blonde, playing on the other side of the table, and he tells Simon that her name is Reb Denning. Reb wins a large sum of money at the tables and leaves. Simon follows her at a distance and as she reaches her car she is attacked by a man. Simon goes to her aid and chases the man off. Simon drives Reb home and she invites him in. There is a lot of noise coming from a party in the next room. As Simon enters the room the door closes, and locks behind him. Simon hears Reb scream in the distance. The party noise was coming from a tape recorder – the room is empty. A voice on the tape tells Simon that he will be held prisoner for a couple of hours and then released. Simon does not plan to stay that long, so he looks around and finds a way out of the room. He searches the house and finds it empty. Suddenly, he hears a noise upstairs, and as he reaches the top of the stairs, a man jabs him with a 'hypo'. Several hours later he recovers and as he makes his way out of the house he finds a dying man, whose last words are 'stop them, Friday night'. Simon gets to his car and drives off. As he drives along the country road he is followed by a car, and suddenly a second car pulls out in front of him. He is confronted by a man with a gun. The man, Ramon, accuses Simon of breaking into Brett Sunley's casino and stealing £100,000. He takes Simon back to the casino, where Sunley questions him about the money. Simon is taken to a cellar room and tied to a pipe. Sunley threatens to kill him unless the money is returned. To give himself time, Simon sends them off on a false trail. Simon manages to free himself from the cellar just before Sunley returns. He drives off but his only clue to Reb's whereabouts, is her exclusive perfume. He traces the shop and persuades the assistant to give him her address. Simon goes to her apartment and outside her door he hears voices. He enters the room via the window, and finds Ramon and another man about to attack Reb. He overpowers them and is about to free Reb when Sunley arrives. Simon lets Sunley leave with the money, while he unties Reb. She tells Simon that she works for the C.I.A., and that Sunley is a banker for several European spies. She planted the clues that led Sunley on to Simon so that she could throw suspicion away from herself. Simon agrees to help her recover the money from Sunley and stop them. The double crossing is not yet over as Simon discovers when he accepts an invitation to danger.

THE BEST LAID SCHEMES (1969)

Simon Templar	Roger Moore
Arlene	Sylvia Syms
Dr Ormsby	Paul Daneman
Diana	Gabrielle Drake
Inspector Mitchell	Norman Bird
John Everett	Fulton Mackay
Skinner	John Tate
Ballard	Godfrey Quigley
Captain Fleming	Francis De Wolfe
Mrs Haggerty	Olive Milbourne
Andrew	Jonathan Elsom
Joe Carney	Frederick Abbott
Coroner	Geoffrey Lumsden
Dr Russell	John Ringham
Nurse	Joanne Dainton
Sailor	Erik Mason

Original Screenplay by	Joseph Morhaim and A. Sandford Wolf
Directed by	John Moxey

THE SAINT is driving along by the sea. As he stops to look at the waves crashing against the rocks, a young girl runs along the beach with her dog. Suddenly, she stops as there in the water is a body. She screams and Simon rushes to her aid. The girl, Diana, tells Simon that the body is her uncle, Captain Fleming, who disappeared a week ago. After the funeral, Simon talks to Arlene, the wife of the dead man. The phone rings and Arlene

Roger Moore discusses the next scene with director John Moxey

answers it. The voice on the other end is apparently her 'dead' husband. Arlene faints and Diana looks after her. Later Simon and Diana go to see Andrew, the nephew of Captain Fleming, and the man who identified the body. They return to the house as Dr Ormsby is giving Arlene a sedative. She tells Simon that her husband was well liked except for his business rival, Ballard. Simon questions Dr Ormsby about Fleming's health and the state of his mind the last time Ormsby saw him. Simon then questions Diana about her uncle, and decides to stay a few days and investigate the case. The next day he drives to Fleming's offices and speaks to his business manager, John Everett. Everett says it's possible that Fleming committed suicide. Simon questions one of the fishermen who tells him that there is a fierce rivalry between the Ballard and Fleming fisheries. Simon follows John Everett when he leaves the offices to a car park where he meets Ballard. That evening as a storm rages outside, Arlene is awakened by a noise. She goes downstairs to find her husband's raincoat dripping wet on the chair, and the rest of his clothes strewn all over the place. She goes into his study, where his pipe has been left smoking on the table. Simon is called in. He thinks that someone is trying to drive Arlene crazy. Simon searches the room and according to Diane the only thing missing is Fleming's passport. Dr Ormsby is called in and says that Arlene is close to a breakdown. Simon asks Diana for a copy of Fleming's will. The person who will gain the most if Arlene is committed is Andrew. Simon goes to see Andrew to discuss the will, and he asks him what he would do if he inherited the fisheries. He says that he would sell instantly to Ballard. Simon goes to the wharf to see Ballard to question him about the rivalry between the two companies. Ballard gets angry, and a couple of his men jump Simon. Ballard joins in and Simon tackles the three of them. The police turn up and take Simon to the local station. Inspector Mitchell questions Simon and The Saint gives him a list of the murder suspects. That evening Everett sneaks in to the Fleming house and he goes through Fleming's papers. He leaves with an envelope but outside the house he runs into Simon. The Saint questions Everett and discovers that Ballard put him up to it. Simon questions Mrs Haggerty, the housekeeper, about the Captain, and she insists that the Captain was murdered. Simon goes to the local pub used by the fishermen, where he is given a hostile reception. He tries to question a man called Carney, one of the last people to see the Captain alive. Carney pulls a knife and The Saint knocks him down. Arlene is convinced that the Captain is alive, and she is on the verge of a breakdown. Dr Ormsby sends her to a sanitarium for a rest. Can The Saint unravel the mystery of the 'dead' captain, or are there too many red herrings in the plot?

LOCATE AND DESTROY (1969)

Simon Templar	Roger Moore
Coleman	John Barrie
Maria	Francesca Annis
Ingred	Julia Arnall
Karsh	Victor Beaumont
Nathan	Maurice Kaufman
Jacob	Alan Lake
Bloom	Harry Landis
Salter	Simon Lack
Captain Rodrigues	Roger Delgado
Dr Lopez	Wolfe Morris
Gonzalez	Andreas Malandrinos
Merkin	Harvey Hall
Dr Pinda	Gordon Whiting
Nurse	Katerina Holden
Peon	Richard Montez

Original Screenplay by	John Stanton
Directed by	Leslie Norman

THE SAINT is in Lima, Peru. He is sightseeing and is looking around an antique shop, when two men enter. They draw out guns and hold Simon and the owner at gunpoint. They are waiting for a man called Coleman to arrive. Coleman arrives to collect a painting, and suddenly one of the men points a gun at him. Simon jumps the second man and the owner rushes off to call the police. Simon and Coleman tackle the two men, but they make their getaway in a car. Later at the police station Captain Rodrigues and Simon question Coleman about the attack. Coleman asks the Captain and Simon to forget the incident, and as Coleman is a wealthy influential man the Captain complies. Coleman returns home and he telephones Karsh, his foreman, and asks him to bring along another man called Salter. At that moment Salter receives a call from Nathan, one of the men who attacked Coleman. Nathan warns Salter to get out quickly, but before he can leave Karsh arrives to take him to Coleman. Coleman questions Salter about the attack, as Salter was the one who telephoned the antique shop to say that Coleman was coming over, and at what time. Coleman attacks Salter and his man Karsh drags him off to Coleman's mine. Simon returns to the antique shop to question the owner to see if he knows why Coleman was attacked. Meanwhile Karsh tortures Salter to find the name of his accomplices. Ingred, Coleman's wife questions her husband about the incident with Salter but he will not speak about it. Simon stops off at the Coleman house and is invited to stay for dinner. Salter manages to free himself and makes a desperate bid to escape. Karsh organises a search party, and goes to inform Coleman, who apologises to Simon saying that there is trouble at the mine. Simon pretends to leave and then sneaks back in to the house to examine the painting that Coleman collected from the antique shop. He is disturbed by Ingred. Simon tells her that the picture is worth over £200,000, but Ingred says that it's just a good copy. Simon leaves, and on the way he comes across Salter, and takes him to the local Doctor. Meanwhile Coleman's men trace Salter to Dr Lopez, but they arrive too late, because Simon has already left for the local hospital with Salter and Dr Lopez's nurse.

his daughter. Maria. On his deathbed Salter gives Simon an address to go to. Karsh arrives at the hospital to find Salter dead, and outside the hospital Karsh spots Simon leaving and decides to follow him. Simon goes to the address that Salter gave him and runs into the two men that attacked Coleman. A third man arrives with Maria, held at gunpoint. Nathan tells Simon that they are not crooks but agents of the Israeli government, and that Coleman is really a Nazi. They have been on his trail since the war ended. Karsh and his man sneak in and start shooting. Two of the agents are killed and Nathan is shot in the arm. Simon takes over and chases after the men, but they escape, back to Coleman. Maria removes the bullet from Nathan's arm, while he tells Simon that Coleman is really Hans Kroleich, a torturer of many Jews during the war. Captain Rodrigues says that there is nothing that he can do, but gives Simon 24 hours to sort things out. Maria returns to the surgery to her father, who suddenly receives a phoney emergency call and leaves. Karsh sneaks into the surgery and kidnaps Maria taking her back to Coleman's mine. Dr Lopez returns to find Simon waiting for him, and they enter the surgery to find Maria gone. Simon tells Lopez to call the police while he sets out after Coleman and his men. Simon returns to the Coleman house where he tells Ingred the truth about her husband. She then takes him to the mine. Simon arrives just in time as Coleman is about to torture Maria. He holds Coleman and Karsh at gunpoint, but suddenly a third man arrives and Simon is outnumbered. Simon is taken to the edge of a pit 1,000ft deep. Can The Saint excape in time, and revenge the victims of Kroleich's crimes?

John Barrie and Victor Beaumont are held at gunpoint by Roger Moore as The Saint

THE SAINT ON WHEELS

W HAT DASHING hero hasn't got his own recognisable form of transport? The Lone Ranger had Silver, Batman his Batmobile, James Bond his remarkable Aston Martin DB5 and the Saint . . . well The Saint has had a variety of vehicles over the years.

Early on in his career, Charteris sent The Saint into battle in a powerful speedster called the Furillac. This car, a lean, blue monster straight out of Charteris's imagination, comes to a heroic end, as it blocks the getaway of some villains who merge their yellow sedan with the speedster

(*The Last Hero* 1930). But almost immediately Templar is behind the wheel of an even meaner machine, the vast gleaming Hirondel that accompanies him on most of his adventures. The Hirondel is more usually driven by Roger Conway in early escapades but after the demise of the Furillac, Templar is just as often to be found behind the wheel of the beast. Actually there seems to be more than one Hirondel – possibly Conway, Templar and later Peter Quentin share a couple between them. Certainly independent descriptions would indicate more than one car – mostly the colour is given as silver, but occasionally it is described as being red and cream. The other fabulous roadster that The Saint can sometimes be found racing is called a Desurio and is from a similar stable as the other two. None of these power-packed monsters seems capable of travel at speeds below 80 mph and they spend their entire working lives as screeching blurs narrowly avoiding head-on collisions, streams of bullets and fatal plunges off cliff-top roads. Templar, however, does drive other less ferocious cars in his written adventures including 'Hildebrand', an inconspicuous, unremarkable Ford roadster he uses when he wishes to make a less dramatic journey.

In the movies Simon Templar could be seen in a number of vehicles considered stylish and elegant at the time. In *The Saint in London* in particular the society cars are marvellous and George Sanders seems quite at ease stepping onto the running boards of moving saloons. But it was on TV that The Saint obtained the car that was to become synonymous with him in most people's eyes.

When the Roger Moore series was being set up in 1962 the producers wanted a sleek, powerful car for The Saint to cruise around in. The obvious choice was Jaguar's new E-Type, which had been launched the previous year at the Geneva Motor Show. The producers approached Jaguar and asked if they would be willing to lend one of the beautiful, speedy E-Types to the company in exchange for the publicity it would receive as The Saint's transport. But Jaguar declined the offer, saying they didn't need the publicity as the car was selling as fast as they could make them anyway. The second most eye-catching sports car of the time was the sensational new Volvo P1800 Sports Coupé, so Volvo were approached and offered an association with the production. Volvo were more than happy to oblige and when they realised they didn't have the model in white in Britain, as the producers had requested, they air-freighted one in. It's impossible to calculate just how much Volvo benefitted from its association with *The Saint* but to say they were pleased would be a massive understatement. Indeed when Moore was so impressed with the vehicle he acquired it for his own use, the company provided an identical one. Years later when Jaguar was approached again, this time to provide an XJS for Ian Ogilvy's Templar, the company gratefully accepted. The latest Saint, Simon Dutton, drives a hand-made 7½ litre Jensen Interceptor with the license plate 1ST.

RETURN OF THE SAINT

ROGER MOORE was now James Bond and his version of The Saint, though fondly remembered, would only occasionally turn up in repeat runs. Producer Robert S. Baker always thought there was still a lot of mileage in the series when they stopped production in 1968 and there was certainly still a demand for the show in the US. He approached Lord Grade with the idea of making a new series of Saint adventures, this time starring the son of Simon Templar, who picks up the halo and carries on where his father left off. Grade gave the go-ahead for the idea and Baker's theory that there was still an interest in the character was borne out by the immediate media and public interest in the project. This time there was no drawn-out casting process, as Baker had already had an actor in mind to play Templar Jnr, Ian Ogilvy. Ogilvy was in his early thirties, a slightly-built, traditionally handsome leading man who had been seen occasionally in films and on TV. As preparations for the series progressed, the idea of Ogilvy playing Templar's son was dropped as plenty of other famous characters (notably James Bond) had survived being played by the same actor in a similar style. So the show's title was changed from *The Son of The Saint* to *The Return of The Saint*.

Baker got many of the original Saint crew back together and off they went – this time to much more foreign location work than there had been in the old series. Sensibly Baker played up the strengths of the original series, tight plots, pretty girls and frequent fight-scenes – although this time the emphasis was not so much on fisticuffs as karate. Many of the writers and directors from the first series were re-employed and any newcomers were certainly of an equal pedigree, but things just didn't quite work. Roger Moore proved a hard act to follow and although Ogilvy was, if anything, closer to Charteris's original conception of the character physically, he never managed to evoke that sense of authority so important to the role. Possibly he looked too young as well, for he could have easily passed as someone in their early twenties at the time, and had an almost trendy air which didn't suit the character. Possibly he could have used these traits as 'the son of The Saint' but they seemed at odds with the, by now, popular image of Simon Templar. Of course these observations are easy in hindsight. At the time Baker and his crew worked hard on the series and if it wasn't for Templar's earlier TV incarnation, Ogilvy's version would have been received more fairly – as a competent, efficient, well-up-to-standard entry in the action/adventure series stakes. As it was, it suffered in comparison to its predecessor and only 24 episodes were made.

THE RETURN OF THE SAINT –
EPISODE GUIDE

Many of the same crew were reassembled for this new series. New writers included Terence Feely, Leon Griffiths (later creator of *Minder*) and George Markstein. The first episode (*The Judas Game*) was credited to Leslie Charteris.

Charles Crichton and Sam Wanamaker were among the directors who hadn't worked on the previous series.

In the US the series was run by CBS, who also later bought the original series and ran that during the same period as the new show aired, although on different nights, as part of *The CBS Late Movie*

THE JUDAS GAME (1978)

Simon Templar	**Ian Ogilvy**
Selma Morell	**Judy Geeson**
Vlora	**Olga Karlatos**
Wilcox	**Maurice Roeves**
Dame Edith	**Mona Bruce**
Quirko	**Marino Mase**
Xexo	**Verantino Venantini**
Algernon	**Richard Wyler**
Buckingham	**Moray Watson**
Screenplay by	**Morris Farhi**
Directed by	**Jeremy Summers**

THE SAINT is mountain climbing in the Alps with Algernon, an operative with British Intelligence. He tells Simon that he is wanted by Dame Edith, a section head with MI6. Dame Edith tells Simon that an old friend, Selma Morell, has been kidnapped by the Albanian Secret Police while on holiday in Yugoslavia. She tells Simon that unless he helps, Selma will end up being tortured, and eventually killed. Selma is being held in a high-security mountain prison that only an expert climber could reach. Simon goes along to the British Embassy to see Buckingham, the head of the Embassy. Simon realises that he has no choice, because if he does not rescue Selma, she will either be killed by the Albanians or by Algernon, a hit man for British Intelligence. Simon sets out to rescue Selma and is met by Vlora, a local agent sent to help him. Simon is able to enter the prison, and find Selma. Can The Saint escape with Selma, and also find out which of Dame Edith's men is a double agent?

THE NIGHTMARE MAN (1979)

Simon Templar	**Ian Ogilvy**
Gunther	**Joss Ackland**
Gayle	**Kathryn Leigh Scott**
Livia Moreno	**Moira Redmond**
Canfield	**Norman Eshley**
Carmelo	**Sharon Mughan**
Di Vallesi	**John Bailey**
Dalby	**Stanley Lebor**
Dillon	**Roy Evans**
Concierge	**Olga Lowe**
Margareta Di Vallesi	**Juilette James**
Mila	**Zienia Merton**
Victor	**Trevor Ward**
Screenplay by	**John Kruse**
Directed by	**Peter Sasdy**

THE SAINT IS in Paris. Late one night he hears a muffled scream coming from the hotel bedroom next to his, and on investigating, Simon finds that the woman who screamed is Margareta Di Vallesi, who was just having a nightmare.

Margareta tells Simon that she was dreaming about her husband, Dr Bernardo Di Vallesi, who has just been appointed the new Italian Ambassador to Britain. Margareta tells him that in her dream she saw her husband being murdered while travelling in an open coach. Margareta describes the scene so accurately that it is obviously Parliament Square in London. Simon realises that the dream will become a reality when the new Ambassador is presented to parliament in a week's time. He will ride through London in an open coach passing through Parliament Square. Simon flies back to London to prevent a murder, and there he meets Di Vallesi, and his wife, but the woman is not the one he met in Paris. The 'nightmare' is just beginning because Simon is about to meet a deadly assassin Senor Muerte – Mr Death.

Judy Geeson and Ian Ogilvy prepare to say goodbye in a quiet moment from *The Judas Game*

DUEL IN VENICE (1978)

Simon Templar	Ian Ogilvy
Sally	Cathryn Harrison
Jed Blackett	Maurice Colbourne
Claudia	Carole Andree
Guido	Enzo Fiermonte
Luigi	Armando Bandini
Screenplay by	John Kruse
Directed by	Jeremy Summers

THE SAINT IS in Venice showing the sights of the city to Sally, the attractive daughter of an old friend. The pleasantness of the day is later turned to fear, when Sally is kidnapped by an old enemy of the Saint's, Jed Blackett. Blackett wants revenge over an incident in Kenya, five years ago. He is holding Sally prisoner on a gondola, and talking to Simon via a two way radio. Blackett has placed a garotte necklace around Sally's neck and if it is allowed to snap, death would be in seconds. Time is running out for Simon and so he enlists the aid of Claudia, one of the best gondoliers in the city, and with her help he hopes to trace Blackett before time runs out for Sally.

A high speed chase for The Saint on the canals of Venice

ONE BLACK SEPTEMBER (1978)

Simon Templar	Ian Ogilvy
Captain Leila Sabin	Prunella Gee
Yasmina	June Bolton
Abdul Hakim	Garrick Hagon
Colonel Leon Garvi	Amos Mokadi
Yakovitz	Geoffrey Greenhill
Garton	Aubrey Morris
Rahman	Nadim Sawalha
Caliban	Shango Baku
Gorilla	Ron Tarr
Stem	Reuben Elvy
Screenplay by	John Goldsmith
Directed by	Leslie Norman

THE SAINT is asked to team up with a beautiful Israeli counter-terrorist officer, Captain Leila Sabin to help her trace a notorious terrorist who has defected and is believed to be hiding out in London. Simon reluctantly agrees to help, but Captain Sabin is not pleased to be working with Simon. She finds him too flippant, but she needs his knowledge of London to help her find Abdul Hakim. Hakim is a leading member of the notorious Black September group, and as such he knows all the other members in the anti-Israeli organisation. Colonel Garvi, head of the London arm of Israeli Intelligence, is desperate to know the names of those men. Simon and the Captain have the task of finding Hakim, and handing him over to Colonel Garvi, before the other agents of Black September can find him, and kill him.

THE VILLAGE THAT SOLD ITS SOUL (1978)

Simon Templar	Ian Ogilvy
Boldini	Giancarlo Prete
Guzzi	Loris Bazzocchi
Moreno	Cyrus Elyas
Vincenzo	Tony Calvin
Dolores Streso	Alba Maiolini
Sophia Castracano	Katia Christine
Prince Castracano	Maurice Denham
Screenplay by	John Goldsmith
Directed by	Leslie Norman

THE SAINT is in Italy, in Santa Maria, a remote village high in the mountains. On his arrival, he is warned not to stay, and told it's a bad place to live, and a very bad place to die. It is a warning The Saint ignores. Simon later witnesses a murder, and finds that the whole town is against him, including the local chief of police, Boldini. Simon's only ally is the young and beautiful widow, Sophia, and with her help, Simon finds out about the village's dark secret.

ASSAULT FORCE (1978)

Simon Templar	Ian Ogilvy
Jeanette	Kate O'Mara
Randolph Smith	Neil Stacy
Chula	Burt Kwouk
Surinit	Eric Young
Colonel Dibha	Carolle Rousseau
O'Hara	Bryan Marshall
Screenplay by	Moris Farhi
Directed by	Peter Sasdy

THE SAINT goes to the aid of a beautiful Eurasian girl in trouble, little knowing that he is about to be involved in a case of intrigue and double crossing. The girl Jeanette, asks Simon to help her and her colleagues Chula and Colonel Dibha to kidnap a visiting South-East Asian politician. Simon agrees to help and recruits O'Hara, one of the best mercenaries in the business. With his help they succeed in kidnapping the politician, but then Chula and the Colonel turn the tables on Simon, when they take the politician away from him. Simon discovers that the man he helped kidnap is really the best hope for lasting peace in South-East Asia, and now he is in the hands of terrorists.

YESTERDAY'S HERO (1978)

Simon Templar	Ian Ogilvy
Roy Gates	Ian Hendry
Sandy	Annette Andre
Michael	Matthew Ryan
Cleaver	Gerald Flood
Diskett	Tony Vogel
Inspector Canfield	Norman Eshley
Brigader Danvers	Tony Steedman
Doland	John Rolfe
Security Man	Charles Pemberton
Original Story by	Roger Parks
Screenplay by	John Kruse
Directed by	Roy Ward Baker

A DEAD MAN returns from the grave, and is bent on vengeance. He is after the man who betrayed him during the war. Simon was on a special assignment with three men, Roy Gates, Diskett and Cleaver. At the end of the mission, Gates was captured, and believed by Simon and the others to have been killed. Gates had been captured but not killed. He had been held in prison and tortured for many years but now he is back seeking revenge on the man who betrayed him, Cleaver. Simon reluctantly agrees to help Gates, and along with Diskett, they plot the downfall of Cleaver, now a legitimate and successful arms dealer.

THE ARRANGEMENT (1978)

Simon Templar	Ian Ogilvy
Lady Greer Stevens	Carolyn Seymour
Sheila Northcott	Sarah Douglas
Guy Northcott	Michael Medwin
Sir Trevor Stevens	Donald Pickering
Inspector Stone	Ian McCulloch
Nina	Vikki Richards
Otis	Gregory Munroe
Aileen	Jane Hayden
Dr Evans	Peter Burton
Lou	Reg Lye
Bartender	Brian Pettifer
Hansen	David Healy
Police Officer	Edmund Pegge
Screenplay by	Anthony Terpiloff
Directed by	Peter Medek

THE SAINT becomes involved in the case of two women who arrange to kill one another's husbands. One of the women, Sheila Northcott, thinks it's a joke, and doesn't take it seriously. The other woman Lady Greer Stevens, is deadly earnest. Unknown to Sheila, Lady Greer Stevens is mentally deranged, and goes through with her plan to kill Sheila's husband, Guy. She then blackmails Sheila into going through with her part of the plan. Can Simon help Sheila before another victim is claimed?

THE POPPY CHAIN (1978)

Simon Templar	Ian Ogilvy
General Platt	Laurence Naismith
Scorbesi	Gregoire Aslan
Sandi	Jenny Hanley
Dominic	Jonathan Burn
Robbie	Kim Fortune
Gent	Christopher Timothy
Gent's wife	Zuleika Robson
Inspector Sullivan	Patrick Jordan
Businessman	Paul Gregory
Doctor	Anton Phillips
Screenplay by	John Kruse
Director	Charles Crighton

JANE PLATT, the sister of Simon's current girlfriend, Jenny, dies from a shot of impure heroin. Simon sets out to avenge her, and at the same time prevent Jenny's father, General Platt, from trying to seek justice first. Simon's quest takes him from London to the Camargue in France, where he comes up against the head of a large family which is running the drug racket. The Father, Scorbesi, and his ruthless son Dominic, control the flow of drugs to London, and they do not like Simon's interference. They make plans to have him taken care of.

THE ARMAGEDDON ALTERNATIVE (1978)

Simon Templar	Ian Ogilvy
Fred	George Cole
Lynn Jackson	Anouska Hempel
Commander Denning	Donald Houston
Loader	Frank Gatliff
Parkinson	Gordon Gostelow
Army Captain	Ian Collier
Bomb Squad Officer	Peter Quince
Telex Operator	Brian Houghton
Police Officer	Edward Lyon
Screenplay by	Terence Feeley
Directed by	Leslie Norman

A MAD SCIENTIST is on the loose. A brilliant man turned down for an important government appointment, he decides to seek revenge. He sets a series of explosions, each one bigger than the last. His threat to the British government is that he will destroy London, unless a girl, Lynn Jackson, is publicly guillotined in Hyde Park. Simon Templar joins up with Commander Denning, a tough, uncompromising man in charge of the Special Branch. They must try and locate the madman before he can achieve his mission.

THE IMPRUDENT PROFESSOR (1978)

Simon Templar	Ian Ogilvy
Samantha	Catherine Schell
Emma Bartlett	Susan Penhaligon
Professor Bartlett	Bill Simpson
Cartwright	Peter Childs
Max Boothroyd	Anthony Steel
Pierre	John Moreno
Demmell	Richard Parmentier
Inspector Le beau	Godfrey James
Screenplay by	Terence Feeley
Directed by	Kevin Connor

THE SAINT IS in Nice at the request of Emma Bartlett, daughter of the noted scientist, Professor Bartlett. She asks Simon to watch out for her father whom she believes is in danger. He has just perfected a new substitute for petrol. Professor Bartlett reluctantly agrees to let Simon keep an eye on him, but unknown to the Saint a young lady called Samantha is out to sell his technology to a foreign power. Simon, posing as Sebastian Tombs, is kidnapped at gunpoint by two men working for Max Boothroyd, an operative of British Intelligence, hired to watch over Bartlett. Boothroyd warns Simon that he is responsible for Bartlett, and not to interfere. Simon returns to the hotel where he is approached by one of Samantha's men, and after a short fight, Simon knocks him out, but is then knocked out himself by Samantha. Later, over lunch, Samantha tells Simon that she works for an organisation called Genius Inc. which specialises in selling people with very high IQs to the highest bidder. Meanwhile, Bartlett receives a call from Simon to meet him at the quayside. But when Emma runs into Simon she discovers that the message was a phoney one. Later at Boothroyd's request Simon is arrested by the local police, but escapes by stealing a police car. Simon must then trace the Professor, and his kidnappers before he can be spirited out of the country.

Ian Ogilvy and Catherine Schell

SIGNAL STOP (1978)

Simon Templar	Ian Ogilvy
Janie Lennox	Ciaren Madden
Inspector Grant	Frederick Jaeger
Linda	Sabina Franklyn
Sally	Heather Wright
Sergeant Taylor	Ian Cullen
Plackett	Brian Glover
Billy Bradshaw	Royston Tickner
Ted	George Sweeney
Malc	Ralph Arliss
Smiler	Kevin Selway
Screenplay by	John Kruse
Directed by	Ray Austin

A TRAIN JOURNEY can often lead to adventure and romance, but for The Saint it can lead to adventure and murder. Simon is travelling on a train, and his companion in the carriage is a young girl, Janie Lennox. She tells him that she has just seen a murder take place as the train passed an old, derelict building. When the train stops Simon reports the incident to the local police who investigate the old house, and find it completely empty. The police also tell Simon that Janie has recently been released from a psychiatric hospital. Despite the police evidence he believes Janie's story and continues to investigate on his own. As the story unfolds Simon's life is soon threatened when he uncovers a tale of rape and murder.

THE ROMAN TOUCH (1978)

Simon Templar	Ian Ogilvy
Bruno Walters	Laurence Luckinbill
Diamond	Linda Thorson
The Capo	Daniele Vargas
Michelle	Kim Goody
Inspector Petrucci	Piero Gerlini
Aberlardo	Piercorrado Dugoni
Marcello	Massimo Sarchielli
Signora Marcello	Alina De Simone
Nurse	Andrea Smith
Paolo	Vito Domenighini

Screenplay by	John Goldsmith
Directed by	Jeremy Summers

THE SAINT is in Rome, where he runs into Michelle, a young girl he has known since she was 16, and who is now a budding pop star. She is being menaced by the local branch of the Mafia. Simon uncovers a tale of intrigue as he steps in to protect a young girl threatened by the mob.

A tense moment for The Saint

TOWER BRIDGE IS FALLING DOWN (1978)

Simon Templar	Ian Ogilvy
Ray Dennis	John Woodvine
Sammy	Alfie Bass
Jenny	Fiona Curzon
Buzz Wepner	Paul Maxwell
Inspector Ashton	Stanley Meadows
Mrs Stewart	Sally Lahee
Charlie Stewart	Sam Kydd
Henry	Alan Browning
Andrew	Neil Hallett
Card Dealer	John Wade
Shill	Paddy Joyce
American Tourist	Thick Wilson
Terry	Jackie Pallo
Rex	Terry Duggan
Sally	Jacki Piper

Screenplay by	Leon Griffiths
Directed by	Roy Ward Baker

THE SAINT investigates when Charlie Stewart is found crushed to death on one of his own demolition sites. His daughter Jenny persuades Simon to take the case. She is convinced that her father's business partner, Ray Dennis, not only conned her father out of a large sum of money but also was responsible for his death. The Saint devises an elaborate plan which he is sure will appeal to Dennis's avaricious nature, and with Jenny's help he puts the plan into action.

THE DEBT COLLECTORS (1978)

Simon Templar	Ian Ogilvy
	Supporting cast
Mary Tamm	Diane Keen
Esmond Knight	Anton Rogers
Neil McCarthy	Geoffrey Keen
Bob Sherman	
Screenplay by	George Markstein
Directed by	Leslie Norman

THE SAINT is in Hyde Park when he sees a young girl on a runaway horse. Simon leaps into action and goes to her aid. He suddenly finds himself involved in the middle of an espionage plot. The girl's sister is being used as the centrepiece in a cold-hearted plot to track down a suspected traitor in MI5.

COLLISION COURSE: The Brave Goose (1979)

Simon Templar	Ian Ogilvy
Annabel	Gayle Hunnicutt
George Duchamps	Stratford Johns
Inspector Lebec	Derren Nesbitt
Captain Finnigan	Joe Lynch
Bernadotti	John Hallam
Pancho	Leon Lissek
Oscar West	Edward Brayshow
Beeky	Michael Robbins
Vic	Prentiss Hancock
Franklyn	Wensley Pithey
Genevieve	Michelle Newell
Coroner	Cyril Luckham
Mrs Cloonan	Peggy Thorpe-Bates
Screenplay by	John Kruse
Director by	Cyril Frankel

THE SAINT IS a spectator at a power boat race, where he spots a well-known crook. Shortly afterwards, one of the contestants, Oscar West, a wealthy businessman, is killed when his power boat blows up. Simon decides to investigate. West was a wealthy man, who always spent his money with reckless abandon. All he leaves behind is a wife, Annabel, and a luxury yacht. Annabel sets off for the South of France to collect the yacht, Simon decides to follow her, but unknown to him Oscar's former partners are after Annabel. They believe that she knows the whereabouts of a fortune in gold bullion, the spoils of a robbery that Oscar was involved in. The gang wants the money, and to make her talk they place her in a bullring with a ferocious bull.

COLLISION COURSE: The Sixth Man (1979)

Simon Templar	Ian Ogilvy
Annabel	Gayle Hunnicutt
George Duchamps	Stratford Johns
Inspector Lebec	Derren Nesbitt
Captain Finnigan	Joe Lynch
Bernadotti	John Hallam
Pancho	Leon Lissek
Oscar West	Edward Brayshow
Beeky	Michael Robbins
Vic	Prentiss Hancock
Franklyn	Wensley Pithey
Genevieve	Michelle Newell
Coroner	Cyril Luckham
Mrs Cloonan	Peggy Thorpe-Bates
Screenplay by	John Kruse
Directed by	Cyril Frankel

SIMON RESCUES Annabel from the bullring just in time, but the hiding place of the bullion still remains a mystery. Later on the gang make an attempt on Simon's life, but a policeman is killed by accident. Inspector Lebec arrests Simon on a charge of murdering the police officer, but later releases him when he realises that Simon was the intended victim. Inspector Lebec hints to Annabel that there was an unknown sixth man involved in the robbery, and that it could have been Simon. Simon and Annabel return to the yacht. 'The Brave Goose' and talk to the skipper, Captain Finnigan. He reveals to them that twice a year he took Oscar on a cruise to Corsica, and Simon believes that this could be the hiding place of the loot. 'The Brave Goose' sets sail for the island, with Inspector Lebec following behind waiting to find the sixth man.

Prentiss Hancock and Ian Ogilvy

HOT RUN (1979)

Simon Templar	Ian Ogilvy
Diana Lang	Rula Lenska
Korvis	John Nolan
Maria	Lorraine de Selle
Harland	Barry Andrews
Erhart	Struan Rodger
Screenplay by	Tony Williamson
Directed by	Peter Sasdy

THE SAINT is in Italy on a skiing holiday. Twice a year the Italian resort town of Cortina finds its population doubled overnight by the onslaught of visitors for the skiing season. The Saint has come to Cortina for a rest, but instead he finds murder and intrigue when he comes up against Diane Lang, an American, who runs a ski school, which is really a front for far more lethal activities.

THE MURDER CARTEL (1979)

Simon Templar	Ian Ogilvy
Laura	Britt Ekland
Vidal	Helmut Berger
Lomax	Don Powell
Valerio	Gigi Reder
Hendricks	Roger Browne
Brown	Sergio Doria
Kemal	Marne Maitland
Pietro	Marco Stefanelli
Mario	Roberto Messina
Screenplay by	John Goldsmith
Directed by	Tom Clegg

SIMON IS ASKED by the C.I.A. to work undercover to prevent the assassination of a powerful oil sheik. Simon's mission is to infiltrate and unmask the leader of a powerful and deadly organisation known as 'the murder cartel'. Simon heads for Rome, where he comes up against the lovely but lethal Laura.

VICIOUS CIRCLE (1979)

Simon Templar	Ian Ogilvy
Renata	Elsa Martinelli
Anne	Tessa Wyatt
Antonio	Gianrico Tondinelli
Dr Brogli	Mel Ferrer
Rotti	Luciano Pigozzi
Roberto	Michael Forest
Captain Genarro	Stelio Candelli
Fabio	Silvio Laurenzi
Screenplay by	John Goldsmith
Directed by	Sam Wanamaker

THE SAINT investigates when Roberto Lucci, a former racing driver, is killer in a car crash. His wife, Renata is one of the leading fashion designers in Rome. Was it an accident or murder?

THE OBONO AFFAIR (1979)

Simon Templar	Ian Ogilvy
Colonel Dyson	Jack Hedley
President Obono	Thomas Baptista
Mora	Muriel Odunton
Joey	Paul Medford
Wright	Derek Newark
Rose	Marjie Lawrence
Assassin	Willie Jonah
Mombasa	Oscar James
Publican	Jason Rose
Inspector Thornton	Jerome Willis
Fred Batley	Robert Gillespie
Jim Batley	John Atkinson
Screenplay by	Michael Pertwee
Directed by	Peter Sasdy

THE SAINT is asked to protect a much-hated African President from assassination. Simon is reluctant to help until the President's young son is kidnapped, and then he is persuaded to help by the President's daughter, Mora. Simon discovers that Mora is involved with President Obono's right-hand man, Colonel Dyson, a tough former S.A.S. officer who will do anything for money, and has played a vital part in the President's ruthless dictatorship.

DRAGONSEED (1979)

Simon Templar	Ian Ogilvy
Carla	Annamaria Macchi
Domenico	Sam Wanamaker
Lucia	Barbara Pilavin
Falco	Shane Rimmer
Gabriel	Paolo Malco
Doctor	Michael Graham
Inga	Greta Vayant
Captain George	Bill Vanders
Screenplay by	John Kruse
Directed by	Leslie Norman

WHEN A RICH man's son dies in a helicopter crash Simon Templar investigates, and finds evidence to suggest murder.

APPOINTMENT IN FLORENCE
(1979)

Simon Templar	Ian Ogilvy
Manfred	Stuart Wilson
Ingo	James Aubrey
Lea	Carla Romanelli
Paolo	Rodolfo Bigotti
Karl	Rosalino Cellamare
Helga	Tamara Triffez
Gaby	Nicole Stoliaroff
Christian	Bryan Pinero

Screenplay by	Philip Broadley
Directed by	Peter Sasdy

WHEN CHRISTIAN VAN ESSER, a close friend of The Saint, is murdered by Italian terrorists, Simon vows to bring them to justice.

THE DIPLOMAT'S DAUGHTER
(1979)

Simon Templar	Ian Ogilvy
Marie de la Garde	Lynn Dalby
Pierre	Murray Head
Shriver	Karl Held
Michel	Weston Gavin
French Ambassador	David Garth
Louis	Artro Morris
Hotel Porter	Jean Driant

Screenplay by	Michael Pertwee
Directed by	Charles Crichton

THE SAINT IS driving along a quiet road in France when suddenly another car cuts in front of him. Simon is not pleased by this even though the driver is a pretty young girl. To make matters worse, a few moments later, another car does the same thing. It's obvious to Simon that the young girl is being chased. Later, when Simon has caught up with the girl, Maria de la Garde, she tells him that she is the daughter of a new Ambassador, and that her troubles are a result of her brother's gambling debts, and that he is being forced into a dope smuggling racket using their father's diplomatic immunity.

THE SAINT TV MOVIE

ROGER MOORE had done everything to make the original TV Saint a success and long after the show's demise he was a great ambassador for the series, helping repeat run sales. He maintained an interest in the character, both personal and financial. Moore, who'd enjoyed directing eight of the episodes of the old series, decided in the 1980s that he'd like to direct a feature-length Saint TV movie. In 1984 stories appeared in the press about this new Saint venture, which was to be called *The Saint's Getaway*. Baker and Moore were to produce the film, with Moore directing. It was to be a two-hour adventure, set in the thirties and concerning the theft of some Nazi jewels. Moore was set to play a walk-on part. As for The Saint; a rather long short-list of actors was mentioned: Simon McCorkindale, Charles Dance, Christopher Reeve, Lewis Collins, Jeremy Irons, Ian Charleston and long-time favourite Piers Brosnan.

The idea was presented to CBS, the company which had eventually taken and had success with the earlier TV Saints. They loved the idea of a new Saint movie but didn't go along with Moore's thoughts on the film. The period-piece premise was dropped and with it went Moore's interest as director. Baker (representing Television Reporters International's interest) was installed as co-Executive Producer and the new feature, a D.L. Taffner/Celtic Films/Television Reporters International co-production was underway. The screenplay dealt with an attempt to frame The Saint for the theft of a fabulous diamond tiara, and was written by Peter Gethers and David Handler. The cast search for someone to play Simon Templar resulted in the booking of a relatively unknown Australian actor, Andrew Clarke. The Saint's New York police adversary Fernack was to be played by Kevin Tighe and the Saint's butler Woods by George Rose. It was decided that the feature should be a pilot episode for a proposed series and it was eventually aired as a 60-minute special on CBS on 12 June 1987 called simply *The Saint*, (although latterly, to avoid confusion with subsequent movies in the TV Saint area, it is always referred to as *The Saint in Manhattan*). After the show was aired, viewers were invited to phone in if they would like to see a series based on the pilot. The series never materialised – not in that form anyway, but the partnership of Baker, D.L. Taffner and Celtic Films was still keen in resurrecting The Saint for TV and went back to the drawing board to work on another variation.

THE SAINT (A.K.A. THE SAINT IN MANHATTAN).

D.L. Taffner/Celtic Films/Television Reporters
International Production.
T.V. Movie USA/Canada 1987.

Cast:

Simon Templar	**Andrew Clarke**
Inspector Fernack	**Kevin Tighe**
Woods	**George Rose**
Fran Grogan	**Holland Taylor**

Also featuring Christopher Marcantel, Caitlin Clarke, Liliane Komorowska, Michael Lombard, Raymond Serra and Ben Vereen.

Screenplay	**Peter Gethers and David Handler**
Director	**James Frawley**
Executive Producer	**Denis E. Doty**
Co-Executive Producer	**Robert S. Baker**
Director of Photography	**William Wages**
Editor/Ass. Producer	**Lee Burch**
Music	**Mark Snow**

THE SAINT flies to New York and, slipping out of a side-entrance to the airport, eludes the waiting Inspector Fernack and takes the helicopter shuttle into the city.

A new ballet is about to open on Broadway with a friend of Simon's, Margot, as the leading dancer. In the performance she is due to wear a fabulous diamond tiara, but this is stolen during rehearsals and replaced by a fake, the thief leaving a card bearing the stick-man logo of The Saint. Fernack investigates, accuses Simon and locks him up but without fnding the real tiara he has insufficient evidence to hold The Saint and has to release him.

Later, following a clue, Simon goes to a large department store's toy section. There an assistant he is questioning is shot dead. Simon chases the gunman but he escapes.

Inspector Fernack, acting on a tip-off calls on The Saint and finds the tiara behind a cupboard but just as he is about to arrest Simon, the tiara is proved to be fake.

A few more clues are needed before the mystery is solved in this tale of The Saint in Manhattan.

This TV film was intended as a pilot for a possible series which never materialised (at least not in this form). Andrew Clarke was miscast in the lead role, appearing like some Tom Selleck (Magnum) clone and even having a similar foil to Magnum's Higgins (John Hillerman) in the shape of George Rose as his butler Woods. Viewers were invited to phone in at the end of the show if they wanted it to go to series but the response couldn't have been great enough.

MYSTERY WHEEL OF ADVENTURE

Presenting The Saint

ENOUGH INTEREST was generated among the media and the public by the failed Andrew Clarke Saint pilot that the production company decided to try again. The D.L. Taffner organisation was planning a series of made-for-TV feature length films under the general heading, *Mystery Wheel of Adventure*. Stories from the books of Dick Francis, and the exploits of Leslie Charteris's 'Happy Highwayman', The Saint were announced as the nucleus of the Mystery Wheel adventures.

The Saint stories would be all-new, specially written for the series and were to depict a Simon Templar for the Nineties. Much was made in the press of the decision to make this version a 'green' Saint, concerned about the environment, whose adversaries would be industrial polluters, crooked developers, arms suppliers and the like. But these villains are the logical progressions of the Saint's earliest enemies, for the character had always gone up against those he considered moral criminals but who cleverly managed to stay one step ahead of the law. So the projected enemies of this latest Simon Templar were certainly in keeping with the spirit of the original stories.

But what about this latest Simon Templar, who would have to follow in the footsteps of Louis Hayward, George Sanders, Hugh Sinclair, Felix Marten, Roger Moore, Jean Marais, Ian Ogilvy and Andrew Clarke as the ninth screen Saint? That task befell British actor Simon Dutton, an experienced enough actor, not exactly unknown but not a household name either.

The series was launched in early 1989 and filming began in the spring on the first episode, *The Brazilian Connection*. Six scripts were commissioned initially, all for 2-hour long segments.

1. *The Brazilian Connection* by Anthony Horowitz
2. *The Software Murder* by Peter Palliser
3. *The Blue Dulac* by Peter Palliser
4. *The Big Bang* by John Goldsmith
5. *Wrong Number* by John Goldsmith
6. *Unreal Estate* by Patricia Johnson

Executive Producer for all   **Jacky Stoller**
adventures

Watch for the sign of the Saint, he will return.

INDEX